GORDON OF KHARTOUM

Alexander McKee

SAPERE
BOOKS

GORDON OF
KHARTOUM

Published by Sapere Books.

24 Trafalgar Road, Ilkley, LS29 8HH

United Kingdom

saperebooks.com

ISBN: 978-0-85495-183-3.

TABLE OF CONTENTS

CHAPTER ONE: THE GENERAL'S SON

'I would that all could look on death as a cheerful friend, who takes us from a world of trial to our true home. All our sorrows come from a forgetfulness of this great truth. I desire to look on the departure of my friends as a promotion to another and a higher sphere, as I do believe that to be the case with *all*.' — *Gordon*.

It was three o'clock in the morning. Fifty thousand fighting men crept forward in the darkness like a tide, with no more sound than that of the night sea; there was no moon to gleam on their white robes, the black spear blades, the silver swords. It was half an hour to dawn, outside Khartoum, on the 26th of January, 1885. Miles away, in the camp of the Mahdi, a white prisoner in chains heard the silence broken by the opening of the assault — the harsh, continuous rattle of rifle fire, the sullen thunder of guns, rising to a crest of thunder like a wave about to burst. Then it broke upon the town, and like a wave, instantly the booming thunder died away into a mere backwash of scattered rifle shots. And then silence again, absolute and final.

Weakened by many months of siege, the defences had collapsed. The few defenders who survived the assault remembered only a white-clad human tide bursting into the streets, screaming *Kenisa*! *Saraya*! 'To the Church! To the Palace!' Mad for loot, 50,000 maddened besiegers streamed through the town. Anything human in their way, man, woman, child, was cut down, slashed, stabbed by whirling sword or driven spear. Like stampeded cattle, the inhabitants dashed for shelter in their houses. The doors were smashed in, or the houses set on fire. The men butchered, the children butchered, even some of the women slashed to pieces. Then, the first rage spent, the Arabs started to strip their captives naked, brown-skinned and black, regardless of sex or age, and the processions of destined slaves began to stream back along the path of the assault towards the prison compounds of Omdurman.

In the flickering, golden glare of the fires, a red glow at their heart, a primitive animal orgy of lust and death, of ecstasy and agony, of power and surrender, welded victors and victims alike momentarily together in one fierce, unforgettable union. The hysterical shrilling of children, the moaning of women, merged with the shrieks of the men, flogged, or tortured in unspeakable ways, until they revealed where their wealth was hidden. Four thousand people perished indiscriminately in Khartoum in this fashion, between the hours of three and nine o'clock that morning; but barely half an hour had elapsed, and it was still dark, when the first wave of onrushing Arab fanatics reached the Governor's Palace and saw there on the steps the cause of the siege, of their many, costly, failed assaults, the arch enemy — the white man, the Christian.

There was a pause. They were afraid that the approach across the courtyard was mined, for the white man was an officer of the Royal Engineers and he had used mines extensively against them during the siege. He stood there silently, in his white Governor's dress uniform, one hand on his sheathed sword. But he did not draw it. Then an Arab leader screamed, '*Mala' oun el yom yomek!*' ['O accursed one, your time is come!'] and bounded forward followed by three other men. The British officer made a gesture of disdain. Then a spear crashed into his body, and as he fell, the four Arabs were round him, the air quick with the hiss of rising and falling swords. A moment later, the bloodied corpse was cast headlong down the Palace steps into the courtyard, where it lay for hours, hacked at, mutilated needlessly by hundreds of passing fanatics, before eventually the head was cut off and the trunk thrown down a well.

It was still morning when the white prisoner at the Madhi's camp, in chains, saw a group of Arabs approach, carrying a bloodied cloth. They stopped to jeer, unrolling their cloth. The blue eyes in the severed head were still half-open, but the hair was white. 'Is not this,' they demanded, 'the head of your uncle, the unbeliever?'

'What of it?' replied the chained man. 'A brave soldier who fell at his post. Happy is he to have fallen; his sufferings are over.'

So died General Charles Gordon. But did he? It was dark when the spear flashed and the swords fell. Few were close enough, in the dim light just before dawn, to see exactly what happened. Some tales told in the Mahdi's camp that night spoke of an ending that was not quiet and resigned, but truly the death of a soldier. Gordon, these men declared, had fought his way down the Palace steps, first with pistol, then with drawn sword, until finally cut down by the raving mob, in death his blood mingling with that of his enemies. But perhaps that was how they wanted to see him die, for they admired him as he admired them, in the strange way of men brought closer by war than ever they could be by peace.

In his death, as in his life, there were always two opinions about Charles Gordon. And typically, in death as in life, the reverberations of his actions went much further than, judging purely by his nominal place in the world, they should have done. For Queen Victoria, disregarding protocol, sent an unciphered message directly to the Prime Minister, Mr. Gladstone. 'These news from Khartoum are frightful, and to think that all this might have been prevented and many precious lives saved by earlier action is too frightful.' The 'Grand Old Man' went white when he read that open letter. 'The circumstances,' he circumspectly noted in his diary, 'are sad and trying. It is one of the least points about them that they may put an end to the Government.' In many eyes, Gladstone had now become, not the 'G.O.M.', but the 'M.O.G.'. Branded forever as the 'Murderer of Gordon'.

The Queen wrote to Gordon's family with a sympathy so passionately felt, and shared, that there can hardly be a parallel except with the cry of a Roman Emperor, 'Bring me back my Legions, Varus!' But Gordon at Khartoum had commanded no valuable legions. He had been just a British officer sent virtually alone on a special mission. National security was not hurt, but national pride was, and the people shared the emotions of their Queen. Government thought differently, and although vengeance came in the end, it was a long time coming. When it did, it was final and terrible. Many thousands of human skeletons were to bleach in the desert before Khartoum could boast a Gordon College, in honour of the headless corpse thrown down the well so many years before.

Charles George Gordon was born into a Service family on 28 January 1833. His father, who was to rise to the rank of Lieutenant-General, was in the Artillery, and this fourth child (out of a family which was eventually to number eleven) was born at Woolwich because his father happened at the time to be stationed there. In this he was typical of most Service children. He had, to begin with, no roots except the Service which his father had joined; he grew up in transit, so to speak.

So many years at Woolwich, and in Dublin, and in Leith, and at Corfu. There was change, and interest, and a semi-privileged position even as a child within a restricted circle; for it was normal for not merely the mother, but the children as well, to take the rank and arm of the father. But there was something lost, inevitably — the sense of belonging to a particular place and a particular people, subject only to the slow, almost unnoticeable process of natural life and death. In manhood, the places of one's childhood would be a dream, having no existence except in the mind; and the mind would be restless for further change, more susceptible to outside influences, yet seeking always for an anchor.

The father, Henry William Gordon, came himself of an army family. Most of the Gordons were soldiers, tracing their descent from a David Gordon who went over to the Hanoverians early in the eighteenth century, was taken prisoner at Prestonpans, and fought under Wolfe at Quebec. As is usual, some of the family had chosen the Church in preference to the Army. The mother, Elizabeth Enderby, provided a contrast because her people were prosperous merchants and believers in the Evangelical faith. 'Trade' and the Fighting Services did not ordinarily mix. During the greater part of the nineteenth century, and persisting well into the twentieth, the latter regarded themselves as an élite because they possessed the privilege of dying in battle, and did not care to 'know' the gross fellows who provided the sinews of war, and profited from it. Their codes of conduct were in any case very different and this provided additional insulation for the social barrier, which was stronger in the Senior Service, the Navy, than in the Army.

In any event, Elizabeth Enderby had crossed it and went on to produce eleven children, which made strict discipline in the family next to impossible. Even with servants, she and her husband were grossly outnumbered by their offspring. 'I feel like a man sitting on a powder barrel,' observed their hard-tried father. The children had a wonderful time, not inferior in freedom to that enjoyed by the boys and girls of slum families, and the crowning exploits of his boyhood were always remembered with happiness by Charles Gordon. Some operations were relatively harmless, such as the collection of live mice and the insertion of parties of them, surreptitiously, into the house of their father's senior, the Commandant at Woolwich, to the consternation of the females within. Some were not particularly original, the old game of doorbell-ringing, for instance. A few were quite definitely dangerous, and could have been lethal. As, for example, the turning of a minor part of Woolwich Arsenal into a children's arms factory. The Gordon boys got some of the workmen, in Arsenal time, to turn out squirts and crossbows designed to fire heavy, window-shattering screws; and with these weapons, on one occasion, broke twenty-seven panes of glass, and on another, totally disrupted an Academy lecture in a shower of splintered windows. These forays were well-organised, and the culprits were never detected; but many small boys could boast as much.

In 1848, when he was still fifteen years of age, Charles Gordon entered Woolwich officially as an officer-cadet, intended eventually for the same arm as his father, the Artillery. But he proved highly strung and hot-tempered, and there was a string of incidents which included butting a senior corporal in the stomach so that he went backwards down a flight of stairs and into and through a glass-panelled door; and another in which he was alleged to have struck another cadet with a clothes brush; and yet another, as a result of which he was told that he would never make an officer, which caused Gordon to tear off his epaulettes and throw them at his superior's feet. Because of these and similar undisciplined tantrums, Gordon was ordered to lose six months seniority, so that he spent an extra term at the Academy, lost his chance of a commission in the Artillery and instead, in 1852, became a subaltern in the Engineers, the 'brainy' Corps of the British Army. All Engineers, it was said, were either 'Mad, Married, or Methodist'. Gordon never married, was later to be accused of being slightly mad, and his mother was a Methodist; but at the moment there appeared to be nothing exceptional about him.

During his first home postings, to Chatham and then Pembroke, he proved satisfactory, being particularly good at survey work. But at the latter station, one marked trait first made its appearance. Simultaneously, he became concerned with religion and evidenced boredom amounting to disaster for the normal social life of an officer; he was especially unable to bear formal dinner parties. Any physical hardship was far preferable, indeed almost pleasurable. In these things, he was remarkably similar to two other eccentrics to be thrown up later by the British Army — T. E. Lawrence and Orde Wingate. And like Charles Gordon, they also were able to identify themselves, in varying degree, with a foreign culture and people — Arabia and Israel respectively.

But Gordon was the original. 'Chinese' Gordon preceded 'Lawrence of Arabia' by more than half a century as the prototype leader of alien, irregular forces employed in romantic circumstances and unorthodox campaigns. Undoubtedly, a measure of identification with the human material under command was necessary for success. The differences between these three odd military men were, however, at least as marked as the similarities. Lawrence, one feels after reading him, has erected on the bedrock of the hard, nomadic life he led a structure of intellectual pretension which is more than half a pose; it amused that strange and contorted character to try the effect of full Arab dress on his more straightforward and direct seniors, expecting no doubt the mutters of 'Damme, the feller's gone native', and countering them with a sophisticated, gravely donnish exposition of the depths of Arab philosophy (which no doubt would have surprised the Bedouin, but which the ordinary British officer was in no position to contradict). In short, what was a simple requisite for commanding Arabs turned into an undergraduate joke grown-up, whenever he was in contact with the dull military machine. Wingate, on the other hand, appears genuine in his Old Testament fanaticism; but the very fury of it appals and makes uneasy those who cannot share it. Even here, however, some of the eccentricities seem studied, a calculated copy of Gordon, the prototype. These oddities of behaviour sprung probably from the fact that he was the least talented, militarily speaking, of the strange trio. Wingate owed his position, and much of his reputation, to a series of powerful pushes from the ruling Churchill dynasty. Some of his methods verged upon farce and were so regarded by contemporaries. Irregular operations must always risk derision, and doubly so if they fail. The spectacle of Wingate stuck in the bush with 'Tiger Tim' (as the Emperor of Abyssinia was known), because he had stubbornly refused expert advice that the route was impassable for vehicles, would have been damaging to his reputation had anyone dared report it at the time.

Gordon appeared just as unbalanced, in his own way, as did Lawrence and Wingate; but the mainsprings of his character were quite different. Although he was to allow himself to be photographed in the dress of a Chinese Mandarin and later in the uniform of a Turkish Pasha, he did not, like Lawrence, pretend intellectual admiration or, like Wingate, identify himself with an alien creed already in being. Quite simply, he made up his own religion. He came to certain beliefs of his own accord, and these proved fundamental in his approach to what would now be termed 'underprivileged', or perhaps 'emergent', but were then regarded merely as 'backward' races; and this was a certain ingredient of his successes in dealing with them.

To his eldest sister Augusta, always his spiritual confidant, he was to write revealingly: 'I feel sure that you, like me, want comfort with respect to political affairs, so I will tell you how I try and comfort myself. First, I believe that all worldly events are part of God's great scheme, that He loves all human beings of all nations equally, that He is perfectly impartial and has no favourites: this I consider as *the* great and never to be disputed comfort. That nation A is better than nation B, however backward B may be, I do not think.' This was to be particularly effective at the scene of his greatest military triumphs, in China, because the Chinese regarded the Western unions as 'backward', not to say barbaric, and were much relieved to find that Gordon was only about half as arrogant as the average European or American.

But Gordon was still only a newly-fledged young officer when, in 1854, he went off to his first campaign where, in the desolate wastes of the wintry Crimea, the British and French Armies were waging a singularly useless war with the Russians. He very nearly did not get there, being posted to Corfu instead and suspecting his father of arranging it. Military families tend often to be less militaristic than civilian; they have more realistic views of war, and, besides, their sons will die first.

The first campaign is always the vital one. There is no experience on earth to compare with war; it is just like peace, only more so. The excitement more exciting, the boredom more boring, the horrors more horrible, the sadness more desolate. It is raw, savage, shocking; no man who experiences it is ever the same again. He is forced, whether he wishes or not, to search for, find, and then desperately hang on to his own newly-forged set of values. Every judgement he will ever make from then on will be coloured by what he learnt in the school of kill or be killed. Characteristics which have been potential become actual. The twin main themes of Gordon's life — the Bible and the Sword — were to be put to the test which would either confirm or destroy. The theories of Life and Death exposed to the process of life and death in its most acute form. War.

CHAPTER TWO: AT THE SIEGE OF SEBASTOPOL

'We do not, generally speaking, like the thoughts of peace. I expect I shall remain abroad for three or four years, which, individually, I would sooner spend in war than peace. There is something indescribably exciting in the former.' — *Gordon*, 1856.

Sebastopol was burning. The autumn night sky had the appearance of a strange sunset, quivering and glowing, and every now and then it was almost daylight as a violent explosion erupted a momentary white glare across the scene of smoking desolation like some monstrous flashbulb. The roar and hiss of the raging fires was a constant background murmur to the thunderous detonations of the Russian powder magazines. When dawn came, the spectacle was truly stupendous and unearthly. 'Beautiful,' wrote Gordon in his diary. He had seen the Acropolis, and been unimpressed, although he admitted that the view had been 'very fine from the top'; only a blazing town, with the Russians retiring in defeat from it, had induced this feeling of awe. He had seen death now, violent and terrible, all around him; and had been unmoved. There was no death, he had decided; man was immortal, only the flesh was clay. Whether death came soon or late, it was not to be feared. Gordon the youth was no more; in nine short months he had come to manhood.

But he had begun the campaign in a distinctive way, refusing to go out to the Crimea in the hired collier appointed to transport his unit, and when he found that he had to pay his own way to the battlefield, became most annoyed. Strictly speaking, he should never actually have seen a battle, as his job was to build huts for the troops as some protection against the appalling Crimean winter; but the best of the British Army had already been destroyed, more by administrative inefficiency than by bullets, and there proved to be room for an energetic and daring young officer.

Gordon arrived at Balaclava on the 1st January 1855, the famous battle now more than two months old. War had been declared in March 1854, between Russia on the one hand and Britain and France on the other. The Allies had invaded the Crimea in September, with Sebastopol as their objective. They had defeated a Russian army of twice their strength at the Alma on the 20th September, and pushing on towards Sebastopol, won another victory at Balaclava on the 25th October, in spite of the blunder which sent the Light Brigade to its doom. Then the Russians went over to the offensive and attacked at Inkerman on the 5th November, concentrating on the positions held by the British; and were again defeated. Three defeats in a row demoralised the Russian Army, and the Allies advanced to the Siege of Sebastopol where their chief enemies, General Winter and General Incompetence, decimated the formidable peace-time veterans, so that the ranks had to be filled up by half-trained recruits. This was the position when, three weeks after his arrival in the Crimea, the hut building chore accomplished, Gordon was ordered up the line to the trenches.

His introduction to war was as a junior leader of a tricky night operation on 14th February. 'Night ops' are always tense, always likely to go wrong; they are especially likely to confusion when Allies of different races, with different languages, are trying a co-ordinated manoeuvre, and if the men in charge have never seen the place in daylight, let alone at night. This was the case on that wintry night in the Crimea. Gordon had never been there before, and when he got into the frontline trench, discovered to his horror that the British captain commanding it was also seeing it for the first time, as the man apologetically explained. Gordon kept silent about his own ignorance, and got on with the job.

The place was at the junction of the French and British forces which at that point lacked forward observation posts in advance of the frontline trenches. The plan was to establish them so as to prevent the Russians creeping forward by night undetected along the weak point, the boundary line between the two Allied armies, and attacking one of them in flank. Out in no-man's-land were a hill and a ruined house, which the French were determined to occupy; they intended also to dig a communication trench up to the hill, so that the newly-established post could be supported from the French lines. Gordon's task was to dig a line of communicating rifle pits from some caves out in no-man's-land, in front of the British lines, up to the ruined house. With some trouble he got eight pick and shovel men and the loan of five pairs of sentries to cover them while they worked, and set off.

The caves should already have been occupied by the British, and Gordon understood that this had been done. When he got there he met only a menacing silence. His first task, therefore, as an Engineer officer, was to do an infanteer's job, and 'clear' the caves, dark, eerie, possibly occupied by Russian infantry already in position. He duly carried out the task, finding the caves to be fortunately as empty of Russian infantry as they were of British, and then went up the hill above to post two covering riflemen. That done, he cut back down the hill and around to the caves again, to post another two sentries actually inside them. But, as he came out of 'dead' ground into the open, two bullets whip cracked past his ears, to slam into the ground nearby. This was followed instantly by a hail of fire from the Russian positions, which now revealed themselves to be only 150 yards away. The two sentries bolted, the working party bolted, and the two sentries just established on the hill also bolted, so fast they left their caps behind. It was these latter two men who had actually fired the first two shots at Gordon, by mistake out of panic, and set the Russian lines in an uproar also. The sentries could not be induced to leave the front-line trench a second time, and therefore Gordon took out his working party without infantry protection and set them to digging the rifle pits. He based with the French on the left, who were out in strength, digging hard, before returning to his own men. 'I stayed with my working party all night, and got home very tired,' he wrote. The only casualty had been a British Colonel who had insisted on going out into no-man's-land in spite of Gordon's joking warning, that if the British sentries didn't get him first, then the Russians would. Somebody at any rate put a bullet through his clothing, which only grazed the officer's ribs, a very lucky escape.

Gordon's own report of the affair, on which the above is based, is not very interesting; being brief, flat, and technical. A typical first time in action piece by a young professional soldier, conscious of the necessity to understate rather than underline the very real emotional side, and rather pleased to be able to show that he had a professional grasp of the finer points from the beginning. He assumes that his readers will be able to read between the lines. Later, when he realised that this was not necessarily so, he became more graphic; but also, perhaps, he had begun to grow up. To others, he certainly appeared very cool and competent. One of his superiors, Sir Charles Staveley, recorded:

'I happened to mention to Charlie Gordon that I was field officer for the day for command in the trenches next day, and, having only just returned from sick leave, that I was ignorant of the geography of our left attack. He said at once, "Oh! come down with me tonight after dark, and I will show you over the trenches." He drew me out a very clear sketch of the lines (which I have now), and down I went accordingly. He explained every nook and corner, and took me along outside our most advanced trench, the bouquets (volleys of small shells fired from mortars) and other missiles flying about us in, to me, a very unpleasant manner, he taking the matter remarkably coolly.'

Gordon had discovered for himself the validity of an old truth: that the only effective way of leading men in action was that which at the same time assured recognition of merit from one's superiors — to take very great risks frequently and to appear disdainful while doing it. Fatalism, religious or otherwise, makes this easier than might appear; but an honest element of enjoyment, if present, of the almost unbearable excitement and tension, is vital. Gordon had it; he liked war. Or, rather, he liked the brief excitement which this kind of campaign gave him. Of the boring months of March, April, and May, he wrote home, grumbling at the inaction: 'It is not my fault, as none of the three nations — French, English, or Russian — will do anything.' Even Garnet Wolseley, who had the same qualities, and with whom Gordon was to be concerned in very grave circumstances later in his career, was astonished at the apparently genuine unconcern for danger of the young soldier. It should be noted that the excitement and tension were of brief duration, breaking spells of boredom; for continual tension, so far from being pleasant, eventually breaks a man. But Gordon was also intensively active and energetic, generating his own inner tension, and the sudden blaze of raw excitement relaxed him. Everyone who has been under fire knows the slightly wild, drunken happiness, at just being alive, which succeeds the actual moments of danger during which life is lived momentarily with an intensity which no other emotion, save perhaps love, can ever equal. And for the worrying kind, whether, as with Gordon, the worry was about the sinfulness of the world and the flesh, or whether, more normally, about one's bank balance and future prospects, there is complete relaxation. When you may not live through the next ten seconds, there is no tomorrow: only this moment.

The Victorians were less reticent than we are about these facets of battle experience: the bitter, murderous misery, too long drawn-out, of the First World War had not coloured their thinking on the subject of military glory, as it was to do with later generations. Psychologically, therefore, Gordon was fitted to excel in his profession; but this by itself is not enough. Very great technical competence is also required. This, too, he had even as a very young officer, as Sir George Chesney noted:

'In his humble position as an Engineer subaltern he attracted the notice of his superiors, not merely by his energy and activity, but by a special aptitude for war, developing itself amid the trench work before Sebastopol in a personal knowledge of the enemy's movements *such as no other officer attained*. We used to send him to find out what new move the Russians were making.' Gordon would make his mark, if he survived.

In May, General Pelissier took over command of the French forces; he had much the same ideas as Gordon, and the following month the latter was able to write:

'On the 6th we opened fire from all our batteries. I could distinctly see the Russians in the Redan and elsewhere running about in great haste, and bringing up the gunners to the guns. They must have lost immensely, as our shot and shell continued to pour in upon them for hours without a lull. Never was our fire so successful. Before seven we had silenced a great many of their guns, while our loss was very small — only one man killed and four wounded. I was struck slightly with a stone from a round shot and stunned for a second, which old Jones has persisted in returning as wounded. However, I am all right, so do not think otherwise. Our fire was continued all night, and the next day until four o'clock, when we opened with new batteries much nearer, and our fire then became truly terrific. Fancy 1,000 guns (which is the number of ourselves, the French, and the Russians combined) firing at once shells in every direction. On our side alone we have thirty-nine 13-inch mortars. At half-past five three rockets gave the signal for the French to attack the Mamelon and the redoubts of Selingkinsk and Volhynia. They rushed up the slope in full view of the Allied armies. The Russians fired one or two guns when the French were in the embrasures. We then saw the Russians cut out on the other side, and the French after them, towards the Malakoff Tower, which they nearly reached, but were so punished by the guns of this work that they were obliged to retire, the Russians in their turn chasing them through the Mamelon into their own trenches. This was dreadful, as it had to be assaulted again. The French, however, did so immediately, and carried it splendidly. The redoubts of Volhynia and Selingkinsk were taken easily by our side. In front of the right attack a work called the Quarries had to be taken (by the British), which was done at the same time as the Mamelon. The Russians cut out and ran, while our men made their lodging for our fellows. We were attacked four times in the night, but held the work; we were driven from the Quarries three times, the Russians having directed all their efforts against them. Our loss is supposed to be 1,000 killed and wounded. Nearly all our (Engineer) working party had to be taken for fighting purposes. The Russians fought desperately.'

The battle swayed back and forth bloodily, the courage of the Russian infantry reinforced by the skill of their general, Todleben, a master of fortification and siege warfare. The young Gordon was not slow to learn, and there was much to learn, because the Crimean struggle came at the technical turning point between, on the one hand, the weapons and tactics of the Napoleonic era, and on the other, the partial introduction of the industrial revolution into warfare — steam-power, railways, iron-clad ships, explosive projectiles. Mixed incongruously with them were the cannon ball, grape-shot, wooden walls, and sailing ships. The next lesson came on the 18th June, after a bombardment which opened the day before.

'At 3 a.m. all our batteries opened,' wrote Gordon, 'and throughout the day kept up a terrific fire. The Russians answered slowly, and after a time their guns almost ceased. I mentioned in my report that I thought they were reserving their fire.' Twenty-four hours later, to the minute, believing that the Russian defences had at last been pounded to rubble, the Allied armies made their great assault.

'About 3 a.m. the French advanced on the Malakoff Tower in three columns, and ten minutes after this our signal was given. The Russians then opened with a fire of grape, which was terrific. They mowed down our men in dozens, and the trenches, being confined, were crowded with men, who foolishly kept in them instead of rushing over the parapet of our trenches, and by coming forward in a mass, trusting to some of them at least being able to pass through untouched to the Redan, where of course, once they arrived, the artillery could not reach them and every yard nearer would have diminished the effect of the grape by giving it less space for spreading. We could then have moved up our supports and carried the place. Unfortunately, however, our men dribbled out of the ends of the trenches, ten and twenty at a time, and as soon as they appeared they were cleared away. Some hundred men, under Lieutenant Fisher, got up to the abattis, but were not supported, and consequently had to retire. About this time the French were driven from the Malakoff Tower, which I do not think they actually entered, and Lord Raglan very wisely would not renew the assault, as the Redan could not be held with the Malakoff Tower in the hands of the Russians. However, at five o'clock, when we had failed at the Redan, we heard a very sharp attack on the head of the creek. The 44th and other regiments advanced, drove the Russians out of a rifle pit they had held near the cemetery, and entered some houses there. The Russians then opened a tremendous fire. The men sheltered themselves in the houses until they were knocked about their ears. Our losses in the four columns are — 1,400 killed and wounded, 64 officers wounded, and 16 killed. The French lost 6,000 killed and wounded, they say! Nothing has occurred since the assault, but it is determined to work forward by sap and mine.'

The technical points of bloodshed Gordon was noting for future use; but he had also come to certain cold conclusions about life and death, arrived at among the torn bodies of his friends that morning. Death was nothing, provided that you could make your peace with God. The body was nothing, only a shell for the soul. 'When we appeared, the Russians lined their parapets as thick as possible, and seemed to be expecting us to come on. They flew two flags on the Malakoff Tower the whole time in defiance of us. Murray, poor fellow, went out with the skirmishers of our column — he in red, and they in green. He was not out a minute when he was carried back with his arm shattered. He bore it bravely, and I got a stretcher and had him taken back. He died three hours afterwards. A second after Murray had gone to the rear, poor Tylden, struck by grape in the legs, was carried back, and although much depressed in spirits he is doing well. Jesse was killed at the abattis — shot through the head — and Graves was killed further in advance than anyone.' After this bloody repulse there was another lull for three months, broken only by an attempt by the Russians to relieve besieged Sebastopol, which was defeated at the battle of the Tchernaya. Gordon took no part in this, but was present in the trenches for the final assault in September 1855, when the British Army failed, the victory being secured by the French.

'We knew on the 7th,' wrote Gordon, 'that it was intended that the French should assault the Malakoff Tower at twelve the next day, and that we and another column of the French should attack the Redan and central bastion. The next day proved windy and dusty, and at ten o'clock began one of the most tremendous bombardments ever seen or heard. We had kept up a tolerable fire for the last four days, quite warm enough; but for two hours this tremendous fire extending (along a front of) six miles was maintained. At twelve the French rushed at the Malakoff, took it with ease, having caught the defenders in their bombproof houses, where they had gone to escape from the shells, etc. The Russians made three attempts to retake it, the last led by a large body of officers alone. However, the Malakoff was won, and the tricolour was hoisted as a signal for our attack. Our men went forward well, losing apparently few, put the ladders in the ditch, and mounted on the salient of the Redan; but though they stayed there five minutes or more, they did not advance, and tremendous reserves coming up drove them out. They retired well and without disorder, losing in all 150 officers, 2,400 men killed and wounded. The French got driven back with great loss at the central bastion, losing four general officers. It was determined that night that the Highlanders should storm the Redan the next morning. I was detailed for the trenches, but during the night I heard terrible explosions, and going down to the trenches at 4 a.m. I saw a splendid sight — the whole town in flames, and every now and then a terrific explosion. The rising sun shining on the scene of destruction produced a beautiful effect. The last of the Russians were leaving the town over the bridge. All the three-deckers, etc., were sunk, the steamers alone remaining. Tons and tons of powder must have been blown up. About eight o'clock I went to the Redan, where a dreadful sight was presented. The dead were buried in the ditch — the Russians with the English — Mr. Wright reading the Service over them. About ten o'clock Fort Paul was blown up — a beautiful sight. The town was not safe to be entered on account of the fire and the few Russians who still prowled about. The latter cut off the hands and feet of one Frenchman. They also caught and took away a sapper who would go *trying* to plunder — for as to plunder there was nothing but rubbish and fleas, the Russians having carried off all else. I have got the lock and sight of a gun for my father, and some other rubbish (a Russian cup, etc.) for you and my sisters. On the 10th a flag of truce came over to ask permission to take away their wounded from the hospital, which contained 3,000 wounded. These unfortunate men had been for a day and a half without attendance. A fourth of them were dead, and the rest in a bad way. I will not dwell any more on it, but could not imagine a more dreadful sight.'

Gordon's education was complete. The French soldier mutilated by the Russians. The thousands of mangled Russians left to moan in agony in the field hospital, because the enemy had abandoned it and the Allies did not know it was there. The torn and shattered corpses, British and Russian together, cast into the ditch for burial with an English chaplain reading out the Service on a bare Crimean hillside. Friends mangled by grape-shot, dying in terrible pain; or crippled for life. Wandering through the burning rubbish dump which had been a town, the wreckage looted of everything except its vermin. British troops failing in the attack, where the French soldiers succeeded. Or grumbling like children at their sufferings, instead of looking out for themselves, as the French did. And all of it for nothing very much; no issue such as might decide the fate of the world for good or evil and thus make the torment and sorrow perhaps worth while.

But he had come to believe that although death was not the end of things, the threat of it in war was 'indescribably exciting'. He was depressed by the thought of the peace, which was eventually signed in March 1856, and began to look round for another war.

CHAPTER THREE: THE BURNING OF THE SUMMER PALACE

'We have seen a great deal of the French engineers; they are older men than ours, and seem well educated. The non-commissioned officers are much more intelligent than our men. With us, although our men are not stupid, the officers have to do a good deal of work which the French sapper non-commissioned officer does. They all understand lines of least resistance, etc., and what they are about.' — *Gordon*, 1856.

Gordon's opinion of the British soldier, formed in his first campaign after the best of the British Army had been killed off, was hardly flattering. But his job was not to be patriotic; it was the waging of war with the material to hand. Of the sufferings in the Crimea he had written: 'There are really no hardships for the officers; the men are the sufferers, and that is partly their own fault, as they are like children, thinking everything is to be done for them. The French soldier looks out for himself, and consequently fares much better.' And on shipboard, he had noted: 'The poor French soldiers, of whom there were 320 on board without any shelter, must have suffered considerably from cold; they had no covering, and in spite of the wet, cold, and bad weather, they kept up their health, however, and their high spirits also, when our men would have mutinied.' And again, he wrote: 'We have capital rations, and all the men have warm clothing, and more than enough of that. They of course grumble and growl a good deal. The contrast with the French in this respect is not to our advantage.'

Gordon, by now a thoroughly professional soldier, instinctively leaned towards the self-reliant subordinate who could and would think and act for himself. The British Army was unlikely to produce such material from Disraeli's 'two nations': on the one hand, the officers who, many of them, took up an Army career more because of the pleasant social life and companionship than as a trade; and on the other hand, the N.C.O.s and men conditioned to obeying only simple drill orders and automatically regarding anything at all complicated as beyond them, a matter for the officers. Fortunately for himself, Gordon was on the brink of a quite different command, where officers and men were if anything too unruly and independent by half, requiring merely control and direction.

The Summer Palace was burning. Captain Gordon was burning it. 'Owing to the ill-treatment the (European) prisoners experienced at the Summer Palace,' he wrote, 'the General ordered it to be destroyed, and stuck up proclamations to say why it was so ordered. It appears that the victims were tied so tight by the wrists that the flesh mortified, and they died in the greatest torture. We accordingly went out, and, after pillaging it, burned the whole place, destroying in a Vandal-like manner most valuable property which would not be replaced for four millions. You can scarcely imagine the beauty and magnificence of the palaces. It made one's heart sore to burn them; in fact, these palaces were so large, and we were so pressed for time, that we could not plunder them carefully. It was wretchedly demoralising work for an army. Everybody was wild for plunder. The French have smashed everything in the most wanton way. It was a scene of utter destruction which passes my description. The people are civil, but I think the grandees hate us, as they must after what we did to the Palace.'

Gordon had arrived in China 'rather late for the amusement, which won't vex mother'. The Taku forts had fallen, and the Chinese utterly defeated in a single battle on the 9th September 1860. Enraged at this set-back at the hands of 'barbarians who live in the remote parts of the earth', the civilised Chinese retired on their capital, Peking, taking the Allied peace envoys with them. The random wrecking of the Summer Palace by the French troops and its systematic and thorough destruction by Gordon and his Engineers ended the war. The gates of Peking were opened and the European envoys — or the bodies thereof — were handed over. For Gordon, it was anti-climax.

The Crimean War had ended too soon for him and then, not feeling 'at all inclined to settle in England and be employed in a sedentary way', he had served, in his capacity as an expert surveyor, with various boundary commissions engaged in marking out the new frontiers. He spent a year in Bessarabia, along the Danube and the Black Sea; then six months in Armenia, during which he climbed nearly to the summit of Mount Ararat; followed by nine months in the Caucasus, not arriving back in England until the end of 1858. He had seen something of the wilder places of the world, and had enjoyed the experience, but his ambitions were for military distinction of a dramatic kind. The flamboyant Garibaldi was soon to be his inspiration. But his correspondence home, during the years 1856-58, contain much normal small talk on normal subjects. 'Our feeding is pretty good, but the drinking is not...' 'The wine was simply execrable...' 'How I wish I could get some partridge shooting!...' 'There is a Miss — here, the nicest girl I ever met; but don't be afraid, the dead do not marry.' Only in the latter statement is there something odd, for the place and the time. Certainly by the time of the Crimean campaign,

Gordon had decided to remain a bachelor for life, and had bouts of disgust at the flesh and of wishing himself dead; and after, of joking about it, and calling himself 'the dead man'. He was feverishly impatient, calm only in the face of death, which he truly did not fear much, if at all; always searching, for a belief, or for himself.

He was soon to find it, in events which had been building up in China even before he arrived, and continued to do so for several years while Gordon occupied his time in uninteresting construction work, for which the most he could say was, 'It's a grand thing being one's own master.' In fact, the decisive event had occurred in the year of his birth, 1833, when a young man from the south of China came to Canton to study for the Chinese equivalent of the Civil Service examinations; and subsequently failed them. Hung-sen-tsuen, as his name then was, contracted religious mania, while in Canton, from an American Baptist missionary, became a schoolmaster, pondered the tracts, and began to hector the neighbours on the subject of their false gods. After a further course of study under another American Baptist missionary, he had a revelation: he was, he found, none other than the younger brother of Jesus. His mission was to convert all China to the true faith and to replace the ruling Manchu dynasty by the Mings, deposed two centuries before. They would be represented by himself, under his new name and title of Tien Wang, King of Heaven. After many years in the wilderness, building up a following, he at last stirred the Peking Government into action and, in 1850, cut their expeditionary force to pieces. This was his cue to proclaim a state of Taiping, or Heavenly Peace, throughout China; and to launch his armies northwards to enforce it. This they did with dedication, slaughtering nearly 30,000 Manchus, men, women, and

32

children, at the capture of Nanking. In England, characteristically, there was a great wave of public sympathy with this new, and virtually Christian prophet, who was clearly leading an oppressed people to freedom, always rather a good thing; in many ways, their feelings resembled those of many Americans in their unconditional sympathy for Anti-Colonialist forces during and immediately after the Second World War. But disillusion was not long in coming. It arrived with the arrival of the Taipings in 1860 outside the walls of Shanghai.

'They first made their appearance in a northerly direction, near Woo-sung, the outpost, burning and sacking the towns and villages, while they brutally murdered many of the innocent inhabitants,' wrote Samuel Mossman, editor of the *North China Herald*, which was printed in Shanghai. 'They continued advancing towards Shanghai, when on the third day their flaunting flags were seen within a mile of the outskirts; while at night lurid flames flashed over the horizon from the buildings and farmsteads set on fire. All was commotion in the settlement. Only a few Indian troops and English soldiers could be assembled to form outposts for defence, while the municipal police patrolled the streets, armed with rifles and sword-bayonets, and the foreign residents had to guard their possessions with revolvers and other weapons in their hands, mustering their Chinese servants for defence, which was adopted at the *North China Herald* office. This anxious state continued for a few days and nights, when a snowstorm of unprecedented severity was hurled on the place from the Tartarian mountains, which providentially protected the settlement and suburbs. It commenced to snow heavily in the afternoon, and continued without interruption, day and night, for *fifty-eight* hours, covering the ground to the depth of *thirty* inches. The consequence was that all traffic on land was stopped, and impeded by ice on the waterways, and the rebels retired to towns a distance off, and formed entrenchments. The snow and ice held fast for three weeks, affording time for the arrival of reinforcements, and the construction of defences around Shanghai.'

The European powers, especially Britain, had just gone to war with the Imperial Government at Peking on a matter of trade, particularly the opium trade. As Lieutenant Thomas Lyster, R.E., was to write in 1862: 'Shanghai is a wonderful place: sixteen years ago it was only a small Chinese town; now it has quite the appearance of a large commercial city. There are no less than 246 ships in the harbour at present. Ports are being opened in the interior, and in a few years our trade in China will have increased enormously…' This could not be allowed to suffer, and, being absolutely neutral and non-aligned, the British drove the Imperial Forces back to Peking with the one hand while in Shanghai, with the other, they aided the Imperial Forces to drive back the rebels thirty miles from the town. When Gordon arrived in China, on his way to the front in 1860, he had seen the newly-severed heads of Taipings hung in baskets from the walls. The British policy was a perfectly consistent one of self-interest: they were intent on furthering their commerce and protecting it; but they were not interested in who governed China, and they did not intend to interfere if they could help it. In the same way, they were maintaining a cautious non-alignment in that other great civil war then raging — the one between the Northern and Southern States of America.

In the beginning, however, although the European regular forces were later to be drawn in, the defence of Shanghai against the advance of the rebels was a local matter for the local merchants, European and Chinese alike, to settle. This became very serious indeed after the fall of Soochow and nearer towns. The ruling Manchus were Mongols, a Tartar people not noted for sweetness and light; but the restorers of the Mings quite rivalled them. The main differences was visual: the Tartar Manchus had the front of their heads shaved, but wore it long at the back in pigtails; whereas, in defiance of enforced Manchu custom, the Taipings wore their hair long in the Beatnik or Beatle style. But there was nothing funny in what happened when they got hold of Manchus, and the city merchants had too much at stake in Shanghai to flee without a fight. As the Chinese Imperial Government maintained no unified standing army (one reason for the success of the rebellion), the defence force would have to be raised locally, in Shanghai, and paid for by the merchants themselves. This was one factor, and the existence in Shanghai at that time of a number of European adventurers and freebooters the other factor, behind the formation of what was eventually to be known as the 'Ever Victorious Army'.

The leading character among the foreign mercenaries was an American civilian, Frederick Townsend Ward, who had a long-standing hankering, and a genuine talent, for military glory; and here saw his chance. According to a contemporary account, 'Ward was born about 1828, at Salem, in Massachusetts, was a man of courage and ability. Probably from poverty he was unable, when a youth, to gratify his desire of studying at West Point; but his mind seems always to have been occupied with military matters, as affording his proper and destined sphere in life. Like not a few of his countrymen, he combined the life of an adventurer with that of a sailor, and had seen a good deal of the world before he came to China. In Central America he had been engaged in filibustering under that celebrated chief of filibusters, General William Walker; at Tuhwantepie he had been unsuccessfully engaged in trying to found a colony for the United States; and at one time in Mexico he had been on the point of taking military service under General Alvarez. Ward seems to have turned up in Shanghai some time in 1859.' In any event, on promise of a large sum of money if successful, in June 1860, he enlisted a fellow American, H. A. Burgevine, and a hundred-odd followers who might vaguely be called European, styled himself 'General' Ward, advanced on the Taiping-held town of Soong-keong, about twenty miles away, and, what was more, took it.

Success, and the high pay offered, as well as the opportunities for plunder, swelled the size of his army to 280 men, mostly from Manilla. The Chinese offered a further reward if he would take the next town, Singpoo, and lent him 10,000 troops from the Imperial Army under General Li-ai-duy. Ward put in a night attack, which he led in person; it was driven off and he himself was badly wounded in the jaw. Ignoring his injuries, he went back to Shanghai to recruit more mercenaries, returning with a hundred men, mostly Greeks and Italians. But before he could storm the town, he was taken in flank and bundled back to Soong-keong by the advance of a considerable Taiping force led by Chung Wang ('General' Chung), the most outstanding of the rebel commanders. Leaving him bottled up in Soong-keong, Chung Wang advanced to the assault of Shanghai, but was repeatedly repulsed from the walls by the detachments of British and French troops stationed there. As the Taipings then had their attentions diverted elsewhere, by the Imperial forces, and as the Europeans were at this point about to advance on Peking to force through their trade treaty with the Manchu throne, operations around Shanghai lapsed for a year; and Ward took advantage of this lull to make another attempt on Singpoo.

The European powers promptly had him arrested, in May 1861, and taken to Shanghai. His force was a standing temptation to their own men to get rich quick (there were said to be 29 deserters from the Royal Navy serving with him at this time); and in any case they did not want to get embroiled with the rebels unnecessarily. Ward was co-operative and ordered his second-in-command, 'Colonel' Burgevine, to desist; but, characteristically, Burgevine made one last attempt on the town. He was beaten by the Taipings, and his force disbanded.

By September 1861, however, Ward was allowed to reconstitute his force on a different basis: the ranks were to be formed of Chinese militiamen and peasants, armed and drilled as European soldiers were, and commanded by European officers. Raised at Soong-keong, where barracks were built for it, the miniature army was known, variously, as the 'Ward Force', the 'Soong-keong Force', or the 'Disciplined Chinese', until the Chinese authorities thought to raise morale by calling it the 'Chun chen chun' — the 'Ever Victorious Army'. Its first engagement was the capture of the nearby village of Quang-fu-ling in February 1862, more or less a Company operation, and by the end of the month, with growing European approval, the 'Army' had increased to the strength of a Regiment — 1,500 men, officered mainly by seamen of many nations, and four 12-pounder mountain howitzers. The rebels were now proving so troublesome that it was decided to clear them away from the immediate vicinity of Shanghai, to a distance of thirty miles if possible. The task was undertaken, initially, by a combined and somewhat motley force consisting of a British detachment of 336 seamen and marines led by Admiral Sir James Hope, a French detachment of 160 seamen led by Admiral Protet, and 600 men of the 'Soong-keong Force' led by General Ward.

Burgevine was wounded, but remained in action, during the taking of the first town, Kachaiou; and was again wounded, this time severely in the stomach, at the taking of the next, Tseedong, from 6,000 Taipings. In consequence of this action the Peking Government decreed, on 16th March 1862, that Ward's men should be known as the Chun chen chun, the 'Ever Victorious'.

In this month there was a change of overall command. The British General, Sir John Michel, went home, and was succeeded by Brigadier-General C. W. Staveley, formerly the commander at Tientsin, where Gordon was also stationed at this time. Staveley backed Admiral Hope's recommendation that a thirty-mile cordon should be drawn round Shanghai, and prepared to enforce it by bringing down more British troops and concluding an arrangement with the Peking Government to provide reliable occupation forces to garrison the towns he intended to capture. This latter force amounted to 9,000 men from Hoonan, who were used to the soldier's trade, regarded then in China as a lowly and brutalising occupation. Their 'transfer fee', paid by the Shanghai merchants, both European and Chinese, was £7 per head. In April, Staveley sallied out and captured three towns, Wong-ka-da, Isipoo, and Kahding, Admiral Hope being wounded at the former place. The latter town was fairly typical, not merely of the province, but of Shanghai also, and its appearance at the time was fully described in the *North China Herald*, edited by Samuel Mossman, who covered the campaign in great detail:

'Kah-ding presents the usual appearance of a Chinese city in the province of Kiang-soo, with crenelated walls forming a complete circle round it, extending six or seven miles, and about fifteen feet high, similar to the dimensions of the wall round Shanghai, and classed in Chinese topography as a "Hyen or Hien", signifying a city of the third order. It has four gates, opening at the cardinal points of the compass; adjoining which are four water channels from Soochow Creek, which intersect the interior with a network of canals, crossed by thirty-two bridges. The thoroughfares of the south-west angle of the city were not built over, and the remainder appeared to have contained numerous well-constructed houses, many of them demolished, while the principal mandarin residences had been preserved for the use of the Taiping chiefs. One of these appeared to have been occupied by the military leader of the insurgents, as two iron guns were placed at the entrance, evidently of English manufacture, and marked "B.P. & Co.," with a crown and date, 1861.' Mossman added, 'But this only represents one of the strongholds held by the insurgents in the provinces covering the Yang-tsze Delta, which at that time numbered about one hundred. Of these the city and port of Ningpo was next to Shanghai in importance. It is the provincial capital of Che-kiang, situated at the confluence of two small rivers, which form a canal from the city to the sea. These streams water a plain encompassed on every side with hills, forming a natural amphitheatre, whose diameter from east to west is about eighteen miles, and some twenty miles from north to south. The plain is densely dotted with villages and hamlets, around which the ground is so level and highly cultivated that it resembles a large garden. It is intersected by numerous canals, formed by the springs that descend from the hills, the principal one being about ten miles long and sixty feet wide. The walls of the city are built of compact masonry, the freestone being quarried in the hills.'

This town was General Staveley's first objective for the sortie which he made in May. Clearly, like the others, it was not an easy proposition: the countryside was simple to defend, consisting of the usual network of waterways; the city itself was ringed by the usual moat and strong masonry walls, mounting seventy guns; and the defenders, some 15,000 strong, were in Mossman's words, 'a formidable enemy to contend with'. Many of them were well-armed, for gun-running was rife. 'Guns were imported by the hundred, small arms by the thousand, and ammunition by the ton,' wrote Mossman. 'One ship, the *Paragon*, was seized with 300 pieces of ordnance in her hold, 100 cases of small arms, and 50 tons of ammunition on board; the arms were all of the best foreign manufacture, with flasks of the strongest English gunpowder.' The people responsible were, he wrote, 'smugglers and foreign renegades, many of them English traders. It is very hard for a brave soldier or sailor to lose his life under an enemy's legitimate weapons and mode of warfare; but when he meets his fate from arms and ammunition of his own country's manufacture, and supplied to the enemy by his own money-grubbing countrymen, it is still harder to bear.' But Ningpo had one weak point: it was one of the former Treaty Ports, with water deep enough to float small warships. Four British vessels and two French dismounted by bombardment the Taiping batteries, and the seamen stormed the town. Halfway through the afternoon of the assault, 10th May, the Union Jack went up on the Salt Gate, the Chinese Imperial forces then joined in, and the rebels fled through the West Gate.

Meanwhile the main land force had simultaneously set out to capture Tsing-pu, another 'Hien', or city of the third order. The British component consisted of 1,429 soldiers with 20 guns and mortars, plus a Naval Brigade of 380 men with 5 guns; the French contributed 800 soldiers and seamen with 10 guns; the 'Ever Victorious' were present to the tune of some 2,000 men; and there were also detachments of the Chinese

Imperial forces. The engineer tasks, particularly the important one of bridging the moat in front of the 15-feet high walls, were entrusted to the Royal Engineers. Gordon, still a Captain, had come down from Tientsin a few days before and commanded them in person. As an essential preliminary to success in assaulting these defended towns was a thorough reconnaissance, this was carried out at the highest level and consisted of General Staveley, Admiral Protet, and Captain Gordon, R.E. In his official despatch, the General wrote:

'Captain Gordon was of the greatest use to me. He reconnoitred the enemy's defences, and arranged for the ladder parties to cross the moats, and for the escalading of the works; for we had to attack and carry by storm several towns fortified with high walls and deep wet ditches. He was, however, at the same time a source of much anxiety to me from the daring manner he approached the enemy's works to acquire information. Previous to our attack on Tsing-pu, and when with me in a boat reconnoitring the place, he begged to be allowed to land in order better to see the nature of the defences; presently, to my dismay, I saw him gradually going nearer and nearer, by rushes from cover to cover, until he got behind a small outlying pagoda within 100 yards of the wall, and here he was quietly making a sketch and taking notes. I, in the meantime, was shouting myself hoarse in trying to get him back, for not only were the rebels firing at him from the walls, but I saw a party stealing round to cut him off.' On the 12th May, the bombardment began, the French gunboat No. 12 bringing great cascades of rubble from the wall with her 64-pounder rifled guns; two breaches were made; two bridges of boats were put across the moat in front of them by the Royal Engineers and the French seamen; and the assault went in. Tsing-pu fell with trifling loss.[1]

The force, travelling mainly by water in an amazing collection of craft, many of them Chinese, some the size and shape of coffins, then moved back nearer Shanghai to winkle out those Taipings who were controlling an area near the walls from the defended villages of Nan-jao and Cho-lin. 'Controlling' is perhaps not the right word: 'marauding' would be better; for a wilderness of flame and smoke and tattered corpses was left behind wherever the Taipings passed: a peace of a sort. But so inappropriate that they were now more usually referred to as 'Chang-mows', the European spelling of the Chinese for 'long-haired ones'. On 17th May, the guns crumpled the walls of Nan-jao; the storming parties rushed forward, the rebels, hidden at the base of the wall during the bombardment, manned the parapets with a yell and a hail of fire; the British light guns replied; and the stormers swept forward again, finding a way in by climbing the walls, as the French did, or crawling in through the embrasures, as the English did. At this point Admiral Protet, at the head of the attackers in spite of his fifty-four years, fell back mortally wounded and died that night. 'The town was a wretched affair,' wrote Gordon, 'and a good many Chang-mows escaped. These Chang-mows are ruthlessly cruel, and have a system of carrying off small boys under the hope of training them up as rebels. We always found swarms of these boys who had been taken from their parents (whom the rebels had killed) in the provinces. I saved one small creature who had fallen into the ditch in trying to escape, for which he rewarded me by destroying my coat with his muddy paws in clinging to me. I

---

[1] The contemporary writers rarely agree as to the English spelling of the names of Chinese towns — Mossman calls it *Tsing-poo*; Staveley calls it *Tsing-pu*; and Hake, editing some of Gordon's MSS regarding the campaign, produces the same sound by writing *Sinpoo*.

started soon after for the attack on Cho-lin. We got our guns in position during the night, opened fire next morning, and assaulted at seven.'

This time, few Chang-mows escaped; they were impeded in their flight by their own barricades. 'They were jammed at one of the gates, where many were shot down,' wrote Mossman. 'The moat appeared full of drowned and wounded, spears by hundreds were floating on the water, and were strewn all over the ground. The frightened foe had even thrown away a number of their muskets, and some double-barrelled guns, a very unusual thing for the Chinese to do. The slaughter was great, as almost every house entered by the victors contained dead and dying rebels.' The stronghold was then destroyed, and the force returned to Shanghai with every appearance of success. But, meanwhile, the Chinese Imperial forces, becoming over-confident, launched an attack on the town of Taitsan. This drew a countermove from the Taiping general, Chung Wang, who virtually annihilated them on 16th May, barely 2,000 escaping, and then drove on to recapture most of the places taken by Staveley's force and garrisoned either by the Imperialists or by Ward's Chinese. These latter the rebels now referred to contemptuously as the 'Cha-Yang-Kweitzer', or 'False Foreign Devils', on account of their European-style dress, equipment, and drill.

'The affrighted villagers were flocking into the settlement for protection in thousands,' wrote Mossman, who was reporting the new rebel advance for his paper. 'The incendiary fires among the farms and villages to the north and north-west were burning to within three miles of the fortified post at Stone Bridge. It was a pitiful sight to see the crowds of poor villagers, chiefly old men, women, and children, trudging along with a scanty supply of food and clothing from their deserted homesteads, and left to the firebrands of the merciless Taipings. The foreigners were no longer looked on as enemies, but friends.' The garrisons cut off by the rebel advance were relieved and evacuated, but not much more could be done. 'By this time the weather was oppressively hot,' wrote Mossman, 'creating malaria in the lowlands and marshes of the Delta; while overhead the sickly south-west monsoon swept along, with the same temperature and humidity during the day and night. A portion of the force marched out with some fieldpieces, to try and come across the enemy. As they proceeded among the farms, and through the fields of corn, they saw numerous dead bodies of innocent country people murdered by the ruthless Tai-pings. Villages were smouldering that these destroyers had set fire to. Every now and then, in front, and on either side, fresh flames and smoke arose, revealing the presence of these blasphemers of the Christian creed. It is simply impossible to seize the cunning, cruel cowards, in the labyrinthine lanes of the Delta. All around they have spies on our movements, so they are comparatively safe in continuing their incendiary tactics within a few hundred yards of our column; then off they escape through ditches and across fields, where it is impossible to get at them. This the rascals are perfectly aware of, especially if pursued by foreign soldiers, encumbered with their heavy equipment. Hunting grasshoppers in a hayfield with foxhounds would be a more sensible occupation than sending soldiers about a country intersected by a network of creeks, in the expectation of catching swift-footed and slippery-skinned Tai-pings.'

How was this problem to be solved?

CHAPTER FOUR: 'HEAVENLY PEACE'

'The Heavenly Father sits on the throne above.
The Heavenly Brother Christ is the next honourable, sitting
on the right of the Father, excelled by no man.
By the Grace of the Father and Brother we sit on His left.
United as one we reign.
Disobey the Heavenly Will and you will be ground to pieces
with a pestle.'

— *Edict of the 'Heavenly King'*, 1862.

'The wonderful marches and conquests of Chung Wang and
the other rebel leaders will be understood when it is explained
that as a rule the Chinese have no standing army; and that the
governors of provinces are also independent of each other.
The rebels' advance was sure to cause the lower classes of the
large cities to become turbulent, being glad of any excuse to
plunder; these men, aided by secret rebel emissaries, spread
alarming reports. Fire would then break out in different
directions and demoralisation take place. The rebels now begin
to advance, burning along the route; and while fires and the
fugitives cause more and more confusion in the city, some
rebels now enter in disguise, and when at length the advanced
guards of the Changmaous (or long-haired) appear, these and
the lower classes rise, and the conquest is complete.

'In proceeding against the rebels at first a district is passed
through where the people are evidently disturbed, but have not
yet left their houses, having their things ready packed; then
comes a district where fugitive country people are hurrying
past, laden with all the household goods they can carry, leading

bullocks, and rushing past in countless numbers — men, women and children in inextricable confusion. Then comes a district quite deserted except by a few who are hanging about in a furtive way about their houses, and who are probably rebel spies or emissaries; then comes a district of which nearly every house or hamlet is on fire, the volume of smoke ascending in every direction, among which are forms running and hurrying here and there, and a stray flag or two appears in the distance; and then comes the rebel forces struggling along by tens or twenties — a set of locusts devouring the country and held in universal detestation by the people. They take a fiendish pleasure in taking life, mutilating if they do not kill everyone they meet, branding them on the face with the characters "Taeping", "Teen Kwokh", or "Heavenly Kingdom of Universal Peace".'

This extract from what is in effect a handbook on antiguerrilla warfare in nineteenth-century China,[2] has a surprisingly up-to-date ring, with many modern applications (unlike the Crimea, where the influence of a now outmoded technology in transition on the form of the fighting left little worth studying). There is a mixture of both Nazi and Marxist methods, particularly the application of the latter to modern China, Malaysia, and Indo-China (Viet-nam and Viet-cong). There is, firstly, the existence of a city proletariat, and, secondly, a weak and disjointed system of government power, exercised by a ruling class which is really a ruling race. Outside, there is the existence of an irregular force composed of natural fighting men, many drawn in by the focus of power and

---

[2] *Events in the Taeping Rebellion*, being reprints of MSS copied by General Gordon, C.B. in his own handwriting, with monograph, introduction, and notes by A. Egmont Hake (W. H. Allen, London, 1891).

plunder, but powered basically by a world-wide revelationary dogma having some of the outward aspects of a religion, but none at its heart. There is the use, in practice, of 'fifth-columnists' and infiltrators of all kinds, to get information, to sow dissemination, rumour, and confusion; to produce an attack on morale from the bottom upwards; as used on a small scale and in a few places by the Nazis, and on an enormous scale, ranging from subtle suggestion and penetration to all-out war, by the Marxists. There is, ultimately, with the victory of the subversive forces, the emergence of rule by terror and torture, which serves also to ease the way to the next step, combined with a rigid insistence on conformity to the new dogma by the crude method of branding on the face, now succeeded by attempts to 'brainwash', or brand the new infallibility on the minds of the conquered. In short, the revolutionary movement appears on-stage with an appeal in both hands: in the left hand 'Loot the shops, rob the rich, down with the ruling classes, all out on the streets'; and in the right hand, to the rulers, 'It isn't any use, you'd better give in, the future is with us.' If the proletariat do come out on the streets, and if the rulers do funk it, then the curtain comes down, not with the hammer and sickle, but with death and a branding iron. And, inevitably, then as now, the fall of the curtain is greeted by prolonged, violent applause, amounting to a 'standing ovation', from a host of well-meaning, humane, tender-hearted, totally irresponsible and misinformed liberals (with a small 'l'). Even Gordon, subjected to the pro-Taiping propaganda barrage before he came out to China, had swallowed some of the guff; and it took reality to change his views.

As in modern times, the propaganda was spread abroad by foreign converts; there was, even then, some sort of organisation behind the phenomenon, centred on the missionaries, mostly American and Methodist. No colonial administrator or soldier has ever yet liked a missionary — except a medical missionary. In their eyes, they are dangerous meddlers. And certainly wrong. The 'right' religion for a native people is their own religion, not a foreign import. This necessarily denies that there is any such thing as a 'world' religion, although not necessarily that each religion might not be a geographically oriented view of much the same thing. The officials of the 'colonial powers' in the century of expanding European empires preferred almost always not to interfere with native rule or customs, and particularly *not* to meddle with their religious beliefs. It was the Taipings, therefore, who were wearing the 'new look', which was to emerge in the twentieth century, upon Organisation-Man, in the form of rapidly won, giant dogma-empires, based on foreign enforced belief. Present-day Russia and China show all of the symptoms, and America some of them. And, as in the present day, there were always misguided fellow-travellers prepared at the drop of a hat to enact the odd spectacle of vegetarians worshipping in a slaughterhouse. Mr. F. W. A. Bruce, the British resident diplomat in China, reported in 1862 to Lord John Russell:

'Mr. Roberts, an American missionary, from whom the Taeping leader Hung se tsuen received some religious instruction, has joined the insurgents at Sou-chow. He has described, in a letter which will no doubt be published, one of their religious meetings at which he attended, having previously dined with their leader Le (styled the "Chung Wang"). It consisted of the offering up of large heaps of provisions before an altar erected in honour of Shang-ti. The assemblage knelt in silence for a couple of minutes, then a short prayer was read from a paper, which was burnt, and a hymn was sung. Mr.

Roberts may be presumed to take a favourable view of their religious observances. But at his own request he was permitted to preach, and he states that his discourse was directed against sacrifice, and contained a strong remonstrance against the cruelties committed by the insurgents, as alienating from them the sympathies of foreigners. I entertain little hope of his exhortations producing any effect on the conduct of his friends.'

However, the British, unlike the Taipings, were not in China to conquer it, but to trade; and as soon as possible they withdrew their own men from the fighting and left the rebels to Ward's force, which by the summer of 1862 consisted, according to Mossman, of '1,200 men, drilled in manual and platoon exercise, carrying breach-loading rifles; and with a battery of 12-pounder howitzers and two 32-pounder guns, admirably handled by a corps of native artillerymen, with foreign officers. This, of course, was due to the American, Ward, who, no more than an ordinary civilian, possessed of pluck and perseverance, was proud of his rank as Major-General in the Chinese service, and was said to have ambitious hopes of rising to a higher command.'

Meanwhile, Gordon had been given the task of surveying the area around Shanghai to a distance of thirty miles from the walls (where that was possible). No accurate maps existed and operations were hampered by this fact. This being Gordon's forte, in a short time he had a detailed map of the whole vast area in his head; which was to be of incalculable importance later. 'I have been now in every town and village in the thirty miles' radius,' he wrote. 'The country is the same everywhere — a dead flat, with innumerable creeks and bad pathways. There is nothing of any interest in China; if you have seen one village you have seen all the country. We had a visit from the marauding Taepings the other day. We went against them and drove them away, but did not kill many. They beat us into fits in getting over the country, which is intersected in every way with ditches, swamps, etc. They are rapidly on the decline, and two years ought to bring about the utter suppression of the revolt.'

To aid him with the survey, Gordon was given an assistant, Lieutenant Thomas Lyster, R.E., who had just come out from England. On 28 August 1862, Lyster wrote to his mother: 'There is another Engineer officer here, Captain Gordon; he is a first-rate fellow, and a very good officer. I suppose you know all about the Taipings. They number about 100,000. We could see the smoke from the burning villages as soon as we got into the harbour at Shanghai on Sunday, the 24th. I borrowed a horse and went out. I never saw, or could have imagined, such a sight. The road was covered with unfortunate creatures, who had been driven out of their homes by the Taipings. The poor women were in a most fearful state; there were numbers of them lying by the side of the road, some dead, and others dying from starvation and exhaustion. I was horrified then, but have become used to it now, as it is an every-day occurrence. It is impossible to get near the rebels unless you surround them.'

The Taipings were like ghosts, leaving as the sign of their passing only wraiths of smoke from burning villages rising in the still air. In fact, troops could pass within a few feet of them without being aware that they were there. Already, on 26 August, Lyster had been out with Gordon, trying to catch a raiding band, without much success. 'We got two prisoners; one was taken by our party; he was up to his neck in water (like the old boy in the Pomptine Marshes).' Any ditch or marsh could hide hundreds of them. 'I was introduced to General Ward, the American, who is an officer in the service of the

Chinese Government; in fact, he has been made a mandarin; he is a quiet-looking little man, with very bright eyes, but is a regular fire-eater; he has saved £60,000. He is married to a Chinese.' But on 2nd October, he wrote to his sister: 'Nothing new here, except that we are to remain for the winter. We have not killed any Taipings since, although they have managed to kill General Ward.'

Ward fell at the head of his men, assaulting the third-grade town of Tse-kee, on 21st September. 'Remarks were freely expressed and printed on the character and career of the deceased,' wrote Mossman, 'the most favourable coming from the representatives of his country and countrymen. Without quoting any of these, it may be said all agreed, that, whatever General Ward's antecedents may have been, it was impossible to deny him the possession of sterling stuff, as regards his courage and coolness in battle, together with talents, not merely to have enabled him to attain to the height of a respectable military position, but to keep himself there in spite of enemies among the military mandarins. When in action he never flourished a weapon, but directed his men with a walking-cane, a style of command followed by his successor, Gordon.'

Gordon was one step nearer his destiny: the solution of the difficult military problem presented by the elusive Taipings. The English had had their reservations about Ward, because he was clearly an adventurer, and, what was worse, an American one. Both he and Burgevine were fairly representative of that type which shortly afterwards 'Won the West'; the clumsiest, most incompetent, senselessly cruel slice of empire-building ever committed. Empires were best built and administered by gentlemen, the English felt, and not without reason. The Americans were shortly to try to exterminate their Indians, the few survivors fleeing north to Canada, then a colony managed by English or Scottish gentlemen, who did not find it necessary to commit genocide before taking over control of tribal territory. But Ward had eventually earned their grudging respect; 'Colonel' Burgevine was a different matter, being younger and more impulsive, and suffering still from the effects of his wounds. But, largely because of pressure from the American community, and because he was already known to them, Burgevine was appointed to command the 'Ever Victorious', which for a while he handled most ably.

An early test was on 24th October, at the re-taking of Kahding against not very determined opposition by a combined force. Gordon, who was mentioned in despatches, was in charge of the engineer tasks and Lieutenant Lyster was responsible for building the bridge across which the stormers would enter. 'Engineer' sounds a cushy job; but properly speaking, this was what is now called 'Assault' engineering, in which the engineers precede the infantry, and not the other way round. 'There were about twenty-seven guns, including French and Ward's Chinese troops,' wrote Lyster. 'On Friday morning we opened fire from all batteries at daylight. It was a grand sight to see the shells breaking down the wall and look-out places. I, with a naval officer, had charge of the boats in which were the ladders and bridges.' After ninety minutes' bombardment, Lyster took the boats up a creek to the wall and then moved them 250 yards along the moat until he found the best place for a bridge, firing with a rifle meanwhile at the Taipings on the wall above who were firing down on him. 'We formed the bridge in a very short space of time, and then the storming party got across, and had no trouble in getting into the town, there being only a palisading to clear away. When I got over the wall I found a lot of Taipings within a few yards of me; I sent a shot amongst them, and told them to *"wilo"*, which means "hook it". They all took to their heels, and I bolted after them as hard as I could go, but had to wait in the middle of the town till a soldier of the 67th Regiment and two of Ward's officers came up. We then went on together and took about twenty prisoners. We were very near being cut off, but we hooked behind a house and waited till the main body came up. Ward's men wanted to shoot them right and left, but I saved as many poor wretches as I could. I was obliged to hit a couple of fellows — I was obliged to pepper one in the hams before he dropped his spear. I am happy to say that I did not kill one of them, and tried to save a good many. I told them to "hook it", as I knew the Chinese troops which were coming after us would kill them without mercy. I pitied the poor women toddling away on their little (bound) feet. A soldier near me fired into a crowd of men, women, and children, and killed a nicely-dressed woman. I would not let him fire again, except at single individuals.' It was not until several letters later that Lyster happened to mention that half his party had become casualties during the short time they were erecting the bridge under fire.

Lyster, a long-faced, grave looking young man, embodied most of the best qualities of the British soldier, officer and man, of the empire-building phase. Unlimited arrogance expressed in actions, not words: an engineer, he was first into the town and pushed on without waiting for the storming party; his immediate reaction to the rebels was to shout at them, not shoot them, assuming that the mere appearance of a British officer should be enough to make them bolt, which it did. An aversion to unnecessary bloodshed expressed in actions, not words: the deliberate sparing of life, where possible, and the arrogant overriding of others less scrupulous, combined with genuine pity for the helpless, even when they were part of a not very savoury band of marauders. Anything less like the modern, Hollywood, pulp back, and telly ethic of the 'tough guy' could not be imagined. There can be no argument as to which is the better of the two; and little doubt as to which is really the toughest. Lyster had no need to prove his manhood by putting on an 'act'. Nor was he impressed by the superficially 'desperado' aspect of the Taipings. He 'disliked and despised' the Chinese. He wrote, shrewdly, 'The Japanese are far superior to the Chinese in every way, and if we come to blows we shall have some tough work cut out for us.' An epic prophecy if ever there was one.

Of Burgevine he wrote, 'He seems to be rather a nice fellow. Ward's force is officered by Europeans: a good many are Irishmen, but they are a very bad lot. Burgevine would be glad to get rid of them. Burgevine was educated at West Point Military School; his brother is adjutant-general in the Southern army. I don't know what brought him here; he is married to a Chinese woman. Poor old Ward is buried here in Chinese fashion — his coffin over-ground. He came out to China as mate of a ship, outlawed from America, and has died worth a million and a half. He was often wounded, and people had the idea he could not be shot. The drilled Chinese are officered by civilians, sailors, and private soldiers discharged from our service, *not one* of whom could direct any operations. Kohding is now garrisoned by 5,000 Imperial troops; but they are sure to run away the first time they are attacked. I have no time for photography here, but I have begun to study Chinese. I have a real live prince living with me — Prince Frederick of Wittgenstein.'

The latter, a member of the 1st Prussian Lancer Guard Regiment, was the British General Staveley's aide-de-camp.

Staveley's despatch concluded: 'The recapture of Kohding completes the radius of thirty miles round Shanghai which it was decided should be cleared of the Taeping rebels.' This was satisfactory for the European powers, who thereupon entered into an under the counter truce with the rebels, to respect the *status quo* established by military force. It was less satisfactory to the commanders of the Ward Force, as Lyster makes clear: 'Burgevine is very well paid by the Chinese, getting £4,000 a year and a *Kumpshaw* (present) for every city he takes. I do not get any extra pay here, as I am in the Queen's service, but the English officers who are drilling the Chinese get £1,200 a year for it. There is talk of taking Nankin from the rebels. Some English officers may be allowed to direct the operations. If so, the place will probably be taken. I will do my best to go. But I think it is very like that Captain Gordon, R.E., will go. If he does, they have the best man in China to show them the way? Nanking was 200 miles away, and the centre of the entire Taiping revolt; it was rash of Burgevine, on the strength of a single victory, the taking in November of a fortified village, to suggest so ambitious a scheme. But needs must when the devil drives, and several devils were nibbling at Burgevine. First, the merchants of Shanghai, with much of the danger removed, were becoming reluctant to pay heavy sums merely to maintain in a state of unemployment a force which now numbered 5,000 men. Second, they doubted Burgevine's loyalty and suspected him of wanting to set up an independent state of his own in China, ruled by himself. Third, they resented his arrogance and bad manners. Fourth, he resented the way in which their generals had taken the credit for the single victory which he had won. Most certainly, something grand and sweeping had to be proposed.

Gordon summed him up: 'He was a man of large promises and few works. His popularity was great among a certain class. He was extravagant in his generosity, and as long as he had anything would divide it with his so-called friends, but never was a man of any administrative or military talents, and latterly, through the irritation caused by his unhealed wound and other causes, he was subject to violent paroxysms of anger, which rendered precarious the safety of any man who tendered to him advice that might be distasteful. He was extremely sensitive of his dignity? An excellent subject — and hero — for some types of Hollywood film; but not the man to deal with the devious and difficult Chinese, who were the proud hereditary rulers and, besides, held the purse-strings. The 'Ever Victorious' cost £30,000 a month and, since the death of Ward, there had been little to show for it. Early in December 1862 the Futai Li and another senior Chinese official came to General Staveley, and, giving their reasons, asked that he replace Burgevine with a British officer.

Staveley replied that he could not do this without authority from his own Government, to whom he would report their request. Both sides knew that this would take many months, apart from Civil Service delays, because of the length of the sea voyage involved. 'General Staveley,' wrote Mossman, 'from the very first had disapproved of the force and its composition. His ideas were that if the Chinese Government wished to organise their army they should be assisted to do so in a proper manner. Neither he nor Mr. Bruce ever liked these forces, officered by a nobody of men who, however brave, were not all of a class which represent the foreigner in his best light to the Chinese. General Staveley would sooner have seen the force broken up than any assistance given it in this shape. For he saw ahead, and considered what would be the finale of it when the rebellion was over.' Such forces tend to turn 'pirate', but in the meantime there was the immediate danger of the 'Ever Victorious' going over en masse to the Taipings. From commander to private, they were in it for the money, the plunder, and Chinese women. Eventually, it was Burgevine himself who precipitated matters.

'On the 4th of January 1863,' wrote Mossman, 'General Burgevine arrived in Shanghai from Soong-keong, and marched into the Settlement with his bodyguard. Leaving them outside the residence of Ta-kee, a mandarin of considerable wealth and influence, who acted as financial officer to the disciplined corps, he entered the premises in a hostile mood. An altercation commenced immediately between them, which led to recriminations on both sides. A good deal of violent language was used, Ta-kee being able to speak broken English fluently. This ended in Burgevine striking the mandarin in the face with his clenched fist, until he drew blood. Afterwards he called his bodyguard into the Treasury. Then he ordered his men to take £10,000. In the *North China Herald* I commented very strongly on this high-handed, scandalous proceeding, which elicited an explanation from him at a personal interview. He excused himself by declaring that his men were in a state of mutiny, from not receiving their arrears of pay.' The story was much longer and more complicated than that, and may be read both in Mossman's *General Gordon's Private Diary of his Exploits in China* (Sampson Low, 1885) and in Hake's *Events in the Taeping Rebellion*, which includes Burgevine's written defence of himself. But the vital facts are that conduct noble and even heroic when enacted before the cameras in the Honky-Tonk Saloon at Dead Man's Gulch was both inexcusable and foolish when introduced into diplomacy; that Burgevine was summarily dismissed by the Chinese, General Staveley assisting; and that the 'Ever Victorious' would require a new commander — the third in five months.

CHAPTER FIVE: A QUESTION OF COMMAND

'When first the war with China began, Sir James Graham, a sagacious man, warned this house of the danger that must arise from entering into war with a third portion of the human race. What then must be the advantages to this country if it can have unimpeded commerce with one-third of the human race? It is for our interests, therefore, that tranquillity should be restored in China.' — *Lord Palmerston, during a debate in the House of Commons,* May 1864.

There were a number of candidates for the vacant post of commander of the 'Ever Victorious Army'. They included even the ambitious Doctor Macartney, until recently surgeon to the British 99th Regiment. The Chinese preferred a British officer, to be nominated by General Staveley. General Staveley recommended instead that Colonel Forester, an American who had been with the force for some time already, should be given first offer. Forester refused, resigned, and returned to America. Staveley's final suggestion was to leave Captain Holland, of the Marine Light Infantry, a British officer already attached to the force, in temporary command; and to recommend Captain Gordon, R.E., for the permanent command, if the approval of H.M. Government could be obtained. There was no reason to think that it would be. Bruce, the British diplomatic representative, did not want the irregular force to have a permanent British commander at all, because this would in effect commit H.M. Government to intervention in the Chinese Civil War. Instead, he suggested that a Prussian should have the permanent command; the German States, unlike Britain, had no great commercial trading stakes in China which might be hazarded. The point at issue was that, within the agreed thirty-mile limit round Shanghai, the British were merely defending their legitimate interests, a point well understood by the rebels. But if serving British officers headed a drive which might lead to the Taeping capital, they would be irretrievably involved in war with the rebels. And if the Taipings won?...

The British force in the Far East was small and thinly stretched, for simultaneously there was trouble of a similar sort in Japan, which was soon to require the attentions of a naval force. As Lieutenant Lyster told his brother: 'There is a slight chance of our being sent to Japan to arrange some difference between the natives and resident merchants. A question has arisen as to the legality of the indiscriminate slaughter of the latter by the former. It has not been settled yet, and there is a likelihood of there being more noise about it than is generally calculated on.' This fundamental point, that the British wanted trade not territory, and were uneager to fritter away limited forces in interminable profitless wars, was to recur continually and have a decisive effect on the fortunes of Gordon in later years. It sprang, of course, from the unalterable fact that Britain was basically a small island with great, but unbalanced resources, which had to trade or die.

While the mails went by sea to London, and London considered, Captain Holland took over command of the 'Ever Victorious' and Gordon went on with his survey of the delta. Lyster wrote of the map they were making: It is an immense thing... The General is delighted with it, and everyone says the Engineers deserve a great deal of credit. My share was small, but Gordon worked day and night,' The work was exciting and the method was to penetrate the country through the maze of small waterways, protected by an armed escort; then return after ten or twelve days to plot in on the master map the details of each tour. No recognisable maps of the area then existed. Lyster was less enchanted with Captain Holland: 'He actually told me, when I was at Sung-Kiang, and had an argument with him about the last French and Austrian campaign, that he did not believe in *tactics*! He had no idea beyond brute force. My idea is, that with a small number of drilled Chinese against a large number of rebels, you should take every advantage of superior knowledge.'

However, administratively, the 'Ever Victorious' was put on a much more sound footing. Holland worked in liaison with a Chinese military mandarin; the system of payment was put on a trouble free basis; the unchecked, unaccounted for spendings on immense and unnecessary military works was curtailed; the soldiers were no longer 'outside the law', and able to bully and plunder as they pleased; and the unnecessarily large 'tail' of the force, its unskilled labourers and junks, was rigorously trimmed down. The numbers were reduced to a fixed 'war establishment' of 3,000 rank and file, 300 labourers (or Pioneer) corps, 100 boatmen and the crews of the war steamers, exclusive of the foreign officers, hospital staff, and interpreters. The mobile field artillery consisted of twenty-eight 12-pounder howitzers, two 8-inch mortars, four Cohorn mortars, and two 32-pounder siege guns, with 300 rounds of ammunition apiece; there were two 18-pounders and four 32-pounders for the static defence of their base at Soong-keong, also with 300 rounds each. The 'punch' provided by this artillery was a vital factor in overcoming fixed defences manned by overwhelmingly large numbers of rebels, some 30 per cent of whom were armed with modern European rifles and revolvers, and had artillery of their own. Another vital factor was the movement of such heavy and unwieldy equipment, ammunition, and stores across a marshy delta crisscrossed only by small paths and canals. To be successful, a general would need thoroughly to understand the siting and use of artillery, know the country thoroughly, and be an efficient staff and administrative officer. A man who was merely a dashing company commander would not do.

'Respecting the equipment and small arms of the force, these were found to be excellent,' wrote Mossman. 'First in order was the bodyguard of 100 men, who were armed with the short French rifle and sword-bayonet. These men were the *élite* of the corps, selected for distinguished gallantry in the field and general good conduct. They had never misbehaved either in action or in garrison; and had been repeatedly employed in suppressing disturbances among the other soldiers. The rifle battalion, 650 strong, was armed with the German government rifle and bayonet; and the remainder of the infantry with the new British Tower musket, recently imported from London. The whole force had been rearmed, and equipped throughout with buff-leather belts and other accoutrements, exactly the same as are worn by British infantry of the line.

'The uniform was made easy and suitable for the climate. A bright green turban formed the head-gear of all ranks. The jackets of every branch of the service was made of English cloth, and cut in shape something between those of the Zouave and Highland regiments. Those of the bodyguard were dark blue, with scarlet facings and green shoulder-straps, bearing their designation in Chinese characters. Those of the artillery were light blue with the same facings, scarlet shoulder-straps, and a broad scarlet stripe down the trousers. The infantry wore a rifle-green uniform; the different battalions being distinguished by the colours of the shoulder-straps, on which were stamped the wearer's regimental number in English and Chinese. The whole force wore knickerbocker trousers the colour of their jackets; and as they preferred the Chinese shoes with satin uppers and thick felt soles, under gaiters, to any foreign boots or shoes, they were allowed to wear them. This was the winter uniform. In the summer they were clad in a white dress with red facings, similar to the *kakee* clothes worn by British troops in India. They wore a coloured blanket, red or blue, on ordinary occasions, like a Highland plaid, thereby adding greatly to the picturesque appearance of the uniform, which was pronounced to be one of the most convenient and serviceable worn by any native corps in Asia. The pay of the private soldier was eight dollars per month, out of which he supplied himself with rations and fuel, except when on the line of march or in the field, when these were furnished by the Government.' A similar method of rationing was used by the British Commandos during the Second World War, the object being to encourage self-reliance and initiative.

The force looked to be a good one, and the appointment of Holland, a professional soldier, to be an advance on Ward and Burgevine, who were civilians and therefore merely amateur soldiers. Mossman thought so, and as he wryly admitted, committed himself to his opinion in print at the time. Almost immediately on 4th February 1863, the Futai, the provincial governor representing the Chinese Imperial authorities, asked General Staveley for permission to send the 'Ever Victorious' against the third-class city of Taitsan, held by between 7,000 and 8,000 Taipings. The Imperialists already had 8,000 of their own soldiers in the area, holding fortified towns, and believed that the amnesty they had offered to the rebels a few weeks before should have had its effect. But Taitsan was just beyond the agreed 30-mile limit from the walls of Shanghai, so Holland was allowed to go only as 'adviser', in double-harness with a Chinese commander. Consequently, there was a slackness of direction. When 2,300 men of the 'Ever Victorious', with 22 guns, arrived before Taitsan on 13 February, rebel reinforcements from their local base at Soochow marched in to aid the defenders, but no reconnaissance of the defences was made. Holland took the word of the Imperial generals that the defences were weak, consisting only of a dry ditch instead of the expected moat, in front of the walls. Therefore, when the guns had made a breach in the wall, no bridging material was brought up; instead the engineer party ran forward with ladders for scaling the walls. As they did so, they cheered; the assault columns thought the cheer was a signal to attack, and they also rushed forward. They were all, engineers and infantry alike, brought to an abrupt halt a bare 40 yards from the walls of Taitsan by a 6-feet deep moat, 20 feet wide, where they presented a vulnerable, near point-blank target to the Taipings. Very bravely, they tried to cross the obstacle; but failed. Then Holland botched the retreat as badly as he had botched the assault. 'If a cadet from Woolwich had the direction he would have done better,' wrote Lyster disgustedly. 'When General Holland told me he was going to retreat, I asked him not to do so, and showed him what to do; but he said he could not depend on his men to remain an hour longer with him. So he retired to Sung-Kiang, losing two guns. General Ward, who was not a professional soldier, would have acted better.'

'Oh, how we laughed,' a Taiping leader is reported to have said,[3] 'as they advanced nearer to the creek with no bridges to throw over! and how we laughed as we saw the ladder they had thrown over getting weaker and weaker beneath them, and at

---

[3] *Events in the Taeping Rebellion*, pp. 240-2.

last fall into the creek, leaving half the party on one side, and half on the other. "What general is he," cried our chief, "who sends his men to storm a city without first ascertaining that there is a moat." "And what general is he," cried another of our leaders, "who allows a storming party to advance without bridges? See, O chief, these unfortunates!" So we jested, as we saw the slaves of the Tartar usurper advancing to destruction. But our chief was wroth when he saw the handful of men who had come out against him. "Do they think we are cowards, even as the impish soldiers of the mandarins, to bring out hundreds against our thousands?" "Not so, O chief," replied a valiant captain, "but they have forgotten that they had foreigners to aid them in Kahding and Najaor, Cholin and Wongka." And we arose as one man; the cry of "Blood!" was in our mouths, and the thirst for blood consumed us; we sallied forth on the "Ever Victorious" troops, and behold, they retired so soon as they saw the brandishing of our spears. Many fled, flinging away their arms in their haste; their ammunition and their belts also they cast upon the ground in their fear. There were English officers too. O recorder of events, how they ran! One of them flung away his pistol and his sword, and swam the creek in his haste. Another also lost his sword, which the Sunkiong men picked up. I will be just, though, and true. Many of the Sunkiong men fought bravely, and their officers as heroes. They tried long to carry off their two guns, but could not stand our fire. Can you believe it, O recorder of events? the English *Chuntae* removed the smaller guns first, instead of leaving them to the last to protect the removal of the big ones. We thank him for the 32-pounders he had left in our hands. Then, too, we were surprised to see him leading the retreat in his boat. We know that such is the practice of the impish mandarins; but we thought that English officers always sought the post of danger. But let not the mandarin slaves think that in their service alone are foreigners employed, and that they alone reap the benefit of their warlike experience. Numbers of them have joined us; many were in Taitsan, and a Frenchman pointed the gun which carried death into the ranks of the foes. We, too, have disciplined troops; and we, too, have European firearms, as the imps found to their cost. They thought they could take Nankin, but they failed before Taitsan.'

Apart from the lost guns, 290 Chinese were killed or wounded, and the casualties among the European officers were severe in proportion to their numbers — 5 killed, 15 wounded, plus 4 marines of Holland's bodyguard wounded: 20 casualties among a total of 46 European officers showed that the failure was not due to the lower ranks of leadership. Gordon's own comment was: 'The causes of the failure were the too cheap rate at which the rebels were held. The force had hitherto fought with the allies with them (except at Tsingpu). They now had to bear the brunt of the fighting themselves, the mistake of not having provided bridges in spite of the mandarin's information, and the too close proximity of the heavy guns to the walls, and the want of cover they had, and finally the withdrawal of the lighter guns before the heavy guns, whose removal they should have covered. There is little doubt that the rebels had been warned by persons in Shanghai of the intended attack, and that several foreigners, who had been dismissed by Captain Holland, were with the rebels defending the breach. Burgevine's acquaintances were not sorry to see the first expedition of the force under an English officer fail.'

The same month there was another failure, also just outside the thirty-mile limit, at Shao-shing, where a force of French disciplined Chinese, under Tardiff de Moidrey, aided by a 'motley company of foreigners' ranging from Frenchman to black man and supported, quite unofficially and against orders, by a British naval party trailing a 68-pounder gun, lost heavily but without taking the town. De Moidrey was shot in the head, at the head of his troops, and from behind, presumably by accident; and a British naval officer was also killed. Part of the Ward force had been involved in this defeat also, and the men were in a semi-mutinous state. As a result of a shipwreck, Gordon was finally appointed to the command. Staveley, who was a relative, had recommended him; but Bruce, on diplomatic grounds, had not wanted a British officer in charge. Bruce's letter, but not Staveley's, had been sent with the mails in the S.S. *Colombo*, which was wrecked off Ceylon in November 1862. The British Government, therefore, had not heard the objections to the appointment of a British officer when they made their decision. The formula used, however, in effect loaned British officers to the Chinese for a period of eighteen months; during which time they were considered to be in Chinese service, took Chinese rank, and were paid by the Chinese (at a rate two or three times that of their last rank in the British Army or Navy). Consequently, when Gordon, now a brevet-Major, was appointed to command the 'Ever Victorious' at the end of March 1863, he became a military mandarin and was supplied with the requisite uniform.

'I hope you do not think I have a magnificent army,' he wrote to a military friend. 'You never did see such a rabble as it was; and although I think I have improved it, it is still sadly wanting. Now both officers and men, although ragged and perhaps slightly disreputable, are in capital order and well disposed.' When Gordon arrived to take over, they had been anything but well disposed. Many were Americans, who suspected that an English officer would probably get rid of them. Besides, many Americans at this moment felt even more strongly anti-British than usual; the raider *Alabama*, handed over to a Confederate crew by the British, was at the peak of her commerce-destroying career, and bitter notes were passing between the Northern Government and the British Government. Just as unhappy was the Chinese Governor of the Province, the ambitious and efficient Li Hung Chang, who had gathered, that, although Gordon was prepared to work with the Chinese liaison officer, Li Adong, there was to be no doubt about who was going to do the crowing on that particular dunghill. About the only enthusiast was the Irishman, Lieutenant Lyster, whom Gordon wanted with him. 'Major Gordon is just the man I would go anywhere with,' he wrote. 'I am not sure that I should join if they were under any other officer.'

But on the fateful day that Gordon joined, only one British officer went up with him from Shanghai, Lieutenant Wood, R.A. 'On the 25th of March we rode up to Sung-keong with Major Gordon. It was somewhat doubtful what sort of reception that officer might receive, as it had been industriously rumoured that they would have no one but Burgevine. However, we arrived and took up our quarters in safety in the Headquarters House, and the next day Major Gordon assembled the officers and non-commissioned officers, told them plainly that they might fear no sweeping changes, or anything that might injure their future prospects. This had the desired effect, and the threatened outbreak did not take place.'

Mossman noted, at the time just before Gordon took up the command, the 'mildness of his manners and the pleasing expression of his features, especially about the eyes; many remarked that he was more suited to adorn a drawing room than to command troops in combat. Yet to my knowledge he refused all invitations to evening parties; and on any occasion when the limited list of ladies in Shanghai were assembled, he seemed to avoid their society. He said that his time was better employed than spending it in "spooning".'

But what impression would he make on the Chinese with whom he would have to work? The Governor, Li Hung Chang, who was also a military mandarin, was prejudiced to begin with, and understandably so. 'I hate all these foreigners,' he wrote in his diary. 'But it would not be wise to let them know. It is not the men personally that I dislike, it is their airs of wonderful superiority. Each and every one sings the same song, "I will do this and I will do that ... I'll make your army more glorious than ever; but you must let me have my own way and not interfere with me."' On 27th March, after meeting the new commander of the 'Ever Victorious', he noted, however: 'It is a direct blessing from Heaven, I believe, the coming of the British Gordon... He is superior in manner and bearing to any of the foreigners I have come into contact with and does not show outwardly that conceit which makes most of them repugnant in my sight. Besides, while he is possessed of a splendid military bearing, he is direct and business-like. Within two hours after his arrival he was inspecting the troops and giving orders; and I could not but rejoice at the manner in which his commands were obeyed.'

Gordon referred to this interview in his diary, which he later gave to Mossman, editor of the *North China Herald*. It was a typical Gordon entry: '25 March, '63. G. takes command. Told Footai eighteen months would see end of rebellion.' Gordon was wrong. It was to take him seventeen months. 'From what I had observed in his correspondence,' wrote Mossman later, 'I inferred that he was of a pious disposition, from seeing the initials (D.V.) for *Deo volente*, in brackets, when intending to do anything particular. So I hinted that he might not be so zealous in the cause of the "heathen Chinee" as of a Christian people. On the contrary, I ascertained that it was chiefly from feelings of pity for the people, that he was induced to accept the offer … and that though the mass of the Chinese profess Buddhism, his sympathies were with them, and not with the upper classes, or Mandarins, who hold the tenets of Confucianism.'

The Governor, or Futai of Kiang-soo Province, Li Hang Chung, asked immediately for an expedition at once against Fushan, 60 miles north-west of Shanghai, which was breaking the thirty-mile limit with a vengeance. General Staveley, who had asked the War Office for a specific ruling on this point, was away; the War Office had not yet replied; and the other senior British officer, Admiral Hope, had left Shanghai for good. Gordon simply said, 'Yes', made his preparations, and was away on 31st March.

On 6th April, Lieutenant Lyster wrote: 'We are all most anxious about Major Gordon, who has made his first campaign with the disciplined Chinese. He has gone to take a place called Fushan, which the Imperialists attacked, but failed at three times. I trust he will get through it all right; he is so regardless of danger it makes one uneasy.' That, in view of recent experience, the success of the whole expedition was doubted, is made clear by Lyster, who added: 'I was out with the English troops, who were 4½ miles from the place, so that if Gordon were beaten he could fall back on them.'

CHAPTER SIX: 'THE EVER VICTORIOUS ARMY'

'G. at Fushan on 2nd April. Captures place on 4th April, with loss of one officer, and three men killed, and five wounded. Rebels fell back from around Chan-zu in the night of the 4th, and are not to be seen on the 5th. The Ever V. return to Soon-Kiong on the 7th of April.' — *Major Gordon's war diary.*

Fushan (or Foo-shan) was a walled city of the third order, situated on a branch of the estuary of the Yang-tsze Kiang. It was already invested by a small force under Major Tapp. In the city and in the area around there were an estimated 20,000 Taipings. When Gordon arrived, his force numbered 1,700 of all arms, with six 12-pounder howitzers, one 32-pounder gun, and one rocket launcher (rockets had been used by the British Army from the Napoleonic Wars onwards). While a force of 8,000 Imperial troops covered his operations, Gordon made a personal reconnaissance of the defences, and then placed his artillery very carefully, sited for concentrated fire on a weak point from a position where there was plenty of cover for the guns and the men serving them, and also for the storming party to hide and add a 'pepper pot' thickening up with musket and rifle fire of the main bombardment.

According to the Gordon MSS edited by Hake: The two rebel stockades of Fushan were situated on the banks of a creek which runs from Chanzu to the Yangtze. They did not appear strong; but there were heavy masses of rebels in rear and on each flank. At 9 a.m. on the 4th April we opened fire. The rebels answered feebly, and by degrees dropped off firing;

they, however, reinforced the stockade from the rear. The 32-pounder continued to bring down the wall of the stockade in masses, and after three-quarters of an hour, on the "advance" being sounded, the rebels left and the troops poured in. The rebels made a feeble effort to return, but with the exception of wounding a gallant officer, Captain Belcher of the 5th Regiment, did us no harm. The stockades were held that night, and communication opened with Chanzu through spies. The European officers already knew something of the realities of Chinese warfare, for the heads of three of the British officers killed in Holland's disastrous attack had been cut off by the Taipings and sent around as evidence of victory. Now, they were to see that some aspects of the Christian story at any rate had been paralleled by the Taipings.

'The next day there were no rebels to be seen; they had left during the night. We walked on, therefore, to Chanzu. About halfway we passed a dreadful sight. Near a large joss-house were thirty-five Imperialist soldiers crucified in different ways. They had been burnt in various places before death. On inquiry we found that they were the crew of some gunboats that had been wrecked previous to our arrival, and had been taken prisoners by the rebels.' The correspondent of the *North China Herald*, accompanying Gordon's expedition, added professional details: the bodies had been 'mutilated, branded with hot irons and crucified — that being a cruel method of torture and death prevalent in China'.

The force then marched on to Chiang-zu (or Chanzu), where an Imperialist garrison (formerly rebels) had been besieged by more faithful Taipings for three months, had run out of ammunition, and had had during that time news only of continuous defeat for relieving forces. After Holland's disaster, the three European heads had been shown to them, and the two captured 32-pounder guns fired at them. The mandarins looked careworn, having been in a considerable state of suspense,' wrote Mossman. But there was no battle of Chiang-zu — the rebel siege lines were abandoned, with scaling ladders and equipment left lying. So complete a success, at so tiny a cost, completely stumped Burgevine, who had gone to the capital, Peking, to state his case, and had done this so ably that he returned with an Imperial order for his reinstatement as leader of the 'Ever Victorious'. The Futai backed Gordon, and the British authorities backed the Futai. Burgevine only had three days to agitate in Shanghai, and then Gordon left in command of another expedition. Had he been given longer, Burgevine might have taken most of the 'Ever Victorious' with him in his next move.

Gordon's move was towards the cities of Taitsan, where Holland had been defeated, and Quinsan. Negotiations for the rebel garrison of Taitsan to come over to the Imperialists were in progress, and the Futai thought that an attack on Quinsan might help them to make up their minds. But he had been deceived, as Gordon very shortly found out. He was marching towards Quinsan when an Imperial courier arrived with news that the rebels in Taitsan, on pretence of negotiation, had lured an Imperialist force into a trap, capturing, killing, or wounding 1,500 of them. Gordon turned on Taitsan.

His diary entry gives the best evidence for the ferocity of the struggle, remembering that he never wasted words and was coldly accurate. 'Force marches across country to Taitsan. Carried stockades on the 30th April, and the city on the 1st May, after a determined resistance. The breach at the West Gate held by picked men. Rebel loss not severe. Ours heavy indeed. Ornamental arch at West Gate pitted with bullets.

Holland's breach was at the South Gate. Very great doubts of success. Struggle lasted on breach for twenty minutes.'

What happened took longer than Holland's assault, because it was methodical. Gordon first destroyed the outlying stockades, then chose the West Gate, and not the South Gate of Taitsan, for his attack. Two bridges were taken intact, then he moved his guns steadily forward, from the 600 yard mark to within 100 yards of the walls, protected by wooden mantlets and covered by flanking parties of riflemen against counter-attack. When the enemy fire began to die away, he ordered his gunboats up the canal to form a bridge of boats across the moat directly in front of the place where his guns had torn a wide breach in the wall. But there could be no concealing the point of attack, and the mass of the Taipings had concentrated here, keeping out of sight and fire. As soon as the storming party rushed forward, and Gordon's guns dared fire no longer, they opened a tremendous fire and masses of them rushed down to the breach, defiantly waving their battle-flags. The stormers were driven back, and a gunboat captured, in a hail of incendiary and smoke-bombs hurled down by the rebels. Then reinforcements came up, and another assault was made, with howitzer support. Major Brennan's 5th Regiment rushed over, was checked momentarily before Captain Schinkoff's company planted their colour on the top of the wall. The snake-flags of the rebel chiefs wavered, and then gave way. The Taipings were running, but it had been a very near thing. Gordon told Lyster that they had nearly had a repetition of Holland's fiasco. 'He said he never saw such stiff fighting even in the Crimea; for twenty minutes there were two crowds waving to and fro — the stormers and defenders of the town.'

Twenty minutes of hand-to-hand fighting, such as this was, is a very long time indeed; even ten minutes should be considered a severe struggle. And the casualties reflected it — at least 8 per cent of the entire force of 3,000 men killed or wounded. Among the rebel dead in the breach, where they had stiffened the defence, were two Americans, two Frenchmen, and three Indian soldiers from a British regiment. There was also a deserter from the 31st Regiment, Private Hargreaves, now severely wounded by a shell splinter. 'Mr. Gordon! Mr. Gordon, you will not let me be killed,' he shouted. 'Take him down to the river and shoot him!' rapped Gordon, before quietly giving instructions for the wounded man to be taken to his command-boat for medical attention before being sent down to Shanghai (where he got a few months' imprisonment for deserting).

Gordon would have liked to have moved on Quinsan at once, to follow up the effect of his dearly-bought victory; but that was not customary in the 'Ever Victorious Army'. Normally, the force virtually dissolved after a battle, to dispose profitably of the plunder. Gordon could not entirely check it, so he marched the greater part of them back to garrison at Sunkiong, and reorganised. In his diary, he noted: 'Force starts for Quinsan, after a great row with the officers and G., de mortuis nil nisi, etc.' Actually, it was more like a trade union dispute in industry. Gordon appointed a British officer to control the issue of rations and stores, with temporary rank of Lieutenant-Colonel. The majors, mostly Americans, did not like a British officer being appointed over their heads, and demanded an interview. They got the interview, but not their demands. They then resigned in a body, but said they were prepared to go to Quinsan. This was the night before they were due to leave. Next morning, only the 100 men of the bodyguard fell in on parade. They were marched off to Quinsan on their own. Gordon then had the N.C.O.s of the non-fallen-in units put under close, indeed chained, arrest. Two majors withdrew their resignations. The men were informed that there would be a roll-call partway to Quinsan; any man not on it would be dismissed. At the roll-call they were all there, but it had been another near thing; and something would have to be done about it, after Quinsan.

This proved to be as easy (for Gordon), as Taitsan had been difficult. Lyster wrote: 'Quinsan was taken by manoeuvre with very little loss…' Gordon's war diary, with sketch, summed up the situation in military shorthand. 'Aspect of Quinsan: isolated hill, surrounded by wall; very wide ditch. City very strong at East Gate. Every manoeuvre seen at top of hill, and telegraphed to (rebel) chief. Determined to surround the city. We have already Chiang-zu, at north, belonging to us. Rebels (in Quinsan) have only one road of retreat — towards Soo-chow, twenty-four miles. Reconnoitre the country on the 30th May. Found this road can be cut at Chun-ye, eight miles from Quinsan, sixteen miles from Soochow, point of junction and key to the possession of Quinsan held by rebel stockades. Detour of twenty miles in rebel country necessary to get at this point. Value of steamer. Worth at least 10,000 men. Moral effect.'

The steamer was the *Hyson*, a paddle-wheeler 60 feet long with a beam of 24 feet, captained by Davidson, a reliable and gallant American seaman. She drew only 3½ feet of water, and could paddle along on the muddy bed of a creek in less than that, using her paddle-wheels as tanks use their tracks. She was virtually unstoppable, dealing with barriers of stakes or sunken junks either by charging them head-on or pausing to drag them away. Additionally, she was armed with a 32-pounder gun in the bows, a 12-pounder at the stern, and a whistle. The whistle, against Chinese troops, was probably the most effective. She had the sort of effect on the Chinese that Hannibal's elephants had on the Romans. Except that what Gordon did with her was to bypass Quinsan, in full-view of the rebels, along a canal which was bordered by a road, and so put himself between the Taipings and their main headquarters at Soochow. This caused them to evacuate Quinsan, and their troops retreating towards Soochow along the canal bank met head-on their own reinforcements coming up from Soochow, which caused incredible confusion, into which the *Hyson* poured her fire. There was some fighting at a stockade which blocked the way, but Quinsan did not have to be assaulted; the Taipings were simply manoeuvred out of it. And the explanation was, that Gordon knew this bit of China better than they did, and saw how to make use of the knowledge.

'Knowledge of the country is everything,' he wrote in a letter, 'and I have studied it a great deal. The rebels certainly never got such a licking before, and I think that there will not be much more severe fighting, as we have such immense advantages in the way of steamers.' Another vital factor was the (to the Taipings) bewildering speed with which Gordon carried out his manoeuvre; they had expected to fight another 'set-piece' battle such as Taitsan, but simply had the rug whipped from under their feet. Instead of a land attack head-on at the walls, they found an amphibious force of steamers and junks, led by the *Hyson*, driving at their canal defences in flank, from the canal. Gordon mounted the bridge of the *Hyson*, between the paddle-boxes, and whipped on the waterborne blitzkrieg. Behind him came eighty steamers, gunboats, and junks, carrying infantry and artillery.

The first defence of the canal was a stockade. The infantry landed and began to advance, while the Imperial gunboats pulled up the stakes blocking the canal. Appalled, the Taipings resisted for a minute, then ran. Some flew back for Quinsan; the infantry pursued them. Others ran for Soochow; the *Hyson* followed these, impeded by numerous boats drifting out of control on the canal, and banging away at the retreating rebel troops going down the road on the canal bank. Then, ahead, loomed the arches of a great bridge, covered by a newly-built stone fort. The *Hyson* charged, blowing her whistle. An embrasured gun from the fort replied; and the answering shell from the steamer went slap into the embrasure. Then the bridge engulfed them, so high above that the funnel scraped through under it without having to be lowered. As the steamer, paddle-wheels clanking and beating the canal water to foam, went whistling under the bridge, the rebels on the roadway it carried above were streaming pell-mell for Soochow.

Urging on the rebel rear with shots from her 32- pounder, the *Hyson* passed several stone forts from which not a round was fired at her. At one point, she stopped to take 150 prisoners, who far outnumbered her crew. 'Soon after this,' wrote a witness, 'four horsemen were descried riding at full speed about a mile in rear. They came up, passed the steamer amid a storm of bullets, and joined the rebel column. One of them was struck off his horse, but the others coolly waited for him, and one of them stopped and took him up behind him. They deserved to get off.' By 6 p.m. the *Hyson* was less than a mile from the main rebel base of Soochow, ploughing through sailing boats which panicked at the sight of the red and green steamer, and were promptly run aground by their crews, and thus deserted when the *Hyson* passed. Sheer brass cheek had got them this far, and all the fortifications in their rear had been bypassed, not garrisoned; and besides, they were now in rear of the whole rebel army. Reluctantly, Gordon turned back. Almost immediately, a large band of rebels opened an accurate fire from the cover of a bridge, but were destroyed by grapeshot from the flank. 'Four chiefs, one a Wang, galloped past on horseback, and although not two yards from the steamer they got away. The Wang got shoved into the water and lost his pony. A party of encamped rebels, not dreaming of any further annoyance that night, were accordingly astonished to hear the steamer's whistle, and rushing out in amazement met a shell, which killed two of them.

'It was now 10.30 p.m.,' wrote the witness, 'and the night was not very clear. At this moment the most tremendous firing and cheering was heard from Chumye, and hurried our progress to that place. The Imperial gunboats were drawn up in line on the other side of the creek to the road, and were firing as fast as they could.' Chumye was the position, now held by part of Gordon's infantry, which blocked the only route between Quinsan and Soochow; there could be no escape over the countryside for the rebels, partly because of lake and marsh, partly because the inhabitants were hostile to them. 'The stone fort at the village was sparkling with musketry, from which at times the most astounding yells burst forth,' wrote the witness. 'The *Hyson* blew her whistle, and was received with deafening cheers from the gunboats, which were on the eve of bolting (some had already left). She steamed up the creek towards Quinsan, and at the distance of 200 yards we saw a confused mass near a high bridge. It was too dark to distinguish very clearly, but on the steamer blowing the whistle the mass wavered, yelled, and turned back. It was the garrison of Quinsan attempting to escape to Soochow — some 7,000 or 8,000 men. Matters were in too critical a state to hesitate, as the mass of the rebels, goaded into desperation, would have swept our small force away. We were therefore forced to fire into them, and pursue them towards Quinsan, firing, however, very rarely, and only when the rebels looked as if they would make a stand. The steamer went up to about a mile from Quinsan, and then returned. Several officers landed and took charge of the prisoners, who were extended along the bank, and at 4 a.m. (31st May) everything was quiet.' It was an epic victory at negligible cost.

Gordon wrote in his war diary: 'Loss of rebels, 4,000 to 5,000 killed, drowned, and murdered by villagers, 2,000 prisoners taken, and 1,500 boats captured. Our loss, two killed. Quinsan captured, capable steamer communication in all directions, most valuable key to whole country.' And in a letter he added: 'My occupying this city enables the Imperial Government to protect an enormous district rich in corn, etc., and the people around are so thankful for their release that it is quite a pleasure. They were in a desperate plight before our arrival, as their way led between the rebels and the Imperialists; but they had the sharpness to have two head men or chiefs in each village — one was Imperialist and the other a rebel; these paid the various taxes to both sides. We took nearly 800 prisoners, and they have some of them entered my bodyguard and fought since against their old friends the rebels. If I had time I could tell such extraordinary stories of the way men from distant provinces meet one another, and the way villagers recognise in our ranks old rebels who have visited their villages for plunder. I took a mandarin, who had been a rebel for three years, and have him now; he has a bullet in his cheek, which he received when fighting against the rebels. The rebels I took into my guard were snake flag-bearers of head chiefs, and they are full of remarks of their old masters. The snake flags are the marks of head men in both armies. Whenever they are seen there is a chief present. When they go, you know the rebels will retire. At Taitsan the snake flags remained till the last, and this accounted for a very severe fight. I never did think the rebels were as strong as people said; they do not number many fighting men.'

The Taiping hordes must, of course, have included large numbers of camp followers and non-combatants, giving the impression during an advance of overwhelming numbers; but it was fortunate for Gordon that he was able to recruit their fighting men so easily to his side, for he soon had another and more serious mutiny in the ranks of the 'Ever Victorious'. The basic cause was his decision to make Quinsan their permanent base, in place of Sung-keong, for disciplinary reasons. In his war diary, he wrote: 'G. determines to move headquarters there, as the men would be more under control than they were at Sung-keong. Men mutiny. One is shot at tombstone outside West Gate. Marks of bullets still there. Men then desert, 1,700 only out of 3,900 remain. Very disorderly lot. Ward spoilt them. G. recruits rebel prisoners, who are much better men.' These men had also the advantage of knowing the Soochow district, which was Gordon's next objective, as soon as the most intense heat of the summer should be over. But, before this expedition could leave, Gordon found himself, as had Burgevine before him, in the awkward position of being unable to pay his men because the Chinese authorities would not meet the bills. He tackled the problem in a different manner, however.

CHAPTER SEVEN: THE 'HOUR-GLASS' STRATEGY

'G. determines to attack Soo-chow, not directly, but on the same principle as Quinsan, viz. by cutting communications. Original intention to take Wokong, a town fifteen miles west of Soo-chow on the Grand Canal, and Woosieh, a town thirty miles N.W. of Soo-chow on Grand Canal. Then to hold Ta-Ho Lake, west of Soo-chow, while in possession of Quinsan, to the east of Soo-chow. Idea was that dissension would break out if this was done. This idea was caused owing to Burgevine going to the rebels only in modified form. The same principle being observed as in the original intention. Soo-chow admirably situated to be cut off. Never thought it necessary to take Soo-chow by force.' — *Gordon's war diary.*

Military methods are more a matter of communications than battle tactics, the actual movement of masses of men, heavy guns, and stores to selected points. Even a small force like the 'Ever Victorious' posed a movement problem similar to that of shifting a small-sized town from one place to another. Gordon's solution was based on his possession of armed steamers and a fleet of junks, which enabled him to move on almost any point through the labyrinth of waterways in the Delta and eventually to get into the great lake of Ta-ho (or Tai-hu), which lay in rear of Soochow. The accurate maps he had made previously of the Delta immensely speeded the process, which otherwise would have contained a great deal of trial and error. The principles of movement being agreed upon, the next stage was to decide the basic point against which movement should be made; this was obviously Soochow, where the largest number of rebels were concentrated and the last remaining point from which they could menace Shanghai. Once the Taipings were cleared out of Soochow, the main European objective — to protect their trading rights and interests — would have been achieved, although the Chinese Imperial Government would still have a rebellion on their hands until distant Nanking, the Taiping capital, could be re-taken. After Soochow, therefore, the interests of the Europeans and the Chinese would diverge. Before Soochow, however, there were further decisions to be made, as to the exact line of approach. Gordon's solution was based on his appreciation that the remaining rebel forces held a position which was, geographically, shaped like an hour-glass: he would cut into this in the centre, at the thinnest point, until he had his steamers on the lake behind Soochow.

In detail, his campaign was based on a geographical triangle, the lines of which were waterways, with a city at each corner. The apex was Quinsan, which he held already, and from which a canal led like a spear straight at Soochow; he did not intend to attack this way, merely to threaten. The two bases of the triangle were two cities on either side of Soochow, Wusieh to the north and Wokong to the south, both of them with short and easy access by water to the great lake in rear of Soochow. If they could be taken, then Soochow would be in his pocket: the rebels would either be squeezed out early or be besieged into surrender. It will be seen that actual battle manoeuvring was a secondary matter. Success in fact depended on getting up sufficient artillery, emplacing it correctly opposite a weak point (found by personal reconnaissance), and timing the assault to coincide with its effects. In battle, the troops would merely do as they had been trained to do — and here Gordon, of course, was drawing on the legacy of the training programme carried out by his predecessors, particularly Ward. There are, therefore, no showy or elaborate battle plans to explain. This was because Gordon was showing himself a competent general. A battle is essentially an organised chaos, so that only simple orders really work; anything at all delicate or complicated inevitably breaks down in ruin.

It was on the level of what might perhaps be called 'grand strategy' that the complications occurred; upsetting both the timetable and people's tempers. The British Minister in Peking, Sir Frederick Bruce, backed Burgevine, not Gordon, for command of the 'Ever Victorious'; because it was British policy not to get too deeply involved in Chinese affairs and because Chinese warfare involved what in European eyes would be bound to rank as 'atrocities'. By all means let an American adventurer associate himself with these; but not a serving officer of the Queen. Of course, he did not tell the Chinese this. On 5th June, when he wrote to Prince Kung, of the Imperial Government, he ruled simply: 'Sir Frederick Bruce must decline to allow officers of Her Majesty's Army to take any part in military operations further than may be necessary for the protection of British interests, and his first step, consequently, will be to desire that Major Gordon, and others serving with him at Shanghai, shall not pass the boundary described by the 30-mile radius.' This ruled out altogether any attack on Soochow. To the new British military commander in China, Major-General Brown, he was more explicit: 'The officer who commands the force will speedily find himself in a position which is neither compatible with his professional reputation nor with what is due to the character of a British officer.'

The Chinese view was directly opposed. They wished to get Gordon, the 'Ever Victorious', and the Europeans generally to take Soochow for them by frontal assault, while they themselves merely besieged Nanking, the Taiping capital. Stopping the pay of the 'Ever Victorious' was simply a device to ensure that they would make this assault. The Futai, Li Hung Chang, noted: 'Gordon thinks of nothing but money these days … he says his men will not fight any more unless they are paid. I tell him that, as soon as Soochow is in our hands, there will be funds sufficient to pay all arrears and some good bounty. This is the word that I have from the Viceroy and his promises come from the Throne.'

Gordon's reply was to resign. On 25th July he informed Li Hung Chang of this, and of his reasons, adding, however: 'As my resignation of this command will necessitate the knowledge of the British Minister and General, I have forwarded to them copies of this letter, and have to add that I will remain in command of the force only till such time as I shall have received their replies.' As he was due to march out the following day to make the preliminary moves towards the fall of Soochow, these would continue as planned: Gordon's reason was that he was already committed to this and that the Chinese had paid for part of the preparations.

General Brown did not see eye-to-eye with Sir Frederick, and his reaction to Gordon's letter was to write to H.M. Government: 'I trust, however, that I may be able to do something in the matter to induce Major Gordon to withdraw his application, having no officer at my disposal to replace him, as in this officer are combined so many dashing qualities, let alone skill and judgement, to make him invaluable to command such a force.'

Gordon's intended operations were therefore contrary to the wishes of the British Minister, who was not in a strong position because a ruling on the point had been requested from the Home Government, and had not yet arrived. In the meantime, Gordon stated that he would observe Sir Frederick's wishes only if he was given a definite order to that effect. The Home Government had, in fact, ruled favourably, so the Minister's indecision was justified. On the Chinese side also there were disagreements. The Futai, Li Hung Chang, noted, in regard to the commander of the Chinese Imperial forces which were to co-operate with Gordon: 'General Ching threatens to resign if some curb is not put on General Gordon. Perhaps it was a mistake to tell Gordon that he was under my direct orders and that Ching, although commander of the forces against the rebels, was not to interfere directly with the Ever Victorious Army. Ching is far from being a great military man. Besides, he has a bad temper like Gordon, and they are both quick to say hot words, like myself.'

Under the surface, even deeper trouble was brewing. The Doctor Macartney (later Sir Halliday Macartney) who had resigned his commission in the 99th Regiment in order to apply for the post of commander of the 'Ever Victorious', had found scope for his military ambitions with the Futai and was organising an arsenal and military force at Sung-Kiang, to support the Chinese Imperial Forces directly. On 15th July, less than two weeks before Gordon's campaign was due to begin, he wrote him a warning note: 'I have made further inquiries about Burgevine, and find for certain that he *is* enlisting men for some service or other; three hundred are said to have been enlisted and were to leave Shanghai yesterday.' On 21st July, Burgevine himself wrote to Gordon; 'You may hear a great many rumours concerning me, but do not believe any of them.' Gordon accepted that, and on his recommendation, no watch was kept on Burgevine.

Therefore, when Gordon marched out on 25th July towards Wokong, he himself had resigned, General Ching was threatening to resign, the British Minister disapproved, the Futai had deliberately failed to pay Gordon's men, and Burgevine was plotting mischief. To cap it all, a few hours before he was due to leave, the artillery officers resigned in a body. It was then 5 p.m., the expedition being planned to start at 9 p.m., after dark, so that their approach along the waterways might be undetected. Gordon rounded up the storekeepers, and anyone else who was prepared to serve a gun, loaded them in the boats, and punctually started. After covering a considerable distance, they stopped at a village on the bank, and here the artillery officers caught them up, stating that they were now prepared to serve. Hake says of them: 'They were brave, gallant men, who evinced far more ingenuity and quickness than is shown among the officers of some armies. They were wonderfully sharp in acquiring a knowledge of the country, and, as there always will be, there were some men who did not do much credit to the force, as a rule they were a most efficient body of officers. Their great fault was a belief in imaginary grievances.'

At daybreak on 27th July, unheralded, unsuspected, Gordon's force, led by the armed steamer *Firefly*, emerged from the maze of waterways at Ka-poo (or Kia-poo, or Kahpu) on the Grand Canal. The infantry were put ashore on the flank, the Chinese gunboats demolished the water barrier of stakes, and the *Firefly* burst through, followed by the rest of Gordon's fleet. The two strong stockades covering the water junction were taken with a rush. Soochow was cut off to the south, and a waterway to the great lake of Tai-hu in rear of the city had

87

been opened up. An Imperialist garrison was put into the stockades and to make sure that Soochow was not merely cut off, but remained cut off, in that direction, Gordon moved on the rebel town of Woo-kong (or Wokong) some miles further south. Again, the rebels were driven out of the stockades with a rush, falling back on the town. When Gordon's guns began to thunder against the walls on 29th July, there was no reply in kind, merely a request to be allowed to surrender on terms. Gordon promised to spare their lives, and nearly 3,000 rebels marched out into captivity. Gordon's loss was one officer wounded, two soldiers killed, twelve soldiers wounded.

An attack from any other direction might have meant a fierce resistance, followed by a retreat on Soochow; but Gordon, by taking Ka-poo first, had cut their only road of retreat — the line of the Grand Canal. There were other factors, too. According to the Gordon MSS edited by Hake, the garrison was new and so was the general. 'He had been made a Wang only three days, and we captured a theatrical company who had come up from Hangchow to celebrate the event. These men were all dressed out in their robes, false beards, etc., and were very much perplexed. The new garrison had just come down from Nankin, and consequently knew nothing of the neighbourhood, and were ill provided with rice and powder, hence their bad defence.'

The prisoners were handed over to General Ching, the Imperialist commander, who, contrary to Gordon's promise, executed five of the leaders. Meanwhile, Gordon was carrying out a personal reconnaissance of the Grand Canal route into Soochow from the south. He got part of the way up, beyond the Patachiao bridge, 300 yards long, with 52 arches, capturing the stockade which covered it and a fleet of boats moored nearby. The Taipings reacted strongly, and the small reconnaissance party bolted back across the bridge under heavy and accurate fire from European mercenaries serving with the rebels. 'This was our first interview with the European rebel contingent, who in their rapid and bold advance and good practice showed that we might expect some harder work before long,' wrote Gordon. He then impressed on General Ching the necessity of holding the key stockades at Ka-poo very strongly, with 1,000 men at least, as there was now bound to be an attempt to retake them. Ching was acting as the follow-up to the hard-core striking force under Gordon's command, which actually cracked the nuts. Ching's job was to gather up the pieces and consolidate the positions won, as well as operating in a holding role to pin down rebel forces. Occasionally, he attacked the smaller nuts on his own account; and was anxious to do more, resentful of European overlordship. But his ambitions were too often in advance of his abilities, and Gordon had more than once already saved him from the full consequences of folly. Now, in defiance of Gordon, he executed the five chief prisoners. This was bad policy as well as bad faith, but it was the latter which shook Gordon, and sent him back at once to Shanghai to demand an interview with the Futai, Li Hung Chang.

Sir Frederick Bruce's assessment, that co-operation with the Chinese would involve British officers with distasteful incidents, had been proved correct for the first time; and was to hold good for the future. But, ironically, as Gordon rode back to Shanghai, determined to resign, another letter from Sir Frederick Bruce was on its way to him from Peking. In this, the Minister had written: 'Since I wrote to Major-General Brown of the command of Ward's Force, I have received further despatches from Her Majesty's Government, from which I infer that no objection is felt to a British officer commanding that force in the field, provided he be on half pay and in the service of the Chinese Government. I shall be glad if you are able to continue your operations so as to force the insurgents to abandon Soochow and the line of the Grand Canal, without which Shanghai cannot be looked upon as secure from attack. I would rather see you in command of the Chinese than anyone else, as I think the corps in your hands will become dangerous to the insurgents, without becoming dangerous to the Government and oppressive to the population.' The latter sentence was in fact the argument *against* Sir Frederick's previous policy which, on balance, preferred Burgevine to Gordon, not on grounds of military efficiency, but of political non-alignment. But it was Burgevine who now made Gordon change his mind. As promised, Gordon had carried the first part of the campaign to a successful conclusion; but his demands for money with which to pay his men had not been met, and he intended that the Futai should accept his resignation.

On 2nd August, while Gordon was on his way to Shanghai, Macartney was returning from there to his base at Sung-Kiang in the steamer *Kiao-chiao* (or *Kajow*), a vessel similar to the *Hyson* and *Firefly*. Soon after he had moored her that morning, and gone ashore, she was boarded and seized by a party of about thirty led by Burgevine, and was last seen heading down the creek for Soochow, unopposed. On hearing this news, Gordon withdrew his resignation. He had made himself a guarantor for the American's good conduct, and therefore felt himself directly responsible; he would have to make good the damage. The damage would be irreparable only if Burgevine managed to seize the artillery held at Quinsan, so Gordon rode through the night to get there first.

Alarm at the possible results of Burgevine's action in joining the Taipings was general. 'Apprehension is entertained for Major Gordon's force, in consequence of General Burgevine's popularity with the junior officers and men,' Captain Strode wrote to Vice-Admiral Kuper on 6th August. Colonel Hough, now commanding the British forces in Shanghai, reported: 'Burgevine's terms with the Europeans he has collected here are service one month and money paid down and other information states unrestrained licence to pillage every town they take, even Shanghai itself. The latter would be an idle threat even under the present reduced state of the garrison, but for the alarming defection of Major Gordon's force, who are all, it is said, traitorously inclined to side with Burgevine. The Governor said a report had reached him of Quinsan, Major Gordon's headquarters, having been given up to the rebels by its garrison. Should this be true, the worst may be anticipated — Major Gordon a prisoner, the siege train lost and the speedy advent of the rebels about this place.'

Major-General Brown, on receiving Hough's alarming letter, acted at once, far outside the terms of his instructions from the Home Government. He immediately authorised British officers to join Gordon's force without having to go on half-pay and serve the Chinese, and he sent 200 Indian troops to help Gordon hold Quinsan. Meanwhile, the Minister, Sir Frederick Bruce, was wringing his hands and supporting his previous policy of supporting Burgevine. 'A man who would have been a most useful friend has been thus converted into a dangerous enemy,' he wrote to Lord John Russell on 9th September. He explained that Burgevine had been unfairly treated by the Futai and other Chinese officials. That his own suggestion, that Burgevine be found 'employment at Tientsin', had not been adopted. And that Burgevine, 'despairing of justice, left for Shanghai'. There, 'No employment was offered to him', and he 'entirely failed in obtaining payment of the sums due as pay. Stung by this treatment, suffering in health from severe wounds received in the Imperial service, and ruined in his prospects, he, with a band of desperadoes of all nations, has joined the insurgents.'

Sir Frederick foresaw dire consequences. 'The first effect has been to reduce Major Gordon and the Chinese troops to the defensive, and to put an end to the hopes of the speedy capture of Souchow, which would have given effectual security to Shanghai. I see there is a feeling at Shanghai that Burgevine will endeavour to organise an expedition and strike a blow at Pekin; and success at Pekin would certainly overthrow the present dynasty, whether it led to the establishment of the Taipings or not.' Sir Frederick was first and foremost a diplomatist, and only a diplomatist could reconcile what he had just written about the need for Gordon to take Soochow with his all too recent attempt to prevent Gordon going anywhere near the place. But the real difference of outlook between the diplomatist and the military was revealed in a final sentence which advocated the policy of 'enforcing the observance of treaties by remonstrance at Pekin, instead of by violent action at the ports'. It is of course natural for diplomats to believe in diplomatic solutions and for soldiers to believe in military ones.

But when the Home Government received this letter, which went into great detail, they seized on the point that General Brown had preferred Gordon to Burgevine, and was by inference part-responsible for the latter's defection. The Minister had written: 'It was a pity that the question was regarded as one of the relative qualifications of Gordon and Burgevine. Of the former officer, I have always entertained the highest opinion, but I fear that even his abilities will not compensate for the injury done to the Imperialist cause by the accession of Burgevine to the rebels.' The grave and responsible view, that Peking might fall as a result, alarmed the Government and Lord Palmerston noted on the margin of the Minister's letter: 'General Brown ought surely to be reprimanded for his conduct in this matter.' Lord Russell disagreed. 'I cannot think authorities on the spot, Chinese and English, are to be entirely disregarded,' he said.

The matter had in fact already been settled, but because communications were slow, the writers of these various letters were necessarily considering situations which no longer existed. Burgevine did not attempt to take Quinsan, nor did he even endeavour to retake Wokong and Ka-poo — instead he went for a sail in the *Kajow* on the lake of Tai-hu. He had in fact defected without any plans or organisation, and without concerting with the Taipings whom he was joining. The most important thing he achieved was to steal a howitzer, which was immediately used with effect by the Taipings themselves in an attempt to recapture Ka-poo. But Gordon's second move — the first had been to make sure of his base at Quinsan — was to hurry on to Ka-poo. He arrived only just in time, because Ching had not left the stockades as heavily garrisoned as Gordon wished. The Taipings' attempt was strenuous and long drawn-out, starting on 8th August and lasting until 14th August, when they conceded defeat, burning the villages and retiring on Soochow. But it had been a close-run thing for a while, with the stolen howitzer, manned by European gunners, being rapidly towed from place to place by a donkey team, getting into position, and opening fire; while Gordon's steamers raced up and down the waterways, firing back. One of the gunboats was sunk alongside the *Hyson*, at 500 yards range, but well-aimed grape at the position occupied by the howitzer forced it to retire. Then Gordon's reinforcements arrived, he went over to the attack, took advantage of a faulty siting of the rebels' defences, and tumbled them back towards Soochow.

The Taipings had in fact only realised the vital importance of those two stockades at Ka-poo after Gordon had taken them. They commanded the route by which the rebels normally obtained their arms, ammunition, and other supplies in two days. Now, their only source of supply was Shanghai itself, and that took five days, even if the shipments got through intact. In fact, losses were higher than 50 per cent by this route. Even this route would have been stopped up if the Imperialists had taken Gordon's advice, but they said they had not enough men. In spite of this, Gordon had to stop General Ching from taking the *Hyson* and some gunboats through to Tai-hu Lake, as this would have meant a naval battle with Burgevine who was still cruising about there in the *Kajow* with this object in mind. Such a clash would have been spectacular but, from Gordon's point of view, to no purpose as yet. At this time he was expecting to be reinforced by a British naval fleet of small craft under Captain Sherard Osborn. But once again grand strategy and high policy prevailed. Captain Osborn would co-operate only on terms, and went up to Peking to arrange them. 'I shall advocate,' he said, 'our having joint naval and military powers over all Europeans under arms in China, to be furnished with funds, to render proper accounts — but in no way to be interfered with by Footais, Tootais, and birds of that feather.'

This was a neat and administratively tidy plan, no doubt, having the solitary drawback that it filled the Taoutais (town governors) and Futais (provincial governors) with horror at the extent of foreign interference in Chinese affairs. Hearing of it, the Futai of Kiang-soo Province, Li Hung Chang, went up to Quinsan in September, to try to induce Gordon to attack Soochow before it could possibly come into effect. Gordon refused. The city was too strong for frontal attack, particularly with Burgevine's European force within the walls; and anyway, there were still some preliminary moves to be made, which would in the end render it untenable by the rebels. He had almost broken through into the lake of Tai-hu at a point to the south of the city. He had to break through completely at that point; and then drive another lance to the lake to the north of the city. Then, and then only, would it fall; and probably without much fighting.

Within 48 hours of the Futai's return, disconsolate, from Quinsan, General Brown arrived there to confer personally with Gordon, and agreed that they must remain on the defensive for the moment. 'Should any treachery take place in Major Gordon's force, and his heavy park of artillery fall into the hands of the rebels,' he wrote, 'my position would be most critical to defend Shanghai — having no larger description of ordnance against that which might be brought against me. In company with Major Gordon I afterwards proceeded to visit the stockade of the Chinese General "Ching", posted about a mile and a half from, and facing the east front of Souchow, where Burgevine is now making his stand with the rebels. Souchow is a very large walled city, twelve miles in circumference, and will no doubt be stoutly defended, and taking into account the host of rebels inside, and the number of followers known to be with Burgevine, I consider it would be rash in the extreme for Major Gordon to hazard an attack with his present small garrison, unsupported by Europeans, to lead an assault; for however well-disciplined his Chinese may

95

be, still they must always be led by Europeans to storm a breach.'

Almost immediately, however, Gordon decided to push closer to the city, his reasons being that General Ching's forces facing Soochow were 'out on a limb', and could be cut off if Burgevine's men made a move, and also because his own troops in Quinsan were becoming sickly, this being the height of the hot season. He therefore closed on Waiquaidong, which brought him nearer to Ching, and decided that he could take Patachiao, where the great bridge crossed the Grand Canal. Its fall would give him safe entry to Tai-hu Lake when required, and deny to the Taipings a possible means of interfering with his own water communications with Shanghai. Once again, Gordon acted swiftly and with surprise, moving by night; once again, an unprepared rebel force was driven out with negligible loss; once again, seeing the importance of what they had lost, a very much stronger rebel force, aided by Burgevine's Europeans, came up, too late, to make a determined counter-attack which failed.

It was now the end of September. At the beginning of the month informed opinion had thought that Burgevine might capture Gordon and perhaps take Shanghai; the British Minister, Sir Frederick Bruce, had feared even that he might take Peking, the Imperialist capital, and bring down the reigning dynasty. In the middle of the month, Gordon noted in his diary: 'Burgevine dilatory and sleepy. Goes off to Nankin. Great mistake.' In the last week of September, the American Captain Jones, who now commanded for Burgevine the captured *Kajow*, was talking privately to the American Captain Davidson, who commanded the *Hyson* for Gordon, of ways and means to surrender. And on 8th October, Burgevine met Gordon to negotiate the details of that surrender (which might be tricky, because the Taipings could not be expected to like it).

Mr. Mayers, an interpreter from the British Consulate, recorded: 'On the night of the 8th instant an interview took place between Burgevine, with his comrade Jones, and Major Gordon; and on this occasion the former placed himself unreservedly in Major Gordon's hands, agreeing to surrender, if possible, on the following day, with the steamer *Kajow* and all his force. Burgevine, however, even whilst arranging with Major Gordon the agreement in question (assigning as his reasons for leaving the rebel service his dissatisfaction with their treatment of himself and the failure of his hopes generally), still displayed the extravagance and obliquity of his nature in a proposition that Major Gordon should desert the Imperialist service with his force, whilst he simultaneously left the rebels with his own followers, and that both should join in an independent career of conquest,' Briefly, what had happened was that Burgevine had bungled everything. During the time he could have interfered with effect, thus raising his prestige and giving himself something to bargain with, he had gone to the rebel capital of Nanking and, with few cards, demanded the earth and failed to get it. Then, returning to Soochow, he had promised, and been paid for, the running of an important cargo of arms into that city; and had lost the lot. Now, as far as the Taipings were concerned, he was just a bad smell. Only a bold coup could restore his position and, after sounding Gordon out as to joining forces, began apparently, according to Mayers, to contemplate capturing Gordon and handing him over to the Taipings. But it is one thing to conceive brilliant ideas; quite another actually to carry them out.

The actual surrender was something of a shambles, due to the wilful General Ching, who fully believed that Gordon, like Burgevine, was capable of going over to the Taipings. Gordon was to mount a fake attack on 9th October, under cover of which all Burgevine's men would come over to him; but Ching got in first, attacked at another point, and the Taipings switched Burgevine to that place to repel Ching's men. Consequently, when Gordon's bluff assault began, Burgevine's mercenaries were nowhere near and so were unable to take advantage of it. If the Europeans still wanted to surrender, they would have to fight their way out, giving the Taipings the slip and battling the Imperialists at the same time. What happened to some of them was described by the American Jones, captain of the *Kajow*. 'On the 10th I received orders (from the rebels) to advance towards Chang-zu. We had a brush with the Imperialists, and captured fifteen war-junks. Our steamer, however, blew up, and two Europeans were severely injured. While this was going on, Burgevine was lying asleep in one of these junks. I heard some remarks made about this, and went to him to remonstrate. He asked who had made remarks about him, and on my declining to tell him, he shot me in the face. I said, "You have shot your best friend." He answered, "Yes, and I wish I had killed you!" On the 15th of October we saw Major Gordon's two steamers coming up the canal, and took advantage of the chance of escape. Our party, with twenty-four men, went down the bank and entered Gordon's lines, where we were well received.'

Mr. Mayers was a witness to this surrender, as the two dozen mercenaries, led by Jones and seven other officers scrambled down the bank under heavy fire from the rebels, to which Gordon's steamers replied. 'The leaders were all natives or naturalised citizens of the United States, but the men, who presented a most pitiable appearance, worn, tattered, and sickly looking, were of eight nationalities. Nearly all were armed with rifles, and some attempt had been made to teach them drill; but the great majority were sailors who had been induced by false representations to proceed to Souchow, with no idea as to the service they were actually intended for. The greatest part of these men volunteered to remain with Major Gordon; the remainder, with the leaders, were sent to Shanghai. Burgevine, with forty others, remains within the city, and their fate is as yet unknown. It appears that the total number, all told, of Burgevine's force was never higher than 103, to which may be added twelve foreigners who were already in Souchow. It is evident that Burgevine counted upon a far larger measure of confidence on the part of the rebel chiefs than he actually enjoyed at any time.'

The *Kajow* was no longer a menace, the accidental explosion of some gunpowder having opened her bows and sunk her. The men wounded by the explosion had been taken off by a boat which was carrying gunpowder, and this also blew up almost immediately. It was during these incidents, which took place in the middle of a struggle with the Imperialists, that Burgevine was found asleep and, on being wakened, shot Captain Jones. His remaining officers were now ashamed that they had ever served under him. Thinking that the Taipings might well be glad to get rid of him, on 15th October, the day the Jones party surrendered, Gordon wrote a letter to the two senior Taiping commanders of Soochow:

'To their Excellencies Chang Wang, Mow Wang,
    You must be already aware that I have on all occasions, when it lay in my power, been merciful to your soldiers when taken prisoners, and not only been so myself, but have used every endeavour to prevent the

99

Imperial authorities from practising any inhumanity. Ask for the truth of this statement any of the men who were taken at Wokong, and who, some of them, must have returned to Souchow, as I placed no restriction on them whatsoever. I now ask your Excellencies to consider the case of the Europeans in your service. A man made to fight against his will is not only a bad soldier, but he is a positive danger, causing anxiety to his leaders, and absorbing a large force to prevent his defection. I would ask your Excellencies if it does not seem to you much better to let these men quietly leave your service if they wish it. Your Excellencies may think that decapitation would soon settle the matter, but you would then be guilty of a crime which would bear its fruits sooner or later. As far as I am personally concerned, it is a matter of indifference whether the men stay or leave; but as a man who wishes to save these unfortunate men, I intercede. Trusting you will accede to my request, I conclude, your Excellencies' obedient servant,

C. G. GORDON.'

The letter was placed on a pole in front of the lines, and soon taken in by the rebels. A few days' negotiation followed, then on the afternoon of 18th October a great display of orange-coloured flags was made at the Medo-chiao Port gateway of Soochow, followed by three volleys of musketry. Burgevine and his remaining men were coming out to surrender. And, while these negotiations were going on, Gordon had met and thrown back a very formidable attempt by able Taiping generals to wipe out his former gains at the key points of Wokong and Patachiao. Ling Wang, an energetic rebel leader, well-known by his nickname of 'Cockeye', was only repulsed at the latter place by bringing up the full

100

firepower of the steamers. At Wokong, the now besieged Imperial garrison was only relieved by a series of bitter attacks by the 'Ever Victorious'. According to the Gordon MSS, 'The rebels here fought better than expected, and certainly astonished Commodore Osborne's secretary, who had come up to see Major Gordon. They were commanded by our old friend Wai Wang, the head man of Taitsan, the only chief who could really boast of having repulsed our troops, and, being composed of the troops of the silk districts, were unaccustomed to be beaten, and were well provided with arms. The rebel earthworks were not strong, but their tenacity in holding them was very great. This fight was one of the most hardly fought of any of our encounters, except Taitsan, and cost us as much as all the others put together.'

The situation was now stabilised and Gordon could resume the offensive, to pinch out and capture Soochow, armed this time with full authority from the Home Government and the blessings of the British Minister at Peking.

CHAPTER EIGHT: 'SOOCHOW HAS SURRENDERED!!'

'I feel convinced that the rebel chiefs would come to terms if they had fair ones offered them. I mean to do my best to bring these about and I am sure that, if I do so, I shall gain a greater victory than any capture of cities would be.' — *Major Gordon to his mother.*

Sir Frederick Bruce made graceful amends in his report to the Home Government, discovering that Gordon had talents beyond the purely military. 'His tact in dealing with the difficulties arising from the jealousy and suspicion of the Chinese authorities, in rescuing Burgevine and the misguided foreigners who served in the Taiping ranks, and in thereby obviating the risk of this foreign adventurer element uniting with them, has been not less conspicuous than his personal gallantry and military skill. I feel the more bound to express my sense of his high-minded devotion to the public interests, as I have criticised, in some of my despatches, the system pursued at Shanghai.' This was to be the basis of Gordon's subsequent reputation as the worker of near miracles in an exotic setting, until eventually the legend grew in the public mind to absurd proportions.

Gordon, meanwhile, spent a week getting a still firmer grip on the strategic waterways to the south of Soochow, before feeling free to move up and cut the city's communications to the north also. There was one uncut waterway leading from the Pon-mun, or South Gate of Soochow, into the Tai-hu Lake. It was covered by the rebel stockades at Wulungchow, two miles west of Patachiao. Gordon set out openly with a large force on 20th October — back to Quinsan. As soon as darkness fell, he took a side creek which led to Ka-poo, where they spent a wet and dismal night. Rain dampened Chinese spirits more than European, however. They reached the stockades at eight o'clock the next morning and Gordon's carefully prepared envelopment plan, in which General Ching was to co-operate, was never completed. After ten minutes firing, the rebels wavered, and then bolted. The last waterway was cut, for the loss of two men killed and three wounded in Gordon's force. To do the Taipings justice, Gordon's methods must inevitably have produced a sense of shock. He disliked attacking foes ready, willing, and able to meet him; still less did he like to meet them when they were cornered. He intended with minimum effort and bloodshed, literally to manoeuvre them out of Soochow, bit by bit. He first selected the vital point, concentrated a powerful force, used darkness and feints to conceal his intentions, then struck like a thunderbolt in the morning, behind the roaring guns and screeching sirens of his steamers, so that it was a shocked and shaken enemy who saw his infantry landed from boats on either side of them, and begin to advance around them. There was, Gordon made sure, only one way out — to the rear. They took it.

These stockades had been held by 1,200 men under Mow Wang, one of the Soochow leaders. On 24th October, at dusk, a violent counter-attack was made by troops under the personal command of the overall rebel leader in Soochow, Chung Wang. They drove in the picket thrown forward in a village in advance of the stockades; then the 'Ever Victorious' re-took the village, with the loss of two killed and six wounded. It was the last time the rebels from Soochow were to attempt to retrieve a lost position; henceforward, they remained entirely on the defensive, as the net closed in. Another force of Taipings, from Kashingfu, were however still pressing around the Imperialist garrison of Wokong. On this occasion, unlike the last, the steamers were available and Gordon left the affair to his adjutant-general, Major Kirkham. The rebels resisted fiercely to their front, but as soon as the *Hyson* came thundering down their flank, they upped and ran, or tried to get away in boats. This was fatal, for the road here ran parallel with the waterway, and the *Hyson* was able to pursue the entire fleeing mass, flailing them with shells from her bow 32-powder. A mass of boats and junks were captured, and 1,300 prisoners taken, including a Wang (literally a little 'King', but actually the equivalent of a General). Thus, on 26th October, Gordon and the Imperialist forces were sure in their possession of all the waterways leading out of Soochow to the south. There could now be no rebel sortie in that direction.

Up to now the Imperialist forces under the Futai had been separated from another force to the north commanded by the Futai's brother. Gordon therefore moved the 'Ever Victorious' to fill the gap between them, directly to the north of Soochow, and chose for his first action the stockades at Leeku, which covered two waterways, one of which led down directly from the north to the North Gate of Soochow. Their fall would continue the encirclement of Soochow to the point where the besieging forces lapped round the city in an arc of 330 degrees, leaving one route only for escape — the line of the Grand Canal where it led off north-west to the rebel stronghold of Wusieh. On the last day of October the assault force, led by the *Hyson*, steamed off down the creeks for the stockades of Leeku. From Shanghai to meet them went a witness whose non-military description, published in the *Cornhill* magazine the following year, fills in the colour so often lacking in the bare black-and-white soldierly accounts.

'On a certain bright and chilly morning in the month of October 1863, the writer of this paper, after two days' voyage by the interminable network of rivers, canals, and lakes which extend for many scores of miles westward from Shanghai, found himself traversing a broad and shallow expanse, reed-encircled and curiously silent, showing none of those myriad sails which usually dot the bosom of Chinese waters. To the westward of this the Golden Pheasant Lake stretched; at a distance of some 4,000 yards — farther than the eye could penetrate to right and left in the misty morning — the grizzled walls of Souchow, a city celebrated for ages in the history of China for its size, population, wealth, and luxury, but now stripped of its magnificence, and held by an army of Taeping banditti against the Imperial forces, of which a disciplined corps of native soldiers, under the command of a British officer, formed the only really effective part. To the right and left, mile after mile, rose the line of lofty wall and grey turret, while above all appeared not only the graceful pagodas which have been for ages the boast of Souchow, and the dense foliage of secular trees — the invariable glory of Chinese cities — but also the shimmering roofs of newly-decorated palaces, confidently occupied by the vainglorious leaders of the rebellion.

'Everything lay silent in the morning haze as I approached by a devious course, passing here a flotilla of Imperial gunboats watching the entrance of some creek leading to the city, and there some charred remains of what was once a flourishing village suburb, the headquarters occupied by the British commander of the disciplined Chinese. He had left behind him before entering the lake the entrenchment of the Chinese generalissimo, Ching, who with some 12,000 sturdy irregular troops was investing the east and north gates, whilst in his front a small forest of junk masts, near the south-east angle of the city, indicated the spot on the Grand Canal where Major Gordon had established his position. It was at a point where a channel, communicating with the Golden Pheasant Lake, joined the waters of the Grand Canal that Major Gordon had recently seized three strong fortifications of the rebels, and entrenching himself in an impregnable position at a distance of about 2,000 yards from the angle of the city, cut off all communication on the south and east.

'While my boat was approaching this spot the proximity of the rebel line became apparent with surprising suddenness, for, following their usual custom, they greeted the rising sun with a simultaneous display of gaudy banners above the line of their entrenchments. The mud walls they had thrown up, scarcely distinguishable before, were now marked out by thousands of flags of every colour, from black to crimson, whilst behind them rose the jangling roll of gongs and the murmur of an invisible multitude. Almost at the same moment a dull report and a puff of smoke rising within the lines of banners showed the manner in which this display was greeted from the still unseen lines of the Imperial commander; and as my boat came to anchor in sight of Major Gordon's position, the dull shock of a sixty-eight-pounder, and a shout from the gunners, announced that a heavy shell had been sent on a successful errand of destruction into the opposing lines.

'At the same instant a dark mass of men swarmed through the sally-port of the "stockade" or fort, which guarded either bank of the Grand Canal, and spread in skirmishing line over the fields on each side — treading waist-deep in the deserted rice crop, ripe for the sickle, but now left to be converted into a field of slaughter. In this soldier-like array, accoutred in uniforms of dark serge, and distinguished by green turbans wound around their heads in lieu of caps, armed with Tower muskets, and delivering a regular fire with steadiness and effect, it would have been difficult for a stranger to the events of the last five years to recognise the despised Chinese, to whom the possession of martial capabilities had so persistently been denied. Such a stranger must have viewed with surprise the firm regularity with which these troops executed the ordinary manoeuvres of the field, and the alacrity with which they sprang forward at the bugle-call to encounter an enemy of their own race and language (in many cases their village kindred), who outnumbered them far beyond the proportion of ten to one.'

After setting off in the wrong direction on 31st October, Gordon had doubled back on his tracks during another dismal, rainy night, and at dawn emerged into the canal two miles from the stockades. Another shock assault went in, the infantry and guns pouring ashore, the fire of the first stockade fixed in front while the infantry crept round it, and eventually rushed it, from the sides. The rebels then evacuated the second stockade, losing 30 or 40 men prisoners, for the loss to Gordon's force of three killed and six wounded. On 11 November this position was improved by the capture of Wanti, two miles away, but with much heavier loss, as the attack went wrong in its execution, two columns assaulting without orders and running into a crossfire. More than fifty officers and men were killed and wounded, but the rebels also lost heavily, 400 in prisoners alone.

The turning point of the campaign had now been reached. If Soochow is thought of as the bull's eye of a target, black, densely packed with men, then the 'inner' line of besiegers was stretched very thin, but complete except for the north-west arc leading to Wusieh. If the besiegers made their final move to complete the encirclement, would they have enough men to hold that thin line, or would it snap? Not only was there the danger of the besieged breaking out, but of other large rebel forces to the north, in the Wusieh or 'outer' area moving down the Grand Canal towards Soochow and taking the besiegers in rear. In Wusieh were some 20,000 rebels and in Mantanchow nearby were some 18,000 more. These were partly menaced by an Imperial force of 20,000 to 30,000 men under the command of the Futai's incompetent brother. By merely existing, they could reduce the proportions of the threat from the Wusieh area, but they could not eliminate it. These may be thought of as operations on the 'outer' fringe of the siege.

But the tough central nut which had to be cracked, Soochow, was not only very strongly fortified but held by some 40,000 Taipings, necessarily close concentrated. Around them was only a thin line of besiegers, holding in small numbers a number of key points. The total force available to the attackers consisted of General Ching's 10,000 Imperial troops, 3,100 men of the 'Ever Victorious', and 400 men of a similar, French-trained force; a total of 13,500 men. Of this total, 7,500 Imperialists and 1,000 men of Gordon's force were tied down in static siege roles, leaving only 5,000 men for assault purposes.

In detail, the nearly complete ring around the city was held by, reading from west to east; a mobile blockade force on Tai-hu Lake consisting of Gordon's three steamers *Hyson*, *Tsatlee*, *Firefly*, and 200 Imperial soldiers; 1,000 Imperialists holding the stockades at Wulungchow; 1,500 Imperialists holding the stockades at Patachiao; 4,000 Imperialists closely investing the Low mun, or East Gate, of Soochow; with 200 of Gordon's force at nearby Waiquaidong; 400 of Gordon's force at Leeku; and another 400 of them at Wanti. For all further operations, either to finally cut off the city by taking positions on the Grand Canal between it and Wusieh, or for an actual assault on the walls, there were available only 2,500 of Ching's Imperialists, 2,100 men of the 'Ever Victorious', and 400 men of the French-trained force. Five thousand in all, to combat ten times their number of rebels. On the face of it, to complete the encirclement of the 40,000 rebels in Soochow, while threatened by other rebel forces from Wusieh, was to menace a tiger by attempting to snip off its tail with a pair of nail-scissors. This was the view of the Imperialists.

Gordon's own plans had originally contemplated the taking of Wusieh, but this had been based on the expectation that he would be joined by Captain Osborn's British naval force of small steamers which would give him complete superiority on the vital waterways. However, the diplomatic and military conditions for the use of this fleet had been too stringent, and it was not ever to be available to him. Further, Wusieh could only be effectively attacked if General Ching's forces co-operated with the northern force under the Futai's brother; and as the two men were fiercely jealous of each other, it became apparent that the project was impossible. Therefore, at this time, the first half of November 1863, Gordon intended not to take Wusieh but to mask it. He planned to cut the Grand Canal linking the two cities, not in one place but in two, at Fusaiquan and Monding, which were sufficiently near to be able to support each other, but at the same time sufficiently far away to prevent a simultaneous concerted attack on the 'cut-off' position by rebels from both Wusieh and Soochow. Part of his reasoning was psychological and political. He knew there were dissensions in Soochow between Lar Wang, who commanded the bulk of the troops, and the Mow Wang, who commanded the smaller portion. With the city cut off, the generalissimo, Chung Wang, might not be able to impose such strict obedience as formerly from his subordinate commanders.

Part of Gordon's force was preparing to move off for this purpose on 14 November, when his plans were totally disrupted by news that the steamer *Firefly*, due to return from Shanghai to rejoin the blockade, had been seized by a party of desperadoes led by a renegade British sailor, Lindlay, who had overpowered and were later to kill the small crew of four men left aboard. There was evidence that Burgevine was behind this, while being protected by the United States Consulate; but he failed to benefit for the Futai instantly had him arrested, coldly remarking to the U.S. Consul that he believed 'the crime of piracy to be dealt with among foreign nations with even greater severity than that of joining the banditti in China'. With the powerfully-armed *Firefly* last seen headed for the rebel positions at Soochow, Gordon's plan had to be altered.

He wrote in his war diary: 'This obliged G. to be quick, and forced him to cut the canal at once; which he did at Fusai-kwan by the capture — without loss — of five stockades. Although most important, it was shamefully deserted (by the rebel garrison), after a sharp skirmish in the hills on the 19th November.' On the same day Gordon left for the East Gate of Soochow, the Low mun or Lo Moon, where his siege artillery was already assembled to cover the assault. Soochow was now largely cut off, and, noted Gordon, 'All the exterior defences of the city had now been captured, but a small mountain path was open to the rebels for escape, and the prisoners gave daily accounts of the dissensions in the city. But no time was to be lost, for the *Firefly*, with its unhappy captain, Dollie, and three others, who were taken prisoners, was with the rebels. So G.

determined to attack the city at the N.E. angle. It was, however, necessary to take the inner line of exterior defences, which now were very formidable.'

The assault took place on 27th November, and a few days beforehand, Gordon benefited from the arrival of one of the British officers who, under General Brown's emergency ruling, had been lent to the Chinese. This was Lieutenant Storey of the 99th Regiment, whose 'Reminiscences' were included by Hake in the Gordon MSS he edited. Storey wanted to see active service, but, he wrote: 'Before leaving Hong Kong many of the mercantile community tried to dissuade me from my project; spoke of Major Gordon as a freebooter and in other disparaging terms; said, that to crush this rebellion was a wrong to the Chinese nation; what was the good of our meddling in a national squabble, in which the rebels had proved themselves the better men? etc. etc. I did not know then that the crushing of this rebellion meant a loss of many dollars to my would-be councillors. The word "Boycott" was not coined, but plainly was I given to understand that if I joined Major Gordon I should have the cold shoulder.'

By way of Shanghai and Quinsan, Storey reached the stockades by the Low-mun gate. 'We arrived at about 11 a.m., and learned that Gordon had just returned from a reconnaissance in force on his right front. C— introduced me to a light-built, active, wiry, middle-sized man, of about thirty-two years of age, in the undress uniform of the Royal Engineers. The countenance bore a pleasant frank appearance, eyes light blue with a fearless look in them, hair crisp and inclined to curl, conversation short and decided. This was Major C. G. Gordon.'

After lunch, Gordon showed them the sights, including the view from a 40-feet high lookout tower. Included in the view was one of the 32-pounder guns captured by the Taipings from Captain Holland, which at that moment the rebels were busily preparing to fire, probably attracted by the red coats of the British officers. As they descended into cover, the shot whizzed over their heads, killing two Chinese soldiers 70 yards away. What Storey had seen impressed him with the strength of the rebel defences. 'On the extreme right; 1, a mud stockade about a quarter of a mile from the city, which was encompassed with a broad and deep stream; 2, a formidable-looking stone stockade about 20 feet high, loopholed for musketry, and bordering on to the water edge of the river, and situated about 600 yards to the left of No. 1. On the left bank, at about 300 yards from No. 2, was 3, a large mud stockade built also on to the edge of the river; the ground rose a little towards the proper right of this stockade; beyond it again was 4, a small mud stockade, say about 300 yards from No. 3. All these stockades were in echelon. The country between them and the city was rather swampy, and afforded no cover for us.'

Nevertheless, Gordon could not wait there indefinitely; to bring the dissensions between the rebel leaders within the city to a head, he had to apply pressure, and one of the reasons for choosing the Low mun was that it was held by the troops of Lar Wang, who was contemplating surrender. The attack was due to go in under cover of darkness, at 2 a.m. on 27th November. At nine o'clock the previous evening, a lantern was seen there which deserters said was a sign that Mow Wang was now holding this gate. This, as it turned out, was true; and he had with him in addition to his own men some twenty Europeans, whose presence was one cause of the dissensions and, moreover, he had been warned of the attack. Soon after Mow Wang's lantern was seen in the darkness, an eclipse of the moon took place, which seemed ominous to the Chinese of the assault force. Nevertheless, they moved quietly down to the canal bank.

'To distinguish friend from foe,' wrote Storey, 'Gordon's force were to wear a band of calico round the neck. By 11 p.m. the troops told off were embarked in large cargo boats, very similar to the barges in use on our canals, and in good spirits. The orders were that the steamer *Hyson*, which was fitted up as a gunboat, should go first, and at a preconcerted signal bombard Nos. 1 and 2 stockades; the cargo boats were to drop quietly down till they were about 200 yards from No. 3 stockade, disembark the troops, who were to advance quietly to within 100 yards or so and wait for the signal, and then rush the place, bringing their right shoulders well up. Should the attack be successful, of which there were doubts, as this was the first and last time that Gordon tried his troops by night, these boats were to move higher up the waterway to allow the boat with reinforcements to come in. The night was most favourable to the success of the enterprise, being very dark.

'The attacking party landed, and with supports well up rushed for No. 3 stockade at the signal. When within 70 to 80 yards the rebels opened a tremendous fire. The officers led their men most gallantly, but little did they or anyone know of the pitfall in front of them. The rebels had filled the ditch which invariably surrounded their stockades with water (a most unusual proceeding) by tapping the river bank. Into this death trap the leading column fell by the score. A panic ensued; those not in the water fell back only to meet the advancing supports; the leading boats instead of remaining where they were tried to retreat; they met and fouled the boats coming up, and the waterway became blocked. The rebels took advantage of the confusion and fired into "the crown" of the troops, who could not be got to rally — for some four or five minutes the bullets fell like hail among them, — and then retreated. The loss was heavy. Seven officers killed and drowned in leading the assault, several severely wounded, and the rank and file got heavily punished. Gordon was in the thick of the *melée* and escaped unhurt, he was doing all he could to clear his retreat and the boats out of the confusion they were in. His staff, who ably supported him in these efforts, were equally fortunate.'

The total loss, in killed, drowned, missing, and wounded was nearly 170 officers and men. But, almost within hours of this repulse, Gordon learned from General Ching that Lar Wang, heading a group of lesser generals commanding 30,000 men, was thinking of surrender; and had suggested that if Gordon would attack the Low-mun stockades, where Mow Wang was, in advance of the city walls, he would shut the gates behind him. The assault on the Low-mun stockades would have to be renewed and this time, with delicate surrender negotiations pending, a reverse could not be afforded. Gordon therefore brought up all his siege artillery which, on 29th November, opened fire. There could, of course, be no concealing this attack; no chance of surprise. The Mow Wang manned his stockades and awaited the onslaught.

'At about 6 p.m. Gordon again assaulted No. 3 stockade,' wrote Storey, 'detaching a regiment to hold in check any resistance that No. 4 stockade might give, this time with success. The rebels fought with desperate courage; ere they could be induced to quit, a part of the ditch was filled in, two light guns dragged across into the stockade, and several rounds fired point blank into them. The rebels in No. 4 stockade, when they saw that they were isolated, cleared out, and retreated to the city. On going over these four stockades later in the day one saw that No. 3 was the key to the whole position, and that was the reason for Gordon hammering away at it so persistently. With these stockades in possession Soochow was completely invested, whether they would capitulate or fight it out to the bitter end was the question.' The losses in this attack had been heavier still: Officers — 6 killed and 3 wounded; European bodyguard — 5 wounded; Chinese rank and file — 50 killed, 128 wounded. The way was now clear for the besiegers to close up to the city walls, but those walls seemed enormously strong.

While preparations for the assault on the city proceeded, Gordon was engaged in almost day-to-day negotiations with, on the Imperialist side the Futai and General Ching, and on the Taiping side Lar Wang and other military chiefs. To the Futai, he said that military success in the assault of the city walls could not be guaranteed and that therefore lenient terms should be granted to the rebels as an inducement to surrender. To the Lar Wang's suggestion that Gordon attack the city, but not engage the troops under his command, who would wear white turbans as a form of recognition, Gordon replied bluntly that he was deceiving himself. The troops were too undisciplined; they would run riot during an attack on a city; he could not enforce discrimination. If the Taipings were sincere in their wish to come over, he added, they had better surrender a city gate as a guarantee of good faith; and if that was impossible, then the only alternatives left to them were either to evacuate the city or fight the matter out. He then discussed with the Taiping leader, almost as a valued friend and adviser, the position of the rebellion as a whole, which he thought bound to collapse soon; he advised Lar Wang to come to terms while this was still possible. Chung Wang, the rebel generalissimo, had already escaped to Wusieh, leaving Soochow, the former 'Venice of China', to its fate.

And, on 4 December, Lieutenant Storey was able to write: 'Soochow has surrendered!'

CHAPTER NINE: THE SACK OF THE CITY

'Shang Yew tyen tang,
Hya Yew Soo Hang?

('Above is Paradise,
Below is Soo-chow and Hang-chow')
— *Ancient Chinese Proverb.*

Nanking means 'Southern Court'; Peking means 'Northern Court'. These were the twin capital cities of China, the former at the moment being the capital of the Taipings, the latter of the Imperialists. Soochow, although a provincial city of the first grade, was the capital only of I-tong, the eastern part of the province of Kiang-soo, thus ranking second to Nanking. But, with Hang-chow, it had had something of the gaiety and taste which, in Europe, would be represented by Paris. What would it be like now, after four years' occupation by the Taipings?

On 4th December 1863, Gordon visited the Futai to coordinate the plan under which Lar Wang and some of his own force were to take prisoner the only rebel commander who still wished to hold out — Mow Wang. But he had hardly returned to his own camp when he received news which altered everything. Two Europeans who had been serving with Mow Wang, but had that morning deserted, were brought to him. They were Radinor and Bertrand, formerly *sous-officiers* in the French Zephyr Regiment at Shanghai, from which they had also deserted. But they were good fighting men, having been often seen on the defences of Soochow.

They stated that, at eleven o'clock that morning (it was now late afternoon) Mow Wang had sent for Lar Wang. After an hour's amicable talk, Mow Wang had invited Lar Wang and some lesser military chiefs to dinner. They had offered prayers, then dressed ceremonially in their robes and crowns; except for one lesser chief, Sing Wang. They had seated themselves, then Mow Wang had got up to make a speech. They missed the finer points of this (in fact, it had been extremely insulting to the other chiefs), but it was plainly not being very well received. When, above the commotion, they plainly heard cries of *tsah, tsah*! ('kill, kill!') they left the banquet hall and made for their rooms, which were nearby. Seconds later, his crown gone and his robes torn, a rebel chief, Ning Wang, dashed in and begged them to protect him. Lar Wang, who had been silent at the banquet, now came and barred the doorway, so that the mob could not get at Ning Wang. They then decided to desert and on their way out to the courtyard saw the body of Mow Wang in two separate pieces, the head on one side of the threshold, the torso on the other, and all the rebel chiefs mounting their horses in a great hurry. They made for the Fual-mun Gate, where these events were not yet known, and so escaped into positions held by the Imperialist General Ching.

Subsequently, it was learned that the murder had been planned by Kong Wang and Sing Wang (the latter had not dressed in his robes, in order not to be encumbered for the killing), on grounds of expediency, and against the wishes of Lar Wang. Mow Wang had made it easy for them by praising the faithfulness of his own men, from Kwangsi and Canton, as compared to the irresolution of those from Hoonan and

Hupih. As there was only one other Kwangsi leader present, Ning Wang, tempers flared up against him, he was stabbed in the neck and back, and then decapitated. 'Thus perished by a cowardly assassination a brave and intelligent man who in the midst of his difficulties never despaired,' wrote Hake. 'He was very good to Europeans, but cruel to his countrymen.'

While the Frenchmen were relating to Gordon what they knew of this story, much shouting could be heard from behind the deserted walls of Soochow, but no sound of firing. At dawn next day, 5th December, there was a brief outburst of musketry, Mow Wang's men fighting with those of Lar Wang, all of whom had shaved their heads in token of submission to the Imperialists. During the night, Lar Wang had diplomatically left two gates open, so that those who wanted to escape should have the chance. General Ching behaved with proper discretion, not even occupying a gate of the city until the morning of the 5th; and Gordon intended not to let his own men enter the city at all — he knew, from his experiences at the burning of the Summer Palace, how plunder converted an army into a rabble beyond any general's power to control. But, in lieu of plunder, he asked the Futai to grant them two months' pay as bonus money for their victories; they had received none so far under Gordon, although Ward had paid bonus money at the rate of five dollars per battle. After some wrangling Gordon got one month's pay for his men, and, after a mutinous howl at the news, got them to accept it.

But Gordon himself went into the city, accompanied by some of his officers, including Lieutenant Storey, in order to see Lar Wang and the other rebel leaders. The internal appearance of the once gay and luxurious capital, presented an appalling aspect,' wrote Mossman. 'Along the main street leading to the centre of the city, not an entire dwelling was visible for more than a mile. On each side as far as the eye could see, heaps of bricks were piled in confusion, without a vestige of wood or other building material; and as no signs of fire were visible, it gave evidence of having been destroyed when the Tai-pings captured and devastated the city four years previously,' Storey noted that 'the city was very quiet; it had a deserted look; not a soul in the streets; shops all shut. We passed through a considerable body of rebels to the Yamen, and in a large hall, with their heads newly shaved in token of submission and dressed in valuable furs, it being winter time and very cold, were a number, say twenty, of very distinguished soldierly-looking men. These were the late rebel chiefs in Soochow. The interview did not last very long. We and they left the Yamen at the same time, we to have a look at the city, they to go to the Imperial Chinese headquarters to make their submission to Li Hung Chang. Again we were much struck by the martial appearance of these Wangs as they mounted their ponies and rode off as it turned out to their death, they being all decapitated that afternoon in the audience tent of the Futai.'

After this, the party went to the Yamen, or palace which had belonged to Mow Wang. 'Nearby,' wrote Gordon, 'we found about thirty heads of small boys, averaging from fifteen to eighteen years, and on inquiry found these were Mow Wang's immediate attendants, and had been beheaded by the Wangs after his death. This may seem a very great cruelty, but they were wicked to a degree that would scarcely be believed. One of them, a boy of fourteen years of age, an adopted son of Mow Wang, himself cut off the head of his small comrade, twelve years old, for stealing some trifles from him. The same youth had been guilty of a great many other atrocities, and had tortured two Chinese soldiers of the French force who had been taken at the Patachiao stockades in October.'

Lieutenant Storey went inside the actual palace. 'The sight I saw there will always be remembered by me,' he wrote. 'Picture to yourselves a large hall with a dark-vaulted high wood roof, against the walls a number of gigantic but much disfigured Chinese deities, a table capable of holding about 150 guests, strewn with the debris of a feast, the air redolent with the sickly perfume of a kind of small water-lilies very much withered placed in masses on the table, chairs and stools upset, candlesticks with the candles burnt out, and a deathlike silence and gloom. Halfway down this room was the bulky headless body of a man dressed in gorgeously embroidered silk robes. The outside robe, which was a magnificent specimen of embroidery, I determined to have, stiff as it was with gore, and was proceeding to take it off when Gordon walked in. I had felt something hard in the breast pocket of one of the under garments, put my hand in and drew out a packet of letters in Gordon's handwriting, which turned out to be letters written by him to the Mow Wang relative to the surrender of the city, and guaranteeing if they did so the security of the lives and properties of the inhabitants. We concluded the body we saw must under the circumstances be that of the Mow Wang. Gordon, who was much moved by the incident, remained by the body. I went and brought in a few soldiers, by them it was taken away, washed, dressed, and then decently buried in his robes.'

Gordon's next moves were based on his reluctance to pursue those of the rebels who had fled to Wusieh with a force which had not been properly rewarded; he had threatened to resign and in the meantime ordered his men back to the Quinsan base. They had marched past the Futai's tent, howling with rage. However, without compromising his resignation or calling on the bulk of his force, there was one more thing he could do. In Mow Wang's palace he had found documents showing that the captured steamer *Firefly* was on Tai-hu Lake, and still a potential menace. He decided to send there the *Hyson* and the *Tsatlee*, which were at the moment moored to the canal bank by the Futai's headquarters, on the route which led through Waiqauidong to Quinsan. He therefore ordered them to get up steam, go round the city, and meet him at the gate nearest to the lake. They had already had a small naval battle on the lake, with forty rebel gunboats, in which the *Tsatlee* had been holed in the boiler and had to be towed out of action for repairs by the larger *Hyson*.

But all these plans were thrown out of gear by the increasing disorder in Soochow, as gradually the Imperialist troops got out of hand and groups of surrendered rebels gathered together again to defend themselves. Gordon went back to the Low-mun gate and, looking along the canal bank towards Quinsan, could see a large crowd around the Futai's boat, about 1½ miles away; this he took to be the ceremony of surrender by the rebel chiefs; which in a sense it was. Then Imperialist troops entered the city, shouting madly, and firing off their muskets in the air; behind them came General Ching who, on seeing Gordon there, went very white (for a Chinaman). Gordon immediately questioned Ching about the fate of Lar Wang and his companions, whom he had last seen riding off confidently and merrily to surrender; one of them, Sing Wang, who had helped assassinate Mow Wang, had inexplicably not shaved his head in token of surrender to the Manchu dynasty. Ching was nervous and evasive; he told a muddled story to the effect that Lar Wang had not gone to the Futai at all; that Lar Wang had demanded the right to retain 2,000 of his own men as an organised force, to hold half the city and its gates, and had refused to bring his men outside the walls. The Futai having refused, said Ching, Lar Wang and the other rebel chiefs had run away.

Gordon, believing this, went to Lar Wang's palace in the city, found it gutted and plundered. A man there, an uncle of Lar Wang, asked Gordon (who had only an interpreter with him) to help get the females of Lar Wang's family to his own palace, where they would be safe. When they arrived there, Gordon found some 500 or 600 armed rebels in the courtyard; and, as the uproar in Soochow rapidly increased, they closed all the doors, shutting themselves in for defence. Increasing numbers of rebels and their families assembled round the house for protection as darkness fell. After midnight, the situation in the city outside had become so serious that Gordon wrote a letter which his interpreter was to carry. It was an order for the *Hyson* and the *Tsatlee* to abandon the Tai-hu Lake project, and instead to take captive the Futai, Li Hung Chang, and hold him prisoner until he had given up Lar Wang and his followers. Gordon's bodyguard were to make their way to the house he was in, as the rebels would not let him go; his presence offered them protection against the bands of pillaging Imperialist troops who were wandering around all night.

Then news came that the interpreter had been attacked by Imperialists and that the message had not got through. Gordon was therefore allowed to leave, with a bodyguard of two rebels. This resulted in him being detained as a suspicious character by the Imperial guards on the Pon-mun gate. They released him after an hour and at about dawn he reached his own boat and began to issue orders. One of them was for Lieutenant Storey, who did not have to be woken up, even at 5 a.m., because the tumult caused by the sack of Soochow had prevented sleep for anyone. Storey and another officer caught up with Gordon, who was dashing from place to place, at the west gate of Soochow.

'We found him alone standing on the wood bridge,' wrote Storey, 'sword drawn and beating with the flat of it and driving back all Imperial Chinese soldiers who attempted to pass.' Gordon told Storey and some others, including his provost-marshal, to go to the besieged house where the wives, concubines and children of the rebel leaders were, and get them out. So they went into the city.

'We were in total ignorance of the massacre of the previous day,' wrote Storey. 'What a contrast we saw. The streets were inches deep with clothing, shops broken into and looted, many houses on fire, very many dead bodies of rebels, all ages and sexes, some of them half roasted, and numerous pigs feeding on them. Women and children running about the streets, screaming with terror, pursued by straggling parties of Imperial Chinese troops maddened with lust and excitement, besmirched with blood, who were entering and looting the shops, cutting down with their sharp bill-hooked knife everyone who came in their way irrespective of age or sex, and firing at random at locked doors and closed windows. We found our way to the Yamen, which was about half a mile off; it was then pretty full of rebels of all sexes and ages, and all in a dreadful state of fear and distress,' More refugees were continually fleeing there, pursued by Imperialists. At first, these were in small groups only; the British were able to disarm them, and send them on their way with a boot smartly applied to the seat of the trousers, 'a sound kicking', Storey called it. But eventually they came in such numbers that the gates had to be closed and this party also were besieged until Storey's companion managed to get through to Gordon and bring back a half-company of disciplined Chinese as escort to the refugees, who were then brought safely out of the city. By then, Gordon was mad with rage. He himself had conducted the negotiations and promised these people the safety of their lives and property. 'He was beside himself,' wrote Storey.

Immediately after seeing Storey he had met Captain Bonnefoi with some troops of the French-disciplined Chinese force, and gone with them into the city to prevent further massacre. The bulk of the 'Ever Victorious' were well on their way back to Quinsan, and Gordon was now waiting for the arrival of the *Hyson* and *Tsatlee* before moving on the Futai's headquarters' and, under the menace of their powerful armament, forcibly making prisoner the man who was in effect the Chinese Commander-in-Chief for the whole region. The unfortunate General Ching came up with a bodyguard and tried to speak to Gordon; he was met with such a stream of abuse and threat, in the hearing both of the Imperialists and the rebels, that he vanished back into the city. All he had been trying to say was that he had been obeying superior orders, those of the Futai. When Major Bailey found him a few minutes later, he had just had twenty of his pillaging soldiers shot, and was in tears as he begged Bailey to tell Gordon that what had happened was not his fault.

But what had happened to Lar Wang and the rest of the Taiping generals? Major Bailey did not know, but reported to Gordon that he had the son of Lar Wang in his tent, and would fetch him. The boy told Gordon that his father had been executed, the previous day, on the other side of the creek. As Gordon was planning action, he had to make sure of his ground; he sent his A.D.C., Prince Frederick of Wittgenstein, across to confirm the story, and the Prince reported that there were nine headless bodies lying there. Gordon then could not restrain himself from visiting the scene. He recognised a number of the heads, including that of Lar Wang which, at the son's request, he brought back with him.

Gordon's steamers then arrived, and almost simultaneously a message from Colonel Tumblety, at Fusai-quan, that the rebel chief of Kwangpu had surrendered to him. Gordon ordered him to do one of two things — to give the town back to the Taipings, or to let them join him at Quinsan. They were not to be handed over to the Imperialists. When he steamed up to the Futai's camp, Li Hung Chang was gone, somewhere inside the walls of Soochow. Gordon therefore sat down to write him a letter containing his terms. The Futai was to surrender to him, in order to be handed over for trial by the Imperial authorities in Peking on a charge of treachery; if he did not surrender, every one of the towns which had been captured by Gordon from the rebels would be handed back to them. There is little doubt that he could have done it, for his own force were still inflamed by the Futai's refusal to pay them the full sum which Gordon considered they had earned.

Dr. Halliday McCartney, now commanding some 10,000 men at his newly-organised base arsenal, came up to Soochow and on 7th December was contacted by the Futai, who handed him Gordon's letter and asked him to translate it for him. McCartney read it through grimly and then observed that it had clearly been written under the stress of great emotion and would do better to remain untranslated. 'If so, you had better keep it,' replied Li. He then explained to McCartney, for transmission to Gordon, his side of the story. The reason for his allowing Soochow to be sacked was that his own men, like Gordon's, had not been paid and he had not the money to do it; under their terms of service, they were allowed pillage in lieu of pay; and this he had permitted, to prevent a mutiny. His reason for executing the rebel chiefs, for which he took full responsibility, was that the number of surrendered rebels was very great, presenting a threat, and that their late leaders were not submissive, but made such insolent proposals, and behaved in such an overbearing manner, particularly in not all having shaven heads, that he felt it was not safe to spare their lives. Their deaths might prevent further fighting and save many lives. This was quite possibly true, since his own brother had nearly been killed by Taiping treachery, and 1,500 of his force wiped out, at Taitson, not many months before. It is possible also that General Ching had something to do with it as, if Lar Wang was allowed to join the Imperialists with his troops, he was likely to eclipse Ching in importance.

General Brown thought the matter so serious that he came up to see Gordon on 9th December, followed by an interview with the Futai two days later. To General Brown, in contrast to his attitude to McCartney, Li Hung Chang was unbending, refusing to explain his motives. To Sir Frederick Bruce, the General wrote: 'I speedily ascertained that, though the Futai was prepared to take upon himself the whole responsibility of the murder of the Wangs and the sacking of the city, and fully to exonerate Major Gordon from all blame, he was either unable or unwilling to offer any exculpation or explanation of his conduct, and it only remained for me to express my opinion and future intentions.' It is clear that Li was not prepared to justify himself officially to any foreigner for what he, a Chinese official, had done in China.

The General told him briefly that his actions would be regarded with indignation in England and elsewhere; that they were impolitic, alienating friends and driving the rebels into desperate resistance instead of capitulation; that he would insist on the promised reward of one month's pay to be made to Gordon's force; that he would refer the matter to Sir Frederick

Bruce; and, pending instructions from the Minister, had ordered Gordon forthwith to cease all offensive operations in aid of the Imperialists, although he would still protect Soochow. 'I concluded,' wrote General Brown, 'by expressing my unhesitating conviction, that after what had occurred the Government would withdraw all assistance hitherto afforded to the Imperial cause, recall Major Gordon and all English subjects serving under him, and disband his Anglo-Chinese force.'

This was well-judged, being sufficiently severe to conciliate Gordon, who felt personally smeared, but preventing precipitate action and leaving the door slightly ajar for the time when tempers would have cooled. Meanwhile, history was being written. In *The Times* of 22nd January 1864, came the first news to reach England:

'Major Gordon captured Soochow on December 5th.'

Reports reached the Imperial capital rather more rapidly, taking a week to get there, and the Government-controlled *Peking Gazette* announced: 'Li Hung Chang reports that the army under his command has captured the city of Soo-chow, and exterminated the rebels.' In the long narrative which followed, there was only one reference to Gordon. 'On the 3rd and 4th of December the naval and military forces under Ch'eng-Hsio-Ch'i, Li Ch'ou-pin, and Huang Yi-sheng, attacked the different gates of the city, keeping up day and night an incessant attack, which became more vigorous the longer it lasted. Gordon, also, established himself close to the city walls, and opened a cannonade against them.'

In the Peking 'honours list', however, Gordon's services were acknowledged by a high military decoration and an Imperial gift of 10,000 taels (about £3,300 at the rate of exchange then current). The awards were brought to Quinsan by an important deputation led by a mandarin and carrying a covering letter of thanks from the Emperor. Gordon wrote on the back of it: 'Major Gordon receives the approbation of His Majesty the Emperor with every gratification, but regrets most sincerely that, owing to the circumstances which occurred since the capture of Soochow, he is unable to receive any mark of His Majesty the Emperor's recognition, and therefore begs His Majesty to receive his thanks for his intended kindness, and to allow him to decline the same.'

The return of the money, with thanks, staggered the Chinese; today it would be more nearly equivalent to £30,000 than £3,000. And it silenced the interested parties who were disparaging Gordon as a 'freebooter' in the style of Burgevine and Ward.

CHAPTER TEN: 'THE HOUR-GLASS IS BROKEN'

'All those who take an interest in you are thankful that you have been so mercifully preserved hitherto — and our hope is that the same protecting Arm which took you into this affair, will bring you out of it safe and sound. It would be idle to say that you must take care of yourself; some degree of danger, indeed a very considerable degree of danger, you must run, but you would scarcely be justified in exposing yourself unnecessarily.' — *Sir Harry Parkes to Gordon*, 11 May 1864.

The strategic consequences of the fall of Soochow were considerable. Wu-sieh was evacuated by the rebels on 13th December, Ping-hu surrendered on the 16th, Cha-poo on the 20th, Hai-yuen on the 21st, and Kah-shur on 7th January; Ping-Wang fell to the Imperialists on 9th January, and Hai-ning surrendered on 25th January. On 18th February 1864, Gordon marched out with his force through a devastated countryside deep in snow in a dash for the two towns of Yesing and Liyang, fifty miles apart, which were sited in the narrowest portion of the hour-glass shaped territory held by the Taipings, now some ninety miles across at this point. Gordon judged that if he thus cut the rebel-held area in two, and then turned north to take Kintang, Tayau, and Chanchufu, the Taiping rebellion would be effectively crushed within two months. What remained, including their capital, Nanking, could be dealt with by the Imperialists alone, and the expensive and dangerous 'Ever Victorious Army' safely disbanded. These were his main reasons for continuing in the Chinese service.

This drive of ninety miles into the heart of rebel territory was a very different enterprise to anything hitherto undertaken. Previous operations had been conducted methodically, to force the Taipings slowly back from Shanghai; the attacking force operating always on interior lines of communication and fairly close to base. Now they were to 'up sticks' completely, a self-contained force, with the heavy equipment, ammunition and stores carried in the steamers and gunboats, which had been planked over against musket fire. True, they were striking at the weak point of the Taiping territory, the thin waist of the 'hour-glass'. But, looked at in another way, this meant that the 'Ever Victorious' were to insert themselves between two powerful enemy forces. Whether they were breaking through to victory or merely moving into the lion's jaws was entirely a matter of comparative force, of organisation, and of generalship. Whatever happened, the enemy would be not only in front, but on both flanks, and probably in rear as well. They would be in 'Indian country' throughout, never safe from attack, by day or night. The cold would numb their bodies, the tension tire their minds, the devastated wasteland through which they passed oppress their spirits.

In the middle of January, a month beforehand, a reconnaissance party led by a French officer had returned from nine days in the wasteland. 'Up to our knees in mud and water, eating and sleeping anyhow,' he reported. 'At about ten leagues from Shanghai, as we gradually approached the rebels, we found the ground obstructed with Chinese corpses. The towns were entirely depopulated, and often burned. Sometimes four walls, which represented a house, would be found to contain the bodies of men, women, and children, and the roads were literally strewn with corpses. The rebels had but just left one town which we entered, and we found bodies of women and children still warm, and wet with blood. We were to stop here for the night, and I set about hunting among the brick ruins for some house that still remained standing where I might find a bed. At last I found one, but turning over the coverings of the bed, a sight met my eyes that paralyzed me. A man and woman lay there, assassinated in the most frightful manner. A cord had been tied so tightly round their waists that their intestines protruded through the open wounds. It was horrible. This is what insurrectionary war is in China. The rebels adopt the cruel plan of murdering everyone who has his head shaved.'

Into this hideous desolation marched the 'Ever Victorious Army', the snows of winter containing until the spring the terrible sickly-sweet stench of decaying corpses. With them went the 50,000 men of the Imperialist Kwosingling, while General Ching was detached to attack Kashingfu. North of Wusieh, they found the graves of the four men from the *Firefly*'s crew who had been aboard when she was captured by the renegade Europeans led by the British sailor, Lindlay. Worse sights than this awaited them on the approach to the first objective, Yesing. They entered a Village 'full of the most miserable objects ever seen, of all ages and sizes, in pitiable condition, in the direst want. These people were consuming human flesh, and the babies of those who had died were lying about unburied, with pieces cut out of them by the survivors,' wrote Gordon. They did what they could for these unfortunate by-products of civil war, and on 1st March fought a battle of manoeuvre around the stockades of Yesing. Into the midst of this battle, unawares, poured a host of rebel reinforcements just coming up in support from Liyang. Caught in the open, pinned to a road, by part of Gordon's force, they were driven in indescribable confusion directly on to their own defences;

and the rebel troops they had come to help kept their gates shut fast and opened fire on them. The city surrendered next day, with the better part of its 5,000-strong garrison. Gordon left it to be occupied by the Imperialists, and pressed on for Liyang. His men were becoming increasingly nervous, as their penetration into rebel territory lengthened, and one soldier had to be shot in order to quell a small mutiny.

For once, the line of march did not exactly border a waterway, and from time to time the artillery, which was waterborne, were out of touch with the marching infantry regiments. On 4th March, just short of that day's planned rendezvous of the two components, the cavalry screen of twenty men led by Colonels Kirkham and Rhode were caught in a village by a much larger cavalry force which they had mistaken for Imperialists. They galloped back hell-for-leather, losing two or three ponies and a Chinese sergeant who was taken prisoner. They found him again forty-eight hours later, terribly mutilated, having been tortured to death.

The second objective, Liyang, fell without a fight on 9th March, 15,000 rebels surrendering. The dangerous flank march, which depended on speed to prevent the Taiping forces from combining, had succeeded. Gordon noted in his war diary: 'The place very strong, and well provisioned. THE HOUR-GLASS BROKEN.' He promptly enlisted 1,000 rebels into his own force, to bring the regiments up to strength, and organised another thousand or so Taipings into a regiment of their own, under their own leaders, to serve as part of his army.

Gordon now turned north, to likewise split in two what had been the northern bulge of the hour-glass, as this contained the rebel capital, Nanking, now in its eleventh year of siege by Imperial forces. The campaign was rising to its climax, and undoubtedly the ease with which Gordon had broken the rebel-held territory in two encouraged optimism. The first city immediately to the north was Kintang, on which Gordon advanced with part only of his force — the 1st, 2nd, and 5th Regiments, supported by some of the light and heavy artillery. In wet and dismal weather, on 20th March, they closed up to within 1,200 yards of its walls, which were not protected by any outlying stockades. 'With the exception of a body of horsemen, who rode out from the city, no force was visible,' wrote Gordon. 'The walls were not manned, no flags were flying in the usual Chinese style of defiance; but still there was something ominous in the deathlike stillness which raised a doubt whether it was not evacuated.'

Next day, with the artillery brought up and emplaced opposite the north-east corner of the walls, and ready to open fire, startling news was received from the Imperialists. A striking force of 7,000 rebels had sortied from Chanchufu, to the north-east of Kintang, and moving round the Imperialist flank had driven deep into their territory. Fushan had fallen to them, Wusieh and Kougyin were threatened, and Chanzu, a bare 30 miles from Gordon's base at Quinsan, was being besieged by them. Gordon decided on the bold answer: take Kintang regardless, then drive straight for Chanchufu, the base of the raiding force, which should bring them streaming back pell-mell.

'Up to this time Gordon bore a charmed life, although he exposed himself most fearlessly,' wrote Lieutenant Storey. 'It appeared as if "the bullet that was to be billet" was not cast!' This, in spite of all the odds facing a leader of semi-disciplined, mercenary forces, who had to lead from in front, right up to the breach in the walls, and across it. Ward had been wounded once, then killed, Burgevine wounded twice, Admiral Hope wounded, and two leaders of the French force, Admiral Protet and de Moidrey, killed. To rub home the deadly arithmetic, the Chinese General Ching had been wounded at Kashingfu on 4th March, less than three weeks previously, and was to die on 13th April.

'The early morn of the day that he intended to assault Kintang turned out to be gloomy, cold, and wet,' wrote Storey. 'The troops had been very busy offering sacrifices of gold, silver, and various coloured tissue papers to their gods. By what process they arrived at the decision of these gods — vis. "that they were unpropitious to the success of the day's undertaking" — I failed to learn. The breach in the wall was a small one, and consequently the ascent to it was rather steep; at the base was a foul, stagnant ditch, certainly not more than eight feet wide and not very deep. The advance to the assault was up a paved path, one of the public paths leading from a gate to the country. Down this paved way the rebels fired with great precision, and caused heavy losses in the assaulting column, who went up gallantly enough to the edge of the ditch; there they stopped, electing to be shot down rather than jump the ditch and ascend the breach. Every effort, in which physical force bore a large preponderance, was made to get them to cross, without any effect. Gordon directed his aide-de-camp, Major Brown, a brother of the General, and another officer to take his two flags, on which were emblazoned in Chinese characters the record of his successes, and cross the ditch, in the belief that the troops would be stimulated by the sight and follow. They crossed. Brown received a severe wound in the back and his companion got a severe blow on the head; both did their utmost. At this juncture Gordon was wounded. He was promptly carried to his boat and the bullet extracted. The troops were withdrawn and the retreat commenced.'

The force lost two officers killed and thirteen wounded, among whom were the two French mercenaries from Soochow, Bertrand and Radinor, now Lieutenants. Thirty-five of the rank and file were killed, 80 wounded. The rebels aggressively followed up their success, as Storey recorded. 'The rebel force at Chan-chow-foo (Chanchufu), about twenty miles off, hearing of our repulse and retreat, made a rapid flank march. About 3 a.m. (the following day, 22nd March), they passed through our advanced sentries and pickets and set a light to the tents of one of the regiments ere they were discovered. For about ten minutes there was a scene of wild confusion and brisk fighting; then they retreated with considerable losses on both sides. The temporary commanding officer did not think it advisable to stay and hold his ground, as it was most important to get Gordon to a place of safety, where he could have perfect rest. Gordon did not try conclusions again with Kintang. He proceeded, when recovered, to attack Chan-chow-foo, the most distant city now held by the rebels in the Kiang-su province, knowing by this move that Kinyang would be isolated, and with Chan-chow-foo in his possession it would merely be a question of days or hours possibly ere they surrender. Later events showed how correct he was in the tactics adopted.'

But, in the meantime, it was the Taipings who were on the offensive, able at one and the same time, from their northern base at Chanchufu, to mount simultaneously a 7,000 strong raid into Imperialist territory and a lightning counter-attack against Gordon's defeated forces retiring from Kintang. There were two reasons for this. The first was the character of the Taiping commander of Chanchufu, Hu Wang. Because he had a sinister cast in one eye he was popularly known as 'Cock-eye'. A South Chinese, like the 20,000 fighting men he led, he was a hard and desperate character, one of the instigators of the rebellion. The second reason was a simple case of logistics: the Imperialists had advanced far from their bases, so that the spring had stretched; while every mile of advance tended to compress the spring of rebel resistance. Part of the 'Ever Victorious' were moved back to Wusieh to counter the rebel penetration, leaving the remainder to help garrison the captured towns. Gordon was once again commanding, but it would probably have been better if he had not; he could not walk and had to control the next battle from a bed in the boat which he used as mobile headquarters. He had only 400 infantry with him and the light artillery. Having established that the local rebel command was at Waisso, he advanced towards it, taking several villages on the way.

Reinforcements, in the shape of the regiment of rebels recruited from the prisoners taken at Liyang, arrived; and the force closed in on Waisso. Again, roadway and waterway diverged, and a rendezvous for the boat-borne artillery and the marching infantry was arranged just short of Waisso. But the banks of the canal proved to be so high that the guns could not fire over them, and the boats returned. Almost simultaneously, out of their sight, the infantry under Colonels Howard and Rhode had run into serious trouble. Not expecting very stubborn resistance, they had distributed their men in 'penny packets', by companies, over so wide a front that touch was lost between them. Through the gaps the hard-fighting southern Chinese rebels infiltrated, separated Howard from Rhode, and finally established themselves in rear of both forces. Rhode and Howard decided to retire. 'This began in an orderly manner,' wrote Gordon, 'but when pressed by the rebels the pace was quickened; the walk became a run and a rout. The best regiment of the force and 600 Liyang rebels were in full flight, though well-armed and with plenty of ammunition. The rebel horsemen, some 100, charged into the mass, leaving the bridles of the horses, and, armed with a sword in each hand, cut down the men right and left. No attempt could be made to rally; it was a race for life for three miles up to Lukachow. The loss was fearful. The rebels fought with great determination, and showed considerable tact in luring the men on. If the men had formed square, they knew well enough it would have been all right for them.' This day, 31st March, they had failed completely and suffered 322 casualties in doing so — 7 officers killed and 1 wounded, 252 men killed and 62 wounded. Four hundred muskets were abandoned to the rebels. The failure was due, not to lack of courage, but to the faulty tactics of the officers, both in advance and retreat, which put the soldiers in an impossible position of disadvantage.

Gordon's attitude was that of a technician, as his war diary and general writings reveal. Very occasionally, there is a sharp comment on the methods of a rival, as when he learned at this time of the defeat of the Franco-Chinese force led by D'Aiguebelle, twice repulsed before Hang-chow. 'He,' wrote Gordon, 'for some very wise reason, only known to himself, made his breach at a gate, so as to breach two walls instead of one,' His own defeats were never minimised nor, where the fault was his, excused. For he was learning all the time, striving for perfection. Perhaps for this reason, he made no attempt to project a perfect 'public image', which almost everyone in authority does to some extent or other; on the contrary, in his correspondence he wrote of defeat equally with victory. On this occasion he included news of the reverse in a letter to Lieutenant Lyster, who had just returned to Shanghai after a spell in Japan, and added details of the horrible scenes he had to witness. 'Major Gordon says the rebels are in myriads, and are going about in all directions devastating the country,' noted Lyster in his diary. 'They are very poor, and live by plunder. They commit frightful atrocities on the unfortunate villagers; numbers of children were seen with their throats cut; and Major Gordon says he saw a woman with her hands tied behind her back, her breast cut off. and her body ripped up. The people are starving — actually eating grass. I believe Major Gordon is to be made a Brevet Lieut.-Colonel by next mail. He deserves all that, and far more. He is the finest specimen of a soldier that I have ever seen. I only hope that he will get safe out of this affair. He is a splendid fellow, and it would be a sin if anything were to happen to him in the Imperial service; he is thrown away on such rascals... The Chinese authorities offered Major Gordon a lot of money for the places he took. This is customary, but he refused and said "the services of an English officer could not be bought with money!" He is so fearless of danger — one cannot help feeling anxious for his safety.'

'Gordon's activity, zeal, and energy were wonderful,' recollected Lieutenant Storey. 'For work he was a perfect glutton; dilatoriness and delay in carrying out orders he could not brook.' Gordon kept three or four British regular officers as his personal staff, but they had to be up to the mark. Storey recalled one occasion when he had sent an A.D.C. forward with a message to troops on the far side of a muddy ditch; and the A.D.C., not wanting to soil his uniform, had wandered off to find a bridge. Seeing this, Gordon himself crossed with the message and was waiting for the unfortunate A.D.C. when at length he arrived. The officer was returned at once to his unit. His provost-marshal, the man responsible for discipline in this troublesome force, was Major Brooks, a former boatswain in the Royal Navy. The Navy had also supplied the best of the regimental commanders, Colonel Tapp, who had been a warrant officer before being allowed to purchase his discharge in 1862. These were Chinese ranks, of course, by which reckoning Major Gordon was a General on a Chinese salary of £100 a month. He had fixed the figure himself, so as to make quite clear that he was not out to make his fortune. To his unceasing watchfulness and attention to all details the wonderful successes that attended his force were entirely attributable,' said Storey. 'For months he rarely took his boots or clothes off at night; he would go to his boat and turn into a couple of blankets sewn up in the form of a sack. If there was a disturbance, or the heavy guns fired more frequently or less than he had directed, or the musketry fire got slack or too rapid, he would be out inquiring into the reason. By day he was everywhere. With all this he invariably looked spruce and tidy, and as smart as if clothes were to be obtained at a few hours' notice.

'During the whole time I was with Gordon,' added Storey, 'I never heard of a written order or saw a piece of blue official paper used. If a commanding officer required fresh arms, accoutrements, blankets, clothing, or ammunition, to replace those lost or damaged in action or worn out, he would put his requirements on a piece of paper torn out of his pocket-book (woe betide him who had not his pocket-book about him, for Gordon was always borrowing a leaf of one), get Gordon to put his name to this very informal indent, and then send this paper and some men to the storekeeper at base, who would without further delay comply with the requisition and issue. The storekeeper would place this piece of paper on a file, and there was his authority to issue and receipt for the same. How our military shopkeepers would groan, tear their hair, and declare the service had gone to Hades were such a simple plan adopted by our red-taped, bound and tied army. With them there would be Boards, Courts of Inquiry to be approved or otherwise innumerable, the lost or damaged articles required to be produced, sheaves of letters written on the subject, indents and receipts in triplicate or quadruplicate made out and exchanged, and finally, after a very long delay, the applicant might think himself really very fortunate if he got just half of his requirements. Military men, I think, will admit that such a thing as red tape did not exist in "The Ever Victorious", and that its total absence was in no ways detrimental to its well-being and success, also that Gordon managed these matters in a simple businesslike way.'

Before making another move to clean up the rebel penetration centred on Waisso, Gordon allowed time for his leg wound to heal, called in further reinforcements from among his own units, and liaised with an Imperialist force of some 8,000 men, which was to assist and follow up the bludgeon of his own attack. The rebel force in and around Waisso was estimated at between 8,000 and 10,000 men. Gordon put his battering ram, the 24-pounder howitzers, to fire on the stockades before the south wall of Waisso, which drew the rebels to that point; then he moved his infantry, consisting of the 4th Regiment only, supported by two mountain guns, to the stockades in front of the north wall. The Taipings wavered uncertainly, not sure now where the attack was coming. The 4th Regiment took advantage of this to storm a small breastwork, and, as the rebels fled back from it to the covering stockade behind, the 'Ever Victorious' were either at their heels or actually among them, so that there was no opportunity for the defenders of the stockade to fire at them from cover. There was only a brief encounter, then the stockade was in possession of the 4th Regiment and their guns. From it, they could fire at the flank of the rebel force which was already being bombarded from their front by Gordon's howitzers. The rebels there retreated, leaving a gap in their line through which the 4th Regiment poured. The retreat of those still fighting was thus menaced, they withdrew, and eventually evacuated the town. The rebel loss was small; that of the 'Ever Victorious' precisely nil. It had been a precision manoeuvre, demanding for its successful execution an extremely keen eye for ground and the weak points of fixed defences, together with an almost physical appreciation of the combined will of a garrison to resist and the point at which that will would begin to waver.

The rebel force disintegrated, leaving only a hard core of 2,000 men to withdraw slowly, pressed by the Imperialist troops. As the advance went forward, it overran Yangshui, where more than 150 bodies were found. These were the Liyang men taken prisoner from Gordon's force in the rout of 31st March. It was now 11th April, and as they pressed on over the ground where the rout had taken place they came upon the dead lying where they had fallen, including the seven European officers. Many of the corpses had been beheaded or mutilated after death. During the next few days the rebel hard-core was whittled down to half-strength, with the help of the inhabitants of the district who hunted down the dispersing rebels in revenge for burnt homes and slaughtered relatives. The Imperialists executed all prisoners who were from the provinces of Canton, Hupih, and Kwangsi; and there was no protest from Gordon.

On 14 April Gordon was facing 'Cock-eye's' stronghold of Chanchufu, the mainspring of rebel resistance in the north. He reconnoitred it, and found that it was surrounded on three sides by the Imperialists; the way out to the west and the Taiping capital of Nanking was open along the line of the Grand Canal, the rebel defences covering this escape route consisting of some thirty strong stockades. He decided that the strength of the defences and the spirit of the defenders, many of whom were redoubtable Cantonese fighting men, merited bringing together the whole of the 'Ever Victorious Army' for the assault. His garrison at Liyang were replaced by Imperialists, and he soon had 4,000 of his own men assembled before the city. At the same time, he impressed upon the Futai the need to surround the rebel stronghold completely, so that the blow would be final, allowing no rebels to escape and ravage other districts.

This time it was the Imperialists who began the attack. On 22nd April heavy firing was heard from the West Gate stockades, covering the Grand Canal escape route. It was the guns of Major Bailey, who commanded an artillery force attached to the Imperialists. Twice the Chinese attacked, and twice they were bloodily repulsed; at the third attempt they broke in and the rebels fled. It was just as well for the military mandarins in command, for the Futai had given them the alternative of taking the stockades or being degraded, as they had been ineffectually besieging the city since January. Not all the stockades on the south bank of the Grand Canal fell on this day, however, for they were stubbornly defended. But some deserters came over in the evening and warned Gordon that the rebels were to attempt a major breakout that night. They duly did so, coming on in great numbers for an hour, but were eventually driven back by the ring of besiegers.

Next day, Gordon's men and the Imperialists together finally cleared all the stockades on the south bank, leaving on the north bank a very strong stone fort, covering the Canal. The

Imperialists tried it, and were thrown back. Then 200 of Gordon's ex-rebels from Liyang scrambled over the water to the west, by means of the jumble of boats and junks with which it was crammed, and stormed into the fort from the rear. The defeated Taipings ran for safety to the walls of Chanchufu, but 'Cock-eye' was a stickler for discipline: he had the gates closed and the beaten force fired on. After an hour or so, the better side of his nature took over, and, keeping the gates closed for security reasons, he had the defeated soldiers pulled up to the top of the walls by cords. But, just to show what he really thought of the affair, he had some of the leaders executed for their part in losing the stockades. Such a man would not be easily defeated. Nor was he.

The attack on the city proper would have to be very carefully prepared. While the emplacements were being thrown up, a melancholy discovery was made in the Canal near the fallen stone fort — the remains of the steamer *Firefly*, engineless, and obviously under repair. Her guns had been taken out for the defence of the city, from which now there could be no escape. Meanwhile, events elsewhere were also rapidly moving towards a conclusion. Gordon noted in his war diary: 'Kintang surrenders 25th April, leaving Chanchu-fu, Faijan, and Nanking, the only towns (held by the rebels) in the upper park of the HOUR-GLASS; and Wuchu-fu and Chang-ching, the only towns in the lower part of the HOUR-GLASS.'

A thousand Imperialist soldiers borrowed from the Futai threw up emplacements for Gordon's batteries midway between the east and south gates of the city, where he had decided to breach the wall. The Futai ordered Bailey's artillery to make another breach, between the south and west gates, which would be assaulted by the Imperialists. When completed, on 26 April, the Imperialists twice attacked and were thrown back each time with heavy losses. Next day, there were simultaneous attacks at both breaches, starting at midday, when the pontoon bridges were thrown across the ditch. Two of Gordon's regiments stormed over, with 'Cock-eye' clearly visible amid the rubble of the wall, cheering his men on, and firing down into the assaulting force. Only a dozen officers and men reached the sloping rubble mound, and they were driven back. At 2.30 p.m. another two regiments were sent away to the assault. All the officers mounted to the crest of the breach, but were not followed by the men, who hung back at the critical moment, knowing too well that a blast of musket fire and grapeshot would be waiting for the head of the storming column as it stumbled to the pinnacle of the pile of rubble.

When the stormers came back for the second time, they had lost in officers ten killed and nineteen wounded; 40 of the rank-and-file had fallen, 260 were wounded. And the Imperialists had been similarly repulsed. 'For all that,' wrote Storey, 'so great was their confidence and esteem for Gordon that one hour after the repelled attack the remnant (of the European officers) came and asked permission as a body to make another assault, in which they felt they would succeed. Gordon would not accept this generous offer, much as he appreciated it, but determined to push his parallels closer to the town and thus avoid exposing his troops so much to fire when they left them.' Gordon asked the Futai for the necessary labour force, laid down the guiding tapes himself, and found that the military mandarins 'fully comprehended the work, and executed it in first-rate style in perfect silence'. Night by night, the approach trenches were cut in zigzags nearer and nearer to the ditch, 8 feet deep and 60 feet wide, which encircled the city walls.

'A barrel bridge was constructed,' wrote Storey. 'It was a cumbrous mass to lift, carry out, and lay. To get it into position it was determined to cut through a large piece of the advanced parallel, and to one T—, a plucky ex-English officer, was assigned the task of laying it before 12 p.m. of the day previous to the next assault. It was a lovely starlight night, but cold. I was with Gordon in the advance parallel, a good bit away from the place where the bridge lay, smoking and talking. On our side the heavy guns were firing a round about every five minutes, and the musketry fire slack. From the city there was no reply. Time wore on, and Gordon got fidgety, looking at his watch, etc., etc. I went off to see how T— was progressing, and found him after a little while, told him that Gordon was getting anxious, and inquired when he thought he would be able to lay the bridge. He replied, "The working party, 800 strong, had had the bridge on their shoulders to place it in position, but owing to some miscalculation the passage for its exit was not large enough, and he was hard at work making it larger; also that the bridge would require looking to ere it was laid, as it had wrung a good deal in lifting up and putting down."

'I returned to Gordon, who impatiently asked, "What is T— about?" I told him. He replied, "Go and tell T— if the bridge is not laid in two hours I will make him lay it by daylight." I returned and gave T— Gordon's message. With the extra time granted the bridge was lifted on to the shoulders of the working party, carried out and laid without any casualty. Up to this time the rebels had been very quiet, but were evidently on the alert and in force, for directly this huge mass appeared in the open they opened a heavy fire, just as if hell had suddenly burst up; in addition, flaming stink-pots, fire-balls, rockets, were thrown — in fact, everything that they could to light up the scene.'

The Futai had found out that Chanchufu had fallen to the Taipings under Chang Wang at 2 p.m. on 11th May 1860, and he therefore directed that, if possible, the assault should take place four years later, to the minute. Therefore, all morning on 11th May 1864, Gordon's guns and those of Major Bailey thundered away at their respective breaches, bringing down the adjoining walls in masses. Deserters had warned Gordon that, behind the breach he had to take, the rebels had mounted the 32-pounder gun from the *Firefly*, stuffed to the muzzle with grapeshot — hundreds of musket balls which would sweep the crest of the breach with a spreading hail far deadlier, momentarily, than any machinegun. Nothing could be seen of this at the moment, and nothing very much, in the rolling dust storms caused by the shot, of the spiked obstacles which by now the rebels had laid across the face of the breach. At 11.45 a.m., Gordon's fire-programme changed to shrapnel and grape, to sweep away the rebel riflemen from their positions on the walls, while the steamer *Hyson* shelled the city. Under this cover the unwieldy pontoon bridge, with its floating supports of barrels and casks, was lurched forward to the ditch and launched upon the water, while light field guns were brought close up behind the assault infantry, ready to go forward immediately for close fire support if the breach should be taken.

Meanwhile, opposite the other breach being hammered steadily by Major Bailey's guns, the Imperialist troops were forming up for their assault. 'They turned out without any formation,' wrote Lieutenant Storey, waiting with Gordon's second column of assault infantry. '3,000 or 4,000 men, with dozens of large flags of brilliant hue flying, horns braying, gongs clashing. The scene recalled to my memory an old scriptural picture I had in my childhood, viz. the capture of Jericho by the Israelites; here, in vivid colours and with living figures, was the whole scene reproduced.'

Gordon's men, organised in three dense columns, paraded quietly in a hollow immediately in front of their breach. By 1 p.m., both breaches were declared practicable. At 2 p.m. precisely, a flag waved, the firing ceased, Gordon's 1st Regiment got up and ran forward without a word, and the Imperialists, with swaying banners and blaring of brass, swarmed down to their part of the ditch.

'The first column, under Colonel T—, who had been a private soldier in my regiment,' wrote Storey, 'had moved up, dashed over the parapet, down the slope to the river, crossed the bridge, and made for the breach. The rebels turned up in great force. The breach fairly bristled with spears. Small bags of gunpowder of about 1 lb. each, with a lighted fuse attached, were thrown into their faces, rockets discharged, and fire-balls and flaming stink-pots flung. The rebels had thrown down a number of beams of wood studded with nails in all directions, upon the face of the breach, which materially added to the difficulties of the assault. In spite of these impediments the first column advanced well, and appeared halfway up, when, as if by magic, they all came down just as if a rope had been passed round them and the ends pulled suddenly in the direction they came from, sweeping them off their legs.' That was the critical moment, with the rebels suddenly swarming into the breach, and masses more coming up behind to join them; the first wave of stormers physically decimated, psychologically beaten.

'I was to go with the second column, which by this time had moved close up,' recollected Storey, 'and I was talking to

Gordon, who was in the advance parallel smoking vigorously and occasionally taking a rifle out of the hands of his bodyguard and firing at some rebel who was making himself too conspicuous. Gordon saw the waver, turned to me and said shortly, "Now Storey, go on; you're late; good-bye." A shake of the hand, and over the second column streamed. The first now reinforced rallied quickly, and together the two columns went up and over. Chan-chow-foo was ours. At the moment of gaining a foothold inside the city wall I glanced to my right, and saw that Ching's troops had carried their breach, pouring over the wall, spreading themselves over a large plain, made for the city; our light guns were dragged across, got into position, and fired into the flying rebels.' Storey, as he scrambled over, saw an abandoned gun which had been laid on the breach, but did not recognise it as the *Firefly*'s main armament. 'It was an old 64-pounder loaded with nails and scraps of iron, laid to sweep the point we attacked. Fortunately it could not be discharged, otherwise the chances were that it would have been as deadly for friend as for foe.'

'Cock-eye' was taken prisoner when, hurrying with a large force to support the defenders of the breaches, he met them head-on running away. He was beheaded, but not tortured. The body of the other chief rebel, Tso Wang, was found dressed in burial robes already; he had been killed by a shell during the repulse of Gordon's forces on 27 April. This successful attack, however, had cost Gordon only one officer killed, one soldier killed, and five wounded. The execution of all Kwangsi and Canton rebel prisoners was merciful, they were simply beheaded. This action was official, ordered by the Imperial authorities. So, too, was the sack of the city; unlike Soochow, it had resisted, and therefore by the common laws of war everywhere, had to suffer. This time, Gordon made no attempt to interfere; and the practical result was that the lines of the 'Ever Victorious' promptly became a refugee camp.

'The few hours I spent in the town I saw several horrible cases of disgraceful mutilation of men, women, and children by the Imperialists,' wrote Storey. 'The wretched inhabitants streamed out, giving the Imperialist camps a wide berth, into our lines. Among this crowd one of our artillery officers recognised a rebel who had been a servant to his brother, whom he alleged this man had murdered. He drew his revolver, pointed it at the poor wretch's head, who by this time had stood up, at his back a heavy gun. Three times did that revolver miss fire, but he never flinched. The fourth shot exploded. For a few seconds the body was erect and rigid, then it gradually fell back a corpse.'

With the fall of Chanchufu the last rebel stronghold in Kiangsu province was taken, 'their power gone, their leaders dead', as Storey put it. 'Gordon's promise to clear out the rebels within a definite time fulfilled, and the last shot in anger by the Ever Victorious Army fired.' All that was left could safely be entrusted to the Imperialists, the end of the rebellion in sight. On 13th May 1864, the 'Ever Victorious' marched back to Quinsan to disband. In the event, it was reconstituted as a very much smaller force for the defence of Shanghai, and Gordon eventually handed over to a Major from one of the English regiments stationed there. He was, said Storey, 'a real good officer and gentleman, but not one to our minds fitted for this peculiar post. Well do I remember his telling us that as regards this command he had but two lights to go by — the Queen's Regulations and the Drill Book. Heretofore red tapeism and blue officialism were unknown quantities to us.'

CHAPTER ELEVEN: 'DID YOU SEE ANYTHING OF THE TAEPING REBELLION?'

'I have a box full of letters from Lay, Osborne, Sir F. Bruce, Wade, Parkes, Burgevine, and mandarins, of the most contradictory nature, the perusal of which will show you how divided the people out here were upon the line to pursue. No one could get on here but a man who, without offending the swells, takes a separate and decided course; indecision is our bane. A bad plan, in my mind, followed out without wavering, is better than three or four good ones not so dealt with.' — *Brevet Lieutenant-Colonel Gordon*, 1864.

When Chanchufu fell, the Taiping rebellion had but two months to run. Gordon saw the end, as a spectator of the eleventh and last year of the siege of Nanking, but his active military career was over; and he closed his war diary with the brief note: 'FINALE. To Sir James Hope, Admiral, and Captain Dew, suppression of rebellion is due, not half enough credit given to the latter.' These men had been largely responsible for initially driving the Taipings back to the thirty-mile limit around Shanghai; the Ward force had acted only as their auxiliaries until Holland's disastrous expedition. Captain Dew, commanding a fleet of small naval vessels, had fought a land battle which connoisseurs judged, for results in relation to the forces engaged, to be the nicest ever brought off in China. But, if they had begun the job, Gordon had fairly finished it; and to Gordon went the applause — and the brickbats.

First, the applause. Gordon, now promoted to Brevet Lieutenant-Colonel, was to travel to the Imperial battle headquarters around besieged Nanking in the steamer *Elfin*, commanded by Captain D. Mc.S. Smith. Lieutenants Lyster and Storey were among those who were to accompany him; but first, the bodyguard arrived. 'They had been eighteen months in the field with him,' wrote Smith, impressed, 'and fought at the taking of all the cities from which he drove the rebels. They are armed with Enfield rifles and bayonets, and thoroughly drilled, and about the best specimen of Chinese soldiers that I have seen.' Smith took the *Elfin* 'up to and past Nankin, without getting a shot from the batteries,' and anchored in a creek on the other city of the rebel capital where the 'Heavenly King', vowed to chastity, was taking his last enjoyment of some twenty wives. It was now 26th June, and on the 30th he committed suicide by swallowing gold leaf.

The Imperial commander sent down an escort and horses for Gordon and his staff to make their ceremonial visit. 'Next morning,' wrote Smith, 'the nags having arrived, Colonel Gordon asked me to accompany him, and we landed. The distance from the ship to the General's headquarters was six miles, and the whole of the way was lined with soldiers, in some places two deep and four deep, every soldier with a flag in his hand about a mile and a half of the way up to the stockades. As our procession passed, they fired salutes, and the bands struck up. Colonel Gordon rode in a handsome chair, Lieutenant Lyster, Mr. Hobson and I on horses. There must have been about 13,000 or 20,000 men turned out to receive Gordon. The General is one of the highest in the Empire, and he couldn't have paid his Emperor a greater compliment were he to visit him.'

Gordon was formally invested with the order of 'The Yellow Jacket', a ceremony which took five hours; at the end of it, he was in effect an honorary Field Marshal. No more than a dozen senior mandarins were allowed to wear this array of distinctive uniforms, yellow being the royal colour. But Gordon, the dynamically impatient side of his nature now regretting his new role of Very Important Spectator, was tempted to be in at the death. 'His object in coming to Nankin,' wrote Smith, 'was to see all the Chinese officials and try to induce them to allow him to bring up his siege-train — with which he took all the other cities — and assist them to take the place. He wanted none of the credit, and he told the General that he did not even want his name to appear in his despatches to the Emperor, and that he would guarantee to take the place in three days from the time he got his siege-train up and in position. The General said that he would be very glad to have him to fight with them, but as they were sure of taking the city in a little time, he declined his assistance; but said, in an awfully polite manner, "that he hoped soon to have the pleasure of receiving a visit from him *within* the walls of Nankin".'

'This ceremony over,' wrote Storey, taking up the narrative, 'Gordon began to make arrangements for his return to England. Such a thing as plain clothes he did not possess. His uniform was pretty well worn out, so a suit of "reach-me-downs" and hat were obtained from Shang-hae. No one would guess the process these garments and hat went through ere Gordon would consent to wear them, he having a great dislike to the sheen of new clothes. The hat was concertinaed; it and the clothes were then made into a bundle, tied up with string, attached by a cord to the side of his boat, and flung into the creek. In this way they were towed down till he arrived at Shang-hae, when they were dried and he wore them.

'His departure from us took place after dinner one evening. He made no allusion to it, and wished us "Goodbye" just as if it was only for a few days' absence, darted into his boat, and closed the door to avoid all observation. Our resources were small, but all was done that lay in our power to do honour to our departing chief. Our stockades were illuminated with Chinese lanterns. The Imperial Chinese troops lined one side of the river for about a mile and a half, and carried numerous banners, lanterns, and blazing torches. Volleys of shell were fired, thousands of crackers let off, and horns and gongs brayed and clashed as the fast boat in which Gordon always travelled came along decorated with the flags he had so often and so successfully carried into action. It was many years ere I met Gordon again. I do not ever remember knowing before or since a man of such an extraordinary force of character, indomitable will, and great energy — the latter he imbued his companions with — and honesty of heart in all his actions. Without parading it, one could not help seeing and feeling that all his actions were governed by a strong current of religion; and though no doubt his strong will and temper made him do and say things which he afterwards repented, yet the force of circumstances and the peculiar position he was in must be taken into consideration. With all his love and admiration for the Chinese race, yet he would never allow any insult or affront offered by them to any Englishman to pass unnoticed.'

Gordon arrived in England during January 1865, and went to stay with his parents at Southampton; cutting short his leave, he asked for an appointment and was ordered to Gravesend to supervise the construction of new defences for the Thames Estuary. And there he was to remain for six years, gradually sinking into obscurity, just an eccentric Colonel who spent his spare time energetically distributing religious tracts, spending his salary on helping the poor and the sick in the mean streets of the town, and — a trait already noticeable in China — able to be merry only in the company of urchin boys of all ages, to whom he gave a helping hand, a new suit of clothes, and, where possible, an introduction to a job, very often at sea.

The obscurity was of his own seeking, for he had come home famous, as 'Chinese' Gordon. But he did not wish for promotion out of his turn, and he discouraged publicity. Some of the latter was not favourable, for there are in England, and there always will be, 'Two Nations' of one sort or another. There is a sharp distinction, for instance, between on the one hand, those who can be called crudely 'Little Englanders', and on the other, equally crudely, 'Jingoes'. For the former, England is always in the wrong; for the latter England is always in the right. In the same year in which Gordon returned home, one of the former, a clergyman named Worthington, produced a pamphlet which proved that the Taipings had been a force for liberal and Christian reform until crushed with atrocious cruelty by the murderous freebooter, Major Gordon. He was able to support these assertions with facts and figures. 'Of the 40,000 prisoners who surrendered at Soochow,' he wrote, '32,000 were butchered before the eyes of Major Gordon.' There had, of course, been a butchery (which Gordon had tried to stop with the flat of his sword), but this was merely to take the first number you thought of, double it, then multiply by ten, a method still of current utility.

Cruel to the Taipings, the Imperialists most certainly were, acting almost like Taipings themselves; but behind them came orderly government, stable conditions, and eventually recovery from Taiping rule, which was not government at all, but an infliction of banditti upon the land. On 15th June 1864, at about the time that the Reverend Mr. Worthington was preparing his pamphlet for the press, Lieutenant Lyster was writing home to his mother: 'The people are poor, as the country had only just been taken from the rebels, and they don't allow the country people to till their fields. They were actually eating each other farther up...' The press was full, during this time, of letters of protest from usually anonymous individuals writing under such typical *nom-de-plumes as* 'Observer', 'Eye-witness', or 'Justice and Mercy'. They could all testify to what Gordon and the Imperialists were doing; but, it seemed, they had never heard of a brutal Taiping or even so much as suspected that the rebels were anything other than a deeply religious, Christian people struggling against tyranny in order to be free. This is, of course, a permanent attitude of mind as evident today as it was then. But it produced in the mind of the general public, who were not in China, but in England and could not possibly know, a doubt as to who was in the right and who was in the wrong and, inevitably, the profound thought that there might be nothing to choose between them.

Consequently, there was a subdued hunger for certainty, and an anxious questioning of anyone who had actually been in China at that time and might be able to provide a raft of truth. In 1867, two years after he had come to Gravesend, Gordon became friendly with a Mr. and Mrs. Freese, who helped to run the local branch of the Religious Tract Society. So far had Gordon sunk into his self-sought obscurity, in little more than two years, that he puzzled Mrs. Freese. The young officer's manner was exceedingly breezy and boyish, he seemed young to be a Colonel, and yet, thought Mrs. Freese, from the expression of his face, he 'might have lived a thousand years'. Politely, they invited the stranger to tea.

'When he was sitting at tea in our room,' wrote Mrs. Freese, he said something about China which caused me to remark, "Oh! were you ever in China — do tell us something about life there," and my husband said, "Did you see anything of the Taiping rebellion when you were there?"

"'I should think I did," he said, "why it was I who put an end to it."

'To which my husband replied, "You don't mean that."

'I looked at him and wondered for a second or two if it could be possible this young man was bragging — a vice I should not have expected to find in him. Presently my husband questioned it out of him and we were both greatly interested at the little he told us. Afterwards we heard more, and then we knew that he was a remarkable man and my puzzle about him was cleared up.'

As an example of perfect, unstudied 'one-upmanship' this anecdote both precedes and exceeds T. E. Lawrence's tale of the fall of Damascus in *Seven Pillars of Wisdom*, in which, however, it was he who told the tale, instead of the other party. Oddly, Lawrence also threw away his fame to retire into an almost calculated insignificance. Gordon could never quite do that. Whenever news came of a punitive expedition being gathered to avenge some dark and distant King's misdeeds — such as Napier's into Abyssinia in this same year, and his friend, Wolseley's, into Ashanti — one half of his being longed to be there, as its leader. The other half recognised — and condemned — this worldly longing for action and renown. But the springs which motivated his spirit had twice the energy of an ordinary man; he hummed with it like a dynamo; the charge of current had to find release in action at any cost. That which

157

was near to hand, and perhaps the more congenial because it alleviated the memory of the sufferings he lived among in China, was the care of the poor and sick. In China, he had done what he could, but as commander of a military force it was never enough; to him, the word 'cannibalism' was not a joke, because unbelievable, but an actual situation in which he had endeavoured to bring in rice supplies to savagely hungry human skeletons sustaining a flicker of life from the fresh-cut flesh of dead children and infants. He had indeed lived a thousand years of pity ever since. It had not hardened him, for in self-defence he fell back on the all-conquering answer that every event on earth was God-ordained; it must be so; but it could hardly matter, for beyond was life everlasting.

'Your heart would bleed to see the poor people here,' he wrote of the slums of Gravesend. 'But, thank God, though they look forlorn, they have a watchful and pitying Eye over them. It does so painfully affect me, and I do trust will make me think less of self and more of these poor people. Little idea have the rich of the scenes in these parts. How long, O Lord, how long!' He did not find the easy answer, of hating the rich. But he did continually tell himself that this *must* be God's will. He wrote: 'There is a very beautiful young girl dying tonight, in a few short hours she will glide into a bright balmy land, and see such sights as would pass our understanding. She suffers much poor thing and makes one feel Oh! if I could soften this pang what would I not do. But still it must be true that it is better for her, that she should; otherwise God who loves her so deeply would alter it.'

These sickbeds were for him a running wound, worse by far to endure than the sight of crucified men or corpses charred by fire-torture, commonplace enough in the villages and cities he had captured. Long before Gordon's time in Gravesend was up, he wrote: 'I have a horror of a sick chamber. When a poor partridge or hare has been wounded it gets away from its comrades and dies quickly, and that is what I want to do when the time comes, and my course is finished. The watchings, the whisperings, etc., round a sick bed are great trials, which I must be spared.'

And so, most horribly, in the end it was to be.

CHAPTER TWELVE: 'HIS EXCELLENCY — OF NOTHING'

'I wear Engineer undress, with fez. It is very fine in its effect! I still think it is all a joke, and shall not realise matters till I get up. I have no title, but, as in China, keep my own. Of course, I am "His Excellency" — of nothing.' — *Colonel Gordon, Suakin*, 26 February 1874.

In 1871 Colonel Gordon entered that 'half-world' — neither civil nor exactly military — which was diplomacy in the world's backwaters during the scramble for trade, empire, and financial outlet during Europe's industrial revolution. The people of this tiny continent had annexed most of the world, and were now busily influencing what remained unconquered. What they had, and the others had not, was energy: they simply could not sit still, but had to be up and about, inventing, exploring, and invading. Against this dynamic, nothing could stand. Vast wastes of ocean, or desert, or jungle; resistance by good fighting men, or bad; none of these could permanently halt the penetration. Indeed climate, with which their medical science was as yet inadequately equipped to deal, proved at this time the most formidable foe they had to face. This aggressive drive is still unchecked, reaching into regions still more inhospitable — outer space and the depths of the oceans. And this is the way in which the events of the second half of the nineteenth century are best understood; for to regard the phenomenon merely as a matter of profit or loss (there were both), is to grasp less than the half of it.

But, superficially, Gordon's first appointment after the wasted years at Gravesend (where the forts he had had to build were clearly useless) was to a genuine European backwater, Galatz. Yet another Danube boundary Commission had been formed, and this time Gordon was to be a Commissioner instead of a junior surveyor, representing Great Britain. This pleased him less than it would an ordinary mortal, for he had a contempt for those who too strongly cared for notice and praise, a process which he called 'Hailing the tram of the world.' He considered his predecessor at Galatz 'a very solemn ceremonious old thing who thought of nothing but this Commission, in which he had ruled as a Despot over all the other Commissioners: if you differed with him, it was at once a personal question...' He himself had no wish to 'rule in the Commission except with my knowledge'. Also, he still retained his early dislike of social life, although he accepted that 'there are people who cannot do without such things. Many husbands and wives are bored to death with each other's society, and want new faces and new ideas...' The Truth was, that he possessed an intense inner life of thought, concerned with God's scheme for the universe, and did not want those thoughts disturbed. At Gravesend, he had even tried to sell his camera for this reason; 'it takes up my time from matters of more import, and the pursuit is of such an engrossing nature as to grow on me in a dangerous way for peace and quiet'.

However, it was while visiting Constantinople from Galatz that he met at the British Embassy Nubar Pasha, Prime Minister to Ismail, the Khedive of Egypt. Gordon was asked if he knew of an Engineer officer qualified to take over the Government of the Equatorial Provinces of the Sudan from Sir Samuel Baker; and was eventually asked to take on the task himself. The Egyptians were in fact looking for what would now be called a 'troubleshooter'. Baker, writing at this time, described what had happened to a district which he had last visited in 1864, nine years previously: 'It was then a perfect garden, thickly populated, and producing all that man could desire. The villages were numerous, groves of plantains fringed the steep cliffs on the river's bank, and the native people were neatly dressed in the bark cloth of the country. The scene has changed! All is wilderness. The population has fled! Not a village is to be seen! This is the certain result of the settlement of Khartum traders. They kidnap the women and children for slaves, and plunder and destroy wherever they set their foot.' In fact, the slave-traders had virtually taken over the area south of Khartoum, had defeated an Egyptian expeditionary force, and were showing ominous signs of growing military power which, allied to the corruption of the Egyptian authorities on the spot, was attracting to Egypt the unwelcome attentions of all the earnest 'do-gooders' in England. To appoint Gordon might hobble the slave-trade and should certainly quiet the zealots of the Anti-Slavery Society.

Gordon was soon fully aware that his appointment was intended 'to catch the attention of the English people', but appreciated that behind the humbug was the Khedive's 'terrible anxiety to put down the slave-trade, which threatens his supremacy'. But he accepted the task, subject to the proviso that the salary offered, £10,000 a year, should be reduced to £2,000; and that his staff 'must belong to the A class — i.e., those who come for the occupation and interest it may give them, and who are content if they are fairly reimbursed for their expenses; not the B class, who go for the salary only and who want to make a good thing of it. My object is to show the Khedive and his people that gold and silver idols are not worshipped by all the world. They are very powerful gods, but not so powerful as our God. From whom does all the money come? From poor miserable creatures who are ground down to produce it. Of course, these ideas are outrageous.'

It was some time before the appointment was approved, for the British Government also had to be consulted. 'If I go to Egypt or not is uncertain,' wrote Gordon. 'I hope He has given me the strength not to care one way or another: twenty years are soon gone and when over, it matters little whether I went or not. When religious people reason with you and say what a deal of good you could do, it is an atheistical saying though they do not mean it...' Gordon now cared very much whether he went or not; he was longing for a task which would absorb all his energies, and had already begun to work out what he would do. As always, supreme self-confidence was the keynote: 'My idea would be to get all things ready before going into the interior. What is the use of pushing on and then having to come back? I feel quite sure I can do better without Baker; in a month I would know more than he does; whereas if I take him and do not follow his advice he would be vexed. God has allowed slavery to go on for so many years that it cannot be a vital thing to risk life and success for a few months. Born in the people it needs more than an expedition to eradicate it.'

The only permanent way to abolish slavery was to remove the market for slaves, which would have required a social revolution in the Middle East. In lieu of this, Gordon's plan was to cut off the slavers from their market by controlling the line of the White Nile with a combination of fixed, fortified posts and mobile river steamers. It was not to be as easy as it sounds. The Egyptian garrison troops were incredibly poor material, their civil and military authorities corrupt, the distances vast, the climate almost unbearable, the slavers formidable, and disease even more so. In addition, Gordon made a number of bad mistakes in picking his staff, possibly because he wanted it to be as representatively international as possible. Among them were an American, Colonel Long, a Frenchman, M. Linant, two Germans, and an Italian, Romolo Gessi. Gordon, having arrived in Cairo on 6th February 1874, to take up the appointment, set about recruiting these people in his usual hurried manner. When the American Colonel asked when would Gordon be leaving, the airy reply was: 'Oh, tomorrow night.'

They set off for Khartoum on 21st February. By September, out of his small staff, two were dead, three invalided back to Cairo, and two were laid up with sickness. Out of a detachment of 250 soldiers sent to him, there were, after three months, only 25 left, so hostile was the climate to Europeans and Egyptians'. Two Engineer subalterns for whom he had asked, arrived about this time, Watson and Chippindall. The latter wrote home: 'Really sometimes I think I shall have a row with Gordon; for though he has such a lot of anxiety and worry, he has no right to nag and worry you in return for it. Oh! and how he bores me night after night about the levels and the distances! I should not mind if he would have one good night of it, and settle it; but every night to discuss whether Baker's levels are right; whether the distance is this or that, what you think; then, if you give an opinion to be nailed at once; and your reasons asked and worried at, till out of sheer fag you agree to any proposition he likes to put forward... He really won't let me do anything. He seems always to think that nobody but his blessed self can even screw a box lid on. He is a fearful egotist in that way. But he is devilish kind to one and really I fear he will almost spoil me for future service.'

Gordon was now in his early forties, and probably more set in his ways. However, the trait had been present even in China, for on the occasion on which he was wounded, Lieutenant Storey had noticed that 'even then his anxiety for the safety of the troops caused him to send perpetual orders and inquiries, which rather hampered the temporary commanders'. This was a natural consequence of his having enough pent-up energy in a small body to serve three large men. When he travelled by camel, instead of a steamer, it was hard for the camels, hard even for experienced camel-riders, to stay with him. One hundred miles in two days, in districts where normally the pace of the beast was 4 m.p.h. In this also he preceded T. E. Lawrence, although in a much less self-consciously 'Spartan' manner. He became irritated when lesser men cracked up. Of Colonel Long, he wrote: 'The American is a regular failure. He is so feeble, he can do nothing at all. He lives on what he *has* done, and of course that does not help what has *to be* done now.' Shortly after, however, he was able to note: 'I have now only Kemp, the engineer, and Long, an American in the Khedive's army, who was very useless before he went to Mtesa, but who now is very useful and active. Nothing like suffering to give a man experience.' The experience convinced Long that Gordon was not the man for him, and four days later he had left for Khartoum, where it took him twelve weeks to recuperate. Almost the only senior subordinate who managed to survive the rigors of marching, exploring, and campaigning in that lethal climate was the Italian, Romolo Gessi, and to him much of Gordon's eventual success was due. But even Gessi came in for irritable criticism at times.

It was his eagerness to get on with the task he had set himself that made Gordon sometimes uncharitable to those also engaged in it; but to the dreadful human wreckage he too often found his attitude was different. In a typical letter to his sister, Augusta, he wrote: 'I took a poor old bag of bones into my camp a month ago, and have been feeding her up, but yesterday she was quietly taken off, and now knows all things. She had her tobacco up to the last, and died quite quietly... A wretched *sister* of yours is struggling up the road, but she is such a wisp of bones that the wind threatens to overthrow her... I have sent her some dhoora, which will produce a spark of joy in her black and withered carcase. But when I got up, I saw your and my sister lying dead in a pool of mud — her black brothers had been passing and passing, and had taken no notice of her. I went round, and found another of our species, a visitor of ten or twelve months to this globe, lying in a pool of mud. I said, "Here is another foundling!" and had it taken up. Its mother came up, and I mildly expostulated with her, remarking, however good it might be for the spawn of frogs, it was not good for our species. The creature drank milk after this with avidity.'

For a handful of Europeans, supported by an indolent, cowardly and nearly non-existent administration, to alter this situation was next door to impossible; for they could be only in the one place at the one time. Nevertheless, Gordon's attitude was so different to that of his predecessors that he could stroll unarmed where before an Egyptian official would have required a regiment of soldiers to guard him. Although there were clashes with slave-traders and border raiders, the problem was not basically military; it was constructive rather than destructive, but with straw for bricks.

At one point Gordon decided that the problem was insoluble and pondered resignation. 'Comfort-of-Body, a very strong gentleman,' advised him to go home. 'Mr. Reason says, What is the use of opening more country to such government...' He did in fact go home, arriving on Christmas Eve, 1786. But, after a month of England, he decided to go back, provided that he was made Governor-General of the entire Sudan, so that the levers of what power there was would be in his hands. He returned to Cairo, saw the Khedive Ismail, '…told him all; and then he gave me the Soudan, and I leave on Saturday morning.' A splendid present — a million square miles of mostly desert, ruined by the slave-trade, and as it turned out, the beginnings of a Holy War just discernible. A land of sheep and wolves, the sheep being black and the wolves being the brown warriors who preyed on them; with the levers of power, the corrupt, so-called Bashi-Bazouks, concerned only to profit by the situation; with an army that was worthless; and with a barbaric enemy to the south on the frontier with Abyssinia. It was less than a year since a strong Egyptian force had tried conclusions with the savage warriors belonging to the Negus of Abyssinia.[4] The Egyptian commander had wished to stay on the defensive, but his American adviser, Colonel Loring, had exclaimed contemptuously, 'No! March out. You are afraid!' March out, they did; losing 10,000 men, 10,000 new Remington rifles, and 25 cannon. The British had dealt very thoroughly with the previous Negus of Abyssinia, Theodore, but their generals had not had to rely upon Egyptian troops. This was the situation that Gordon inherited.

He moved into it with some 300 unreliable troops, usually travelling ahead of them, with a single companion, surprising

---

[4] World horror when in 1936 the invading Italians used mustard gas in lieu of mines to secure their mountain flanks, was quite misplaced. It must be realised that, then as now, anyone falling alive (whether wounded or not) into the hands of all such peoples will be obscenely dismembered while still conscious, after their entrails have been first removed. It was British practice, on the North-West frontier of India, to shoot their own wounded rather than let them fall alive into enemy hands. Mustard gas was humane, compared to an Afridi or an Abyssinian-wielded knife.

both the Egyptian garrisons and the trouble-makers. He began to recruit local warriors to his own force, as he had in China, and solved the problem of what to do with freed slaves by taking them into his own ranks. He did not want battle, but sometimes he had to fight and, remembering the fate of anyone who fell into the hands of these people, his calmness was astounding. An Arab chief who had served him at this time told Slatin Pasha two years later: 'Gordon was indeed a brave man. I was one of his chiefs in the fight against the Mima and Khawabir Arabs; it was in the plain of Fafa, and a very hot day. The enemy had charged us, and had forced back the first line, and their spears were falling thick around us; one came within a hair's-breadth of Gordon, but he did not seem to mind at all, and the victory we won was entirely due to him and his reserve of 100 men. When the fight was at its worst he found time to light a cigarette. Never in my life did I see such a thing; and then the following day, when he divided the spoil, no one was forgotten, and he kept nothing for himself. He was very tender-hearted about women and children, and never allowed them to be distributed, as is our custom in war, but he fed and clothed them at his own expense, and had them sent to their homes as soon as the war was over.'

The courage required was of a very high order, very much greater than merely for facing death, of which in truth Gordon was not very much afraid. These people especially like to prolong their victim's agony as much as possible and possess scientific knowledge (based on long experience, of what precisely are the tenderest parts of the human body, male and female. There is no doubt that they obtain pleasure from these practices, which have also an abiding religious significance of the witch-doctor variety.[5] This must be understood as the

---

[5] E.g., the case of the eleven Italian airmen of the United Nations

savage background to all Gordon's operations in the Sudan, and of the British military operations later, during which Kitchener always carried with him a bottle of poison (like a secret agent in modern times) in order to escape, in a certain eventuality, a fate very much worse than the excruciating, but brief, torment of such suicide. It should also be understood that the 'do-gooders' of England took care to know nothing of these things; but were ready as ever with emotional torrents of well-meaning advice, and often criticism, of the man on the spot. They did not know what could be done, and what could not be done; and, again typically, many did not genuinely care for humanity, but were merely working off their excess of bad temper in what they imagined would serve as a 'good cause', advocating a blast of blood and death for the slavers. They, more than anyone else he had to deal with, tried Gordon's patience most sorely.

In the autumn of 1877 he moved out against Suleiman, son of the great slave chief, Zebehr, and succeeded — just. 'I had at Dara,' he wrote, '2,000 troops of only mediocre sort; all were timid, the fort bad, and I had not the least confidence of victory if it came to war. I rode to the slaves' camp with fifty men and saw their troops. I should estimate their number to be about 4,000. I told Zebehr's son and his chief to come to Dara; they came, and I told them I knew they meant to revolt, that I would break them up; but they should be paid for their arms.

---

force in Katanga who fell into the hands of some native allies of the U.N., who put on public sale the more interesting organs belonging formerly to the dismembered Europeans. This occurred as late as 1961. In a slightly different category was the complaint of the Vicar-General of Elisabethville, in 1963, that Ethiopian troops had dismembered a girl after raping her. In a hot climate, 'drawing' a corpse is a sensible hygienic measure, but it appears that in this case the girl was alive at the time.

They left me, and then wrote to give in. Then came three days of doubts and fears. Half were for attacking me, the other half for giving in. The result is that I think they have all given in, and I am on my way to Shaka, their headquarters. I thank God He has given me strength to avoid all tricks; to tell them that I would no longer allow their goings on, and to speak to them truthfully. There are some 6,000 more slave dealers in the interior who will obey me now they have heard their chiefs have given in. You may imagine what a difficulty there is in dealing with all these armed men. I have separated them here and there, and in course of time will rid myself of the mass. Would *you* shoot them all? Have they no rights? Are they not to be considered? Had the planters no rights? Did not our Government once allow slave-trading? Do you know cargoes of slaves came into Bristol Harbour in the time of our fathers?

'I would have given £500 to have had the Anti-Slavery Society in Dara during the three days of doubt whether the slave dealers would fight or not; — on the one side, a bad fort, a cowed garrison, and not one who did not tremble; on the other, a strong, determined set of men accustomed to war, good shots, with two fieldpieces. Then I would have liked to hear what the Anti-Slavery Society would say. I do not say this in brag, for God knows what my anxiety was, *not* for my life, for I died years ago to all ties in this world and to all its comforts, honours, or glories, but for my sleep in Darfour and elsewhere. It is better to be tired and worn than that one poor black skin should have a bullet-hole in it.'

Gordon pointed out that, 'When in 1834 His Majesty's Government abolished slavery, they had an irresistible force, with fleets, troops, etc., at their disposal; also a machinery of magistrates to carry out the emancipation. In my case, I have nothing of the sort. The force I have may be considered antagonistic, or, at any rate, very indifferently disposed to such a scheme.' Those at home, who wrote to him about his 'noble work' for the 'poor blacks', or took the opposite tack, and condemned him for not putting down slavery at once, if not before, were equally deluded, in spite of the fact that they could very plausibly point to what was being done elsewhere. 'I read the Parliamentary papers on the Gold Coast,' wrote Gordon to his sister. They make me smile, for His Majesty gives a proclamation, and it is over. Needless to say, that is not the case in these lands; the state of affairs is not parallel, and I think that, though slave razzias may cease, the holding of slaves will *never* cease under any government, let it be as strong and incorruptible as you like. Certainly, if razzias cease, no more slaves will be made, but those now with the people breed, and their children are slaves.'

He had discovered that what looked like firm ground from a distance, turned out to be on close inspection a morass. 'With my caravans, I expect there are 100 so-called slaves. I ask one man who those seven women are. He says, "My wives." How can I disprove it? Can I risk the imputation of taking away one of his wives? Besides, what could I do with the poor black? I do not want her with me. Another says, "These three boys are my sons." How am I to disprove it? Am I to go into the question whether he did beget them or not?' One of the chiefs of the slave razzias, commanding 400 picked men, was himself a slave, a member of Suleiman's household. What was Gordon to do about him? What he was dealing with was not a simple military situation, but a deep-rooted social system. And indeed, because the people had many children, and because the offspring of slaves was also a slave, the problem was likely to swell in size and complexity every year.

Shortly afterwards, Gordon wrote: 'As I suspected, I am convoying down a caravan of slaves. I came on them today — some sixty women and men chained together. The owner of the caravan had bought them at Shaka. He had not taken them from their homes. That had been done far away by the slave traders in the interior. Was he to blame? The *purchase* of slaves is permissible in Egypt. Would you have hanged him? If you had, you would have incurred just obloquy. Would you have taken the slaves from him? First, it would be robbery in the present state of the law. Second, what would you have done with them? Would you have been able to feed them and care for them? If not prepared to take charge of them, you do them no kindness in taking them from the slave merchants. In all probability you would have done what I did, namely, order their chains to be taken off (as scandalous) and left them with the merchant, who, looking on them as valuable cows, will look after them. Don Quixote would have liberated them, and made an attempt to send them back some forty days' march, through hostile tribes, to their homes, which they would never have reached.

'When a man is internally ill, it is no use poulticing his toes. So with these matters. Let the Anti-Slavery Society get the types ready for "*Increase of Slave Trade*", and for "atrocious", "disgraceful", and "Colonel Gordon".' Gordon boiled over when he thought of the sly, ignorant imputations of the 'do-gooders' (who merely sat at home and offered comfortable advice); he wrote ironically: 'Of *course*, His Highness (the Khedive) is delighted at some 10,000 or 15,000 of his subjects (the slave traders) having been in semi-revolt. Of *course* he, who gains not one farthing, but who is menaced by this state of things, wishes it to continue, and is only using me as a blind.' And he made clear what his target was. 'I do not wish to be hard on individuals, but on the class who are bigots, whether it be on the churchyard or temperance or any such question, who do not consider the other side.' They were, he thought, incapable of producing any effective plan, and the resources to back it, because fundamentally and in spite of their protestations they 'care more for their dinners than they do for anything else.' In fact, Gordon had come to the bitter realisation that he could do little, and that the little he could do would not last.

And he was angry at being advised, by humane people, to be indiscriminately ruthless, to exterminate utterly an entire race, for that is what the slave-raiders (as opposed to the slave-merchants) really were. 'They are,' he wrote, 'in spite of their slave-stealing, a fine brave people, and far superior to the Arab of Lower Egypt,' On the other hand, it should not be supposed that he thought it possible to rule in that land without power of life and death, for he specifically demanded it from the Egyptian authorities. Nor did he like his expeditions to be dubbed at home 'missionary enterprises'. They were for 'geographical discovery and forcible suppression of the slave trade,' he wrote. 'What I declaim against is the hypocrisy of terming my own or any expeditions *apostolic missions* or *missions of philanthropy*. They are not so, and under false colours will never succeed, whatever they may do in the geographical line.'

At this time a British missionary team, passing through Khartoum on their way to Uganda, went to the Governor-General's palace and there met a military figure which far more resembled that of a Montgomery than a 'Lawrence of Arabia'. 'The guard turned out, and several Kavasses ushered us upstairs, and in a large corridor we saw a table laid for lunch, and a little man in his shirt sleeves walking about. I took him for the butler. On looking through the doors opposite I saw a very splendid divan… But on catching sight of us the "butler" rushed up and said, "How d'ye do? So glad to see you! Excuse shirt sleeves. So hot! Awful long voyage. I'll make a row about it. Are you very angry with me?" A hearty grasp of the hand to each, a piercing glance of small sharp eyes accompanied this flow of words, spoken in a clear, sharp but pleasant tone of voice. Yes, it is he indeed, the liberator of the slaves, the ruler of a country half as big again as France, the Chinese Gordon!' Another of the missionaries, Dr. Bernard Allen, was above all impressed, as so many were, by the 'steely blue eyes, which looked at you as if you would not dare to ask him a question if he did not wish you to do so'.

By the spring of 1879, Gessi the Italian had broken up many of the slave-gangs, but needed assistance to complete the matter; and Gordon marched out to his aid, writing to a friend, 'The gate of mercy is shut and locked and the key lost.' It was interminable marching in the heat, along the routes of the slave caravans, marked by the skulls and scattered bones of slaves who had died in chains on the march. By summer, the chief slaver, the young Suleiman, son of Zebehr, was dead, and his band destroyed by Gessi. By August, Gordon could write: 'Not a man could lift his hand without my leave throughout the whole extent of the Sudan.' But, by then, he was being recalled to Cairo, for the Khedive Ismail had fallen from power, being replaced by the Khedive Tewfik.

Gordon had feared this new development ever since, the previous year, he had served unsuccessfully as President of a Commission of Inquiry into the finances of Egypt. The country was hopelessly in debt to the international bankers, paying interest of 7 per cent on innumerable loans; and Gordon's soldier's solution would have cut too sharply into the flesh of the creditors, whom he despised as financial 'sharks' and 'swordfish'. He referred to the Prime Minister, crudely, as D'Israeli, and of the financial experts on the spot, he wrote: 'The Rivers Wilsons, Barings, etc., are a mushroom lot and one would not have to go back to any remote period to find that their family mansions were near the Tower or the Minories, and that the head of the family knew the value of pretty worn apparel.' Gordon, of course, knew nothing of the intricacies of finance, and his appointment was a last desperate throw by the Khedive Ismael, to use Gordon's popularity with the English public as a means of staving off his English creditors. But the latter wanted their money, naturally enough, although the long-term view might have served them better and would certainly have saved the rebellions and bloodshed which were to follow, and which eventually brought the British into Egypt to stay, and Gordon to his death in the Sudan.

The whole of Egypt was now a quicksand, on which no man might build. Gordon was despondent. 'Would my heart be broken if I was ousted from this command? Should I regret the eternal camel-riding, the heat, the misery I am forced to witness, the discomforts of everything around my domestic life? Look at my travels in seven months. Thousands of miles on camels, and no hope of rest for another year. Find me the man and I will take him as my help who utterly despises money, name, glory, honour; one who never wishes to see his home again; one who looks to God; and one who looks on death as a release from misery; and if you cannot find him, then leave me alone. To carry myself is enough for me; I want no other baggage.' But the new Khedive, Tewfik, had one more mission for Gordon — a diplomatic one in Abyssinia, which was a total failure. The Negus was swollen with pride and demanded far more than Egypt would, or could give. Gordon had an uncomfortable and dangerous journey back.

'They are,' noted Gordon, 'a race of warriors, hardy, and, though utterly undisciplined, religious fanatics. I have seen many peoples, but I never met with a more fierce, savage set than these. The King said he could beat united Europe, except Russia.' No doubt the boast sprang from hurt nationalism, for although the Negus had won victories over Egyptian armies, an Anglo-Indian punitive expedition in 1867 had resulted in the death of his predecessor, Theodore.

Gordon returned to England in January 1880, in the last months of the Disraeli government. Lord Salisbury discussed him with Rivers Wilson, the financial expert, who said that for ordinary diplomatic work Gordon was 'impossible'. However, 'If you told him to capture Cetewayo, for instance, he would get to Africa, mount on a pony with a stick in his hand and ask the way to Cetewayo's kraal, and when he got there would get down and have a talk with him.' Shortly after, the Tories were out, and the Liberals were in. Simplified, very crudely and uncharitably, the former represented the forces of Jingoism and international loan finance, the latter stood for the 'Little Englanders' and 'do-goodism'. These elemental and unpalatable alternatives are the reason for much of the 'floating vote' and explain why many Englishmen wish that they could send to Westminster as their representative an unfortunately defunct gentleman named Guy Fawkes, 'the only man who ever went to Parliament with the right intentions'.

The new Liberal administration, intent on swift and dramatic reform, decided on the exciting experiment of appointing Gordon as secretary to the Maquis of Ripon, their new Viceroy of India. It took Gordon less than a week of India to discover that the 'reforms' were so much wallpaper. He landed at Bombay on 28 May and resigned on 2 June. True, he was totally unfitted for a diplomatic appointment of the routine kind, but it took him only three days or so to diagnose that, as he wrote to Miss Florence Nightingale, 'the element of all government is absent, i.e. the putting of the governors into the skin of the governed.' And, for his sister Augusta, he strode his favourite hobby-horse: 'the way Europeans live there is absurd in its luxury; they seem so utterly effeminate and not to have an idea beyond the rupee... All the salaries are too high by half above the rank of captain. It is a house of charity for a lot of idle, useless fellows.' The truth of these fundamental charges would now be admitted generally by those familiar with the subject. Gordon was in fact altogether too much of a reformer for a reforming administration. The brief episode left him temporarily penniless, for he insisted on repaying the cost of his passage money to India.

However, he was not unemployed for long. His resignation was announced in England on 4th June 1880, and on 6th June he received a telegram from Sir Robert Hart, Inspector General of the Imperial Customs, Peking, inviting him back to China, where an internal and international row was boiling up. Gordon believed that the message really came from Li Hung Chang, the former Futai of Kiang-su Province, now one of the highest officials of the Empire; borrowed money; and left at once. He *did* send a telegram to the army authorities in Whitehall, requesting permission, but did *not* wait for a reply, which when it came was unfavourable, but was later countermanded. Once in China, he found himself wrapped inside some very devious intrigue by various parties who were trying to stop the Imperial Government from going to war with Russia by means of fomenting a civil war to be led by Li Hung Chang, with Gordon as the military head of the revolt. This did not suit Gordon at all. He was opposed to a war between China and Russia; but he was also opposed to a revolt by Li Hung Chang or anyone else; and he was certainly not going to lead such an adventure, which was being pressed strongly by the Germans and to a lesser extent by Britain and France also.

Gordon prevented the war party at the Imperial Court from going to war by the simple process of pointing out in detail exactly why China was too weak to do this, and what the consequences would be. When the mandarins said that the Taku Forts were impregnable, and Gordon replied that they would fall easily, it was not just one man's opinion against that of another; Gordon, they had to remember, was not a diplomat — he was a man who had taken countless Chinese fortresses. That he was no diplomat he made clear by taking a dictionary and pointing to the word for 'idiocy' to describe their warlike intentions. In this he was going counter to much Chinese and European opinion, which over-estimated the recovery China had made from the Taiping rebellion and placed too much stress on the unwillingness of Russia to go to war at a point so far from her main centres.

But, in the event that it came to war, his military advice to them was brilliant. It was also timeless, being currently followed in Indo-China, first against the French, and now against the Americans, by the Communists. 'China's power lies in her numbers, in the quick moving of her troops, in the little baggage they require, and in their few wants,' he wrote. 'It is known that men armed with sword and spear can overcome the best regular troops equipped with breech-loading rifles, if the country is at all difficult and if the men with spears and swords outnumber their foe ten to one.' Their superiority would be still greater if equipped with rifles, he pointed out. The mass Chinese armies should never be used for 'pitched battles', but for infiltration and in 'night attacks *not pushed home*';

a 'continuous worrying of their enemies'. For this sort of war he advised the deletion of the arm which had been most important to him — the artillery. Its movement was too slow and confined, so that the infiltrators would be tied to it fatally. Instead, to give covering fire, he advised the use of light rocket projectors, with their ammunition, easily divided up into one-man loads. And he stressed what the Russian-Japanese conflict of 1904-5, and the Great War of 1914-18 were to prove up to the hilt, that 'Infantry fire is the most fatal fire; guns make a noise far out of proportion to their value.'

It was odd that so far-seeing a military adviser, able almost at once to put his finger on the really vital factors in a situation, should think little of any such ability, regarding the conduct of war as a matter of minor importance. 'The stride China has made in commerce is immense, and commerce and wealth are the power of nations, not the troops,' he wrote. 'Like the Chinese, I have a great contempt for military prowess. It is ephemeral. I admire administrators, not generals. A military Red-Button mandarin has to bow low to a Blue-Button civil mandarin, and rightly so to my mind.' In administration, he had pre-Beeching advice to give. 'I wrote the other day to Li Hung Chang to protest against the railway from Ichang to Peking along the Grand Canal. In making it they would enter into no end of expenses, the coin would leave the country and they would not understand it, and would be fleeced by the financial cormorants of Great Britain. They can understand canals. Let them repair the Grand Canal.'

Back in England once more, he elaborated these ideas in the quite different context of the British colonial empire, where in 1879 Lord Chelmsford had been defeated by Cetewayo's Zulus at Isandhlwana, and where Sir George Colley was currently trying to cope with Boer guerrillas. His dictum still was — no cannon, except for static defence of a necessary network of control posts. Cannon tied the regular troops to its defence and also determined both the line of march and the time taken, which could easily be predicted and an ambush worked out. His second dictum was — 'The Individual man of any country in which active outdoor life, abstinence, hunting of wild game, and exposure to all weathers are the habits of life, is more than a match for the private soldier of a regular army, who is taken from the plough or from cities, and this is the case doubly as much when the field of operations is a difficult country, and when the former is, and the latter is not, acclimatised.' These were unwelcome thoughts to an empire-building country whose power lay in industry; they meant that industrial might was not a gain but a loss, where colonial wars were concerned. Gordon's suggested solution was to use guerrilla forces in conjunction with the regulars, working together as the drilled 'Ever Victorious' had with the masses of undisciplined Imperial troops. And also, to make haste slowly. 'All is done on the "*Veni, vidi, vici*" principle,' he wrote. 'It may be very fine, but it is bloody and expensive, and not scientific. It would seem that military science should be entirely thrown away when combating native tribes. I think I am correct in saying that the Romans always fought with large auxiliary forces of the invaded country or its neighbours, and I know it was the rule of the Russians in Circassia.'

This devastating article appeared in the *Army and Navy Gazette* with shattering impact; for on the day previous to publication, Sir George Colley had been killed by the Boers in a terrible defeat at Majuba Hill.[6] The impact had been further

---

[6] The full text of the article will also be found reprinted in *The Life of General Gordon*, written by Demetrious C. Boulger and published by Thomas Nelson in England and America in about 1896.

prepared by a cartoon and word-portrait of Gordon which had appeared in *Vanity Fair* one week previously, 19th February 1881. 'Chinese Gordon is the most notable of living Englishmen,' ran the headline, followed by perhaps the best character-sketch ever of that 'strange little unpretending man'. 'Colonel Gordon is the most conscientious simple-minded and honest of men,' proclaimed the writer. 'He has a complete contempt for money, and after having again and again rejected opportunities of becoming rich beyond the dreams of avarice, he remains a poor man with nothing in the world but his sword and his honour. The official mind, being incapable of understanding this, regards it as a sign of madness. And as it is found that besides being utterly without greed he is also entirely without vanity or self-assertion, he is set down by the officials as being 'cracky' and unsafe to employ in comparison with such great men as Lord Chelmsford, Sir Garnet Wolseley, and Sir George Colley. He is very modest and very gentle, yet full of enthusiasm for what he holds to be right. This enthusiasm often leads him to interfere in matters which he does not understand, and to make in haste statements he has to correct at leisure. But he is a fine, noble, knightly gentleman, such as is found but once in many generations.'

Gordon's reply was to bury himself in Mauritius for a year, to oblige a friend who did not want the post of senior Engineer officer there. In 1882 he was promoted Major-General, and left Mauritius to become Commandant General in the disturbed Cape Colony of South Africa. Oddly enough, he had just written a military paper advocating the advantages of the Cape route over those of the Mediterranean and Suez Canal. Again, his recommendations were simple and shatteringly unorthodox, and more than half a century ahead of their time. He objected to British military bases being sited in colonies with large native populations, 'who may be with us or against us, but who are at any time a nuisance'. For these reasons, he ruled out such existing bases as Hongkong, Singapore, and Aden; advocating instead the construction of bases on virtually uninhabited islands which could be effectively garrisoned by 'a company of soldiers'. And he noted, long before anyone else did, that the existing bases were sited where 'from the colonial feelings they have almost ceased to be our own'.

At the Cape, however, he was an official failure. He was supposed to bring the rebellious Basutos to heel, but decided, uncompromisingly, that the Basutos were in the right and that a settlement was required which would recognise this. In January 1884 he was home again; and now the time-bomb of Egypt and the Sudan, which had been ticking away steadily under Mr. Gladstone's government of 'Little Englanders' for some years, blew up in their faces.

CHAPTER THIRTEEN: THE BROKEN SQUARE

'Our English government lives on a hand-to-mouth policy. They are very ignorant of these lands, yet some day or other, they or some other Government, will have to know them, for things at Cairo cannot stay as they are. The Khedive will be curbed in, and will no longer be absolute sovereign. Then will come the question of these countries... There is no doubt that if the Governments of France and England do not pay more attention to the Soudan — if they do not establish at Khartum a branch of the mixed tribunals, and see that justice is done — the disruption of the Soudan from Cairo is only a question of time. This disruption, moreover, will not end the troubles, for the Soudanese through their allies in Lower Egypt — the black soldiers I mean — will carry on their efforts in Cairo itself. Now these black soldiers are the only troops in the Egyptian service that are worth anything.' — *Gordon*, 1887.

'We neither govern nor take responsibility,' wrote Gordon of the impasse in Egypt; 'yet we support these vampires' (the corrupt Turkish officials). 'We are getting mixed up with the question of whether the interest of £90,000,000 will be paid or not. We are mixed up with the Soudan. We are in constant and increasing hot water with the French, and we gain no benefit from it, for the Canal will remain theirs.' The increased taxes to pay the exorbitant 7 per cent interest on the loan had to come from peasants already wretchedly poor; for the European creditors had rejected Gordon's advice of 1878, to give the shaky economy of Egypt a breathing space. And the real ruler of Egypt now was Baring. So, when the revolt came, 'it partook in some degree of the nature of a *bona fide* national movement', as Baring himself admitted. A group of army officers, led by Ahmed Arabi, mutinied and then took over the Government. The bankers sent a joint Anglo-French note, demanding Arabi's removal, and after the note they sent the Mediterranean Fleet. Furious at further foreign interference, the mobs took indiscriminate vengeance on all Europeans. The British fleet bombarded Alexandria; the Egyptians reacted with an even more furious popular uprising. Their army, led by Arabi, retired on Cairo, threatening to blow up the Suez Canal. And in August 1882, Sir Garnet Wolseley, Gordon's old friend from Crimea days, was landing with an army of 20,000 men. Such was the result of diplomacy conducted by, and for, what Gordon called the 'financial swordfish', 'sharks', and 'cormorants'. And so it was that another Gordon, Corporal John Gordon, from Aberdeen, now of the Black Watch, on 12th September, began to march towards Arabi's entrenchments at Tel-el-Kebir, and his first battle.

'Young men make the best soldiers,' he wrote. 'No man in mature life has the marvellous recuperative power of youth. A night's rest remakes an exhausted young man, fits him to grapple with a task as tremendous as the one which prostrated him the day before.' The march had been through soft sand, reflecting upwards the merciless downpour of heat from the sun; but then, almost within sight of the enemy, they were halted; and not merely halted, but told that they were all off duty for almost the next twenty-four hours. Lord Wolseley had occupied the Canal zone before Arabi, and now intended to destroy his superior forces, formidably entrenched on a four-mile front, by a risky manoeuvre which would largely nullify the Egyptian fire-power — if it worked. At 6 p.m. on 12th

September the men paraded in light marching order, with 100 rounds, two days rations, and cold tea in their water-bottles; they gathered round their company commanders, and were told that they were in for a night attack — or, rather an approach march throughout the night, so precisely timed that the entire force of 11,000 infantry, 2,000 cavalry, and 60 guns would be right on top of the Egyptian entrenchments at first light. They were to rush these with the bayonet — and not a shot was to be fired until the position had been taken. Their battalion, the Black Watch, would be the pivot on which the whole force would align itself during the night march; and with them would go Lieutenant Rawson, R.N., as guide and navigator to the whole army. In Egypt, the time between night and day is very brief; and if they were only minutes late, they would inevitably be mown down.

It was an extremely daring conception, in which much depended on the discipline of the troops; hence the twenty-four hours' rest beforehand, to make sure they were keen and fit. Absolute quiet was essential: orders were to be given in whispers, no weapon was to be loaded (so that there could be no accidental discharge) and no matches were to be struck. By midnight, the exhausting and difficult business of aligning the force exactly had been carried out; rum was issued; then Lieutenant Wyatt Rawson of the *Nepaul* joined them, and the approach march began. 'Solemn, impressive, was that night march across the desert,' wrote John Gordon. 'The muffled sound of rhythmic tread on the sand, the occasional low whispers of command, the now and then accidental clinking of swords warned us that we were approaching blindly but surely our fate at the hands of the enemy. The march became tedious because of frequent halts to reform the line. Our steps had become almost mechanical, we were so completely spent that sleep was trying to master us even while we kept on tramping. All at once a solitary shot roused us.'

It had been fired by an Egyptian sentry, who had detected something of this vast mass of men and animals approaching steadily in the darkness. They had arrived on time, almost on the brink of day. The march was at an end, and without an interval the battle was on. Instantly the whole line of entrenchments burst into one long chain of wicked fire. Who had thought the fierce charge was to be made in the face of a mass of flame? Surely there would not be a man of us left to reach the trenches now not five hundred yards away? In the midst of heat and roar, with the shriek of shot and shell almost deafening us, we received command to kneel and fix bayonets. "O my God, it's hot!" said Lieutenant John G. Maxwell unconsciously, as he stood near me, his sword drawn, ready to lead the charge. On the order, we rushed forward to the sound of bagpipes, cheering as loud as our lungs would allow, the most weird, unearthly noise imaginable; but what wonder, rising from thousands of men in a fighting line dashing at a living chain of fire. We noted the enemy's aim was high. Before we reached the trenches we were in one line of four deep; on the rear slope lay the Egyptians, some twenty thousand of them, pouring the volleys over our heads. Without a halt we leaped across the trench, landed on hard sand, and immediately pushing our way to the top of the breastworks, found ourselves among the muzzles of Egyptian rifles. A desperate hand-to-hand fight ensued a horrible encounter. Thank God, it was quickly over. Most of our killed and wounded met their fate on the parapets, where the enemy had mounted their heavy guns and to protect them had placed their best troops. These troops faced us with unflinching resistance, disputing

186

every inch of ground. My bayonet could have told the horrible experience which I forbear to relate.

'After clearing the rebels out of the main line of entrenchments we followed them so closely they could not make even a momentary stand in their other lines of defence, and soon we had them in full retreat; we knelt down and poured the volleys after them. Soon after, the Scottish Division of our Royal Horse Artillery came dashing towards us. With a lusty cheer we opened our ranks to let them through, and I can hear now their ringing "Scotland forever!" Instantly their guns were about and they opened a tremendous fire of canister and shrapnel shell upon the retreating masses of Arabi's army. An officer, suddenly sighting a train drawing out of Tel-el-Kebir station, gave the gunners orders of direction and distance. We watched the effect of this fiendlike destroyer. The first shell fell short; we could see a cloud of sand arise. Then followed the second, and as if knowing which car to choose, it plunged into the one filled with ammunition. The explosion was tremendous, piling all the cars together, blocking all further traffic. Just then, our cavalry, after marching round the enemy's left flank all night, swept across the plain and charged through the disorganised Arabs, scattering them to the four winds. This was the final touch to the historic, decisive battle of Tel-el-Kebir.'

In the aftermath of victory, one of Wolseley's officers sent him a message from the top of a pyramid: 'Four thousand years look down on you, the conqueror of the Pyramids.' Wolseley's reply was cooling: 'Don't be a fool! Come down.' Egypt had been conquered (which had antagonised the French, because they owned the Suez Canal), but what was to be done with Egypt's colonial territory in the Sudan? Parallel with the nationalist revolt of Arabi, which had begun in 1881, an even more dangerous movement, a rebellion both nationalist and fanatically religious, had broken out among the Arabs in the Sudan and had spread all along the shores of the Red Sea. This movement was both anti-Egyptian and anti-European, and was led by Mahomed Ahmed Ibn el-Sayyid Abdullah who gathered a small group of followers and styled himself the Mahdi, the long-awaited religious prophet whose coming had been foretold by the founder of the Moslem faith. The effect he had on others was no more rationally explicable than that of Gordon. With the latter, it was the power of the blue, honest eyes which impressed; with the former, it was his pleasant smile. That is as near as mere description can get; clearly, these men were power-houses of energy and belief; the impact of their personalities had to be experienced in order to be understood. Like Gordon, the Mahdi had an austere cast of mind; but there were differences. Gordon smoked heavily and indulged in the odd brandy and soda, although aware that these were human weaknesses; the Mahdi, however, believed so strongly in temperance that anyone in his domains found either consuming a glass of liquor or committing blasphemy, forthwith underwent an operation to deprive him of a hand or a limb or some other member, and all without an anaesthetic. Sometimes the operation decided upon was fatal. Another contrast was that, in private, the Mahdi was an unrestrained sensualist; but this was not incompatible with his religion, for the Moslem paradise is a good deal more uninhibited than the Christian. Like Gordon, he was sometimes written off as a mere madman; and it was this sad underestimate which allowed the flame of his revolt to grow almost unchecked.

The force sent to crush him was always insufficient, its leaders too confident; and the desert, the difficulty of the country, their most dangerous enemy, of which the Mahdi made full use. The first large expedition was destroyed in battle on 9th December 1881, losing 1,400 men; and on 7th June 1882, an even more sizeable force of 6,000 men was virtually wiped out. At this time, of course, the Egyptians were hampered by the Arabi revolt and the British invasion; but in June 1883, with Britain (and Baring) firmly in control, a massive expedition was assembled at Omdurman, on the western bank of the Nile, opposite Khartoum. Its leader was the British Colonel Hicks, who had a part-European staff, and their force numbered 7,000 infantry, 120 cuirassiers, 300 irregular cavalry, and 30 pieces of artillery, including rockets and mortars. Two war correspondents went with the expedition in order to report details of the great and crushing victory over the Mahdi. The advance, when it came at last, in October, was slow, ponderous, and known to everybody, best of all to the Mahdi; and the force was accompanied by 6,000 camels and a host of women. It was, in fact, precisely the sort of expedition which Gordon had condemned for use against irregulars; ponderous, predictable, resembling a huge hammer and presenting in fact only a tied-down target. As a final incompetence, the last part of the approach march to the heart of the Mahdi's power was made by a route along which there were no wells, and therefore no water to be had. The men were starting to collapse from thirst when, on 1st November, the Mahdi's forces began a series of running attacks — in and out of the scrub — which lasted until 4 November.

The war correspondents never reported the details to their newspapers, for they did not survive; few did. But Gordon learned some of the facts, when in January 1884 he was sent out again to Khartoum to try to save something from the wreckage of Egyptian rule in the Sudan. 'What a defeat Hicks's was!' he wrote. 'It is terrible to think of over 12,000 men killed;

the Arabs just prodded them to death, where they lay dying of thirst, four days without water! It is appalling. What a hecatomb to death!' The odd thing was, that although the destruction of the Hicks force made clear how powerful the Mahdi now was, controlling over 100,000 fanatical fighting men, Gordon was sent on his rescue mission into the Sudan single-handed, except for a small staff. He had no army. The reason was that the British Government had no policy they could call their own; and were simply hoping for a cheap miracle. But the basis of the tragedy was that no one, not even Gordon, fully realised how thoroughly the Mahdi had transformed the situation within a few years. He was not just another slave-raider on a big scale; every man of his vast army was disciplined and ready to die for him. Consequently, all the bitter political arguments and accusations were based on an appreciation which failed to comprehend the new reality. Gordon came nearest to understanding it.

W. T. Stead, editor of the *Pall Mall Gazette*, and originator of the 'interview' technique of journalism, printed on 9 January 1884, a pronouncement from Gordon which set light to the whole matter. 'The danger to be feared is not that the Mahdi will march northward to Wady Haifa; on the contrary, it is very improbable that he will ever go so far north. The danger is altogether of a different nature. It arises from the influence which the spectacle of a conquering Mahommedan Power established close to your frontiers will exercise upon the population which you govern. In all the cities in Egypt it will be felt that what the Mahdi has done they may do; and, as he has driven out the intruder and the infidel, they may do the same. Nor is it only England that has to face this danger. The success of the Mahdi has already excited dangerous fermentation in Arabia and Syria. Placards have been posted in

Damascus calling upon the population to rise and drive out the Turks. If the whole of the Eastern Soudan is surrendered to the Mahdi, the Arab tribes on both sides of the Red Sea will take fire. I see it is proposed to fortify Wady Haifa. You might as well fortify against a fever. Contagion of that sort cannot be kept out by fortifications and garrisons. In self-defence the policy of evacuation cannot possibly be justified. You must either surrender absolutely to the Mahdi or defend Khartum at all hazards. The great evil is at Cairo. It is the weakness of Cairo which produces disaster in the Soudan.' Gordon proposed that the more distant provinces must be abandoned, but that the Eastern Sudan must be held; and that, in any case, because of the vast distances and the presence of the Mahdi's warriors, evacuation of Khartoum would involve the death of most of the people concerned.

Compared to Gordon's sweeping vision, the thinking of the politicians and the diplomats, although involved and subtle, was simple murderous nonsense. The Cabinet was divided. Gladstone, the Prime Minister, just did not want to be bothered with so intractable and distant a problem; and he was anyway temperamentally opposed to undertaking what, according to his principles, was military aggression. Others, by sending Gordon to the Sudan, thought to force the Government into intervention sooner or later. But over them all hung the paralysis of British politics, the belief in the overriding importance of the parliamentary game as compared to anything else whatever; neither the national interest nor the impending massacre of thousands by the Mahdi made any real impact in comparison. And, consequently, the action taken was thoroughly British, in a long and abiding liberal tradition; like the humane old lady who wanted chicken for dinner, they made half-a-dozen half-hearted attempts to wring the unfortunate bird's neck, thus infinitely prolonging its suffering, and when finally it was dead, the carcase was so mauled as to be uneatable.

Gordon originally understood that his task was to evacuate the threatened Egyptian garrisons at Khartoum and elsewhere, but his written instructions from the Foreign Office, dated 18th January 1884, ordered him "to report on the military situation in the Soudan, and on the measures which it may be advisable to take for the security of the Egyptian garrisons still holding positions in that country, and for the safety of the European population in Khartum. You are also desired to consider and report upon the best mode of effecting the evacuation of the interior of the Soudan, and upon the manner in which the safety and the good administration by the Egyptian Government of the ports on the sea-coast can best be secured.' Gordon was also to see what he could do to prevent any 'stimulus' to the slave-trade; and 'you will consider yourself authorised and instructed to perform such other duties as the Egyptian Government (i.e., Sir Evelyn Baring) may desire to entrust to you'. The old lady had placed both hands, somewhat uncertainly, upon the neck of the chicken.

By 12th February, however, Gordon was no longer to 'report' and 'advise'. The 'Grand Old Man' in person stated that his mission was 'for the double purpose of evacuating the country by extricating the Egyptian garrisons and reconstituting it by giving back to those Sultans their ancestral power'. The old lady was starting to apply strangulation pressures to the bird's neck.

On 19th February, Lord Hartington for the Government stated in the House: 'I contend we are not responsible for the rescue or relief of the garrisons either in the Western or the

Southern or the Eastern Sudan.' The liberal old lady had recoiled in humane horror at what she had been about to do.

Gordon proposed that, prior to evacuation, the administration should be handed over to Zobier,[7] the most influential of the slave-raiders, who, being of the country, understood it and could form some sort of nationally-based government; better an orderly handover to him than just to retire, leaving a vacuum of bloodshed and chaos. The Foreign Secretary replied that 'the public opinion of this country would not tolerate the appointment'. What he meant was that the 'do-good-ing' societies, although tiny, were very vocal; it would cause trouble for the Government in the House, some little embarrassment perhaps. The old lady was afraid of what the neighbours would say. Even Baring, who was opposed to the whole idea of Gordon's appointment, jibbed at this. 'I venture to think,' he telegraphed, 'that any attempt to settle Egyptian questions by the light of English popular feeling is sure to be productive of harm...'

Gordan had set off for Khartoum, from Cairo, on 28 January. When he had arrived and studied the situation, he asked for 200 reliable troops to be sent to Wady Haifa and for a small force of Indian cavalry to go to the other point of strategic importance, Berber. These were very modest requests, essential if the Egyptian garrisons were to be evacuated without heavy loss and the tribes which had not yet gone over to the Mahdi were to be deterred from doing so. The Government, however, declared that they could not do this; for it would constitute military intervention and aggression in the Sudan. The old lady was not really trying to kill the chicken, merely intimidate it. In his memoirs, one member of the

---

[7] Dr. Zebehr. European spellings of Middle Eastern sounds are just as varied as with Chinese.

Government, Sir Charles Dilke, was afterwards terribly frank. On the day that Gordon left Cairo, he judged, 'here ended our responsibility because it must be remembered that Gordon at Khartoum was entirely outside our reach. From this moment we had only to please ourselves whether we should disavow him and say that he was acting in defiance of our instructions.' The whole affair was just an unfortunate misunderstanding, the old lady had only the best interests of the chicken at heart, and had certainly never contemplated any designs upon it.

The odd thing was, that while the old lady was so protesting publicly, she had meanwhile dragged the bird round the corner, and in a fury of flying feathers and frantic squawks, had sought to strangle it quickly, before any of the neighbours could notice what she was doing.

In the Eastern Sudan, bordering on the Red Sea route to India, a powerful slave-trader, Osman Digna, had risen for the Mahdi and cut off an Egyptian garrison near Suakin. General Valentine Baker, a British soldier-of-fortune serving with the Egyptians, was sent to relieve them with a force of 3,500 native troops. On 5th February 1884, he met disaster near the wells of El Teb, losing over half his force to a wild rush of Sudanese tribesmen, the remainder dispersing. Meanwhile, the large British Army of Occupation was sitting, more or less idly by, in barracks at Cairo. But on 12th February the Black Watch were told to be ready for operations, and a few days later they sailed in the *Orontes* as the first unit of General Sir Gerald Graham's force of some 4,000 British troops. So while General Gordon was on his way to Khartoum, Corporal John Gordon of the Black Watch was landing on the shores of the Red Sea at Trinkitat, hard by the scene of the disaster. They were told nothing by their C.O. Lieutenant-Colonel William Green, who put them ashore under cover of night, a prey to morbid fears.

All were oppressed by the 'gruesome thought' of what the savages did to the dead and wounded. 'To be told nothing, to be left entirely out of a commander's confidence,' wrote Corporal Gordon, 'is demoralizing; we felt no co-operation with our leader, ours was a blind obedience. We knew that in the dark we had landed on the site of a recent horrible tragedy, and that is all we knew.'

He noted that in their supporting Naval Brigade, which supplied the brains and the machineguns, officers and men worked closely together, knowing and understanding each other. In the army, they did not; there was a great gulf between Officers and Other Ranks; and, as he was shortly to discover, from the General downwards, although they were brave, they did not know their business. Several stupid mistakes were to be made, including one which was to become famous as the only occasion on which a British square was broken.

On 29th February they marched off, formed in a square, to relieve the Egyptian garrison of Tokar. Six battalions formed the square, and behind came the cavalry under Brigadier Stewart. Near El Teb, they came under fire from Osman Digna's positions, and were ordered to halt and lie down while the Royal Artillery and the machineguns of the Naval Brigade silenced the Sudanese who were using captured weapons, including a Gatling gun. This was a tense and not very useful business, the infantry suffering casualties without being able to reply. Gordon saw a shell coming straight for him, passing directly over his head and landing in the middle of the square, blowing the head off a mule and the arm off a man. Then the men were ordered to get up and advance, the fighting face of the square now consisting of the Black Watch, the 65th York & Lancaster Regiment, and the Royal Marines.

'The Soudanese were still in a state of elation from their recent triumphs over the Egyptian garrisons and the Egyptian troops sent to relieve those garrisons; they were hungrily waiting for our advance,' wrote John Gordon. 'These black, bushy-headed, grinning savages, of wonderful physique, were utterly fearless men, indefatigable fighters, but they were not armed with modern weapons. They had a few trained men with rifles; but outside two batteries of artillery taken from Baker Pasha, weapons of the masses of Soudanese were spears, double-edged swords, crooked knives, boomerangs, and shields of rhinoceros hide; formidable enough, surely; we knew we were up against the real thing; that was indicated by our square formation.'

The British square advanced steadily, directly to the front of the Black Watch being rifle pits and an old sugar mill, with masses of the enemies waiting there for the right moment to charge the square and crumple it up. They came at last, in a mad rush; but the bounding Sudanese were met by the steady crash of drilled volleys from Martini rifles, and were momentarily checked. But they came on again, in 'a rapid succession of charges'. Each charge was broken, the soldiers halting to fire, then marching steadily on, shoulder to shoulder, up to, into, and over the enemy trenches. At this point, the battle was hand to hand, bayonets flashing, spears whizzing through the air, stricken men reeling away and dropping to the ground. The Sudanese guns were captured and turned on their late owners, then a halt was called to reform the square and issue fresh ammunition, for enormous masses of the enemies were gathering in front. At this point there occurred a most astonishing spectacle, the cavalry, having apparently gone mad, charging the mass of unbroken Sudanese, and being cut to pieces for their pains.

The gallop-happy Brigadier Stewart, instead of holding back for the proper role of cavalry — the timed and decisive blow at a beaten enemy which converts defeat into rout, as demonstrated by Wolseley at Tel-el-Kebir — swung his force round the square and charged into the hordes of Sudanese who had not yet been engaged by the infantry. The Black Watch gave them three cheers as they went thundering by, but Gordon recalled that they felt more like shouting, 'What the devil are you doing? Have you gone stark mad?' It was a 'sickening' spectacle, wrote Gordon. 'We could see the black hordes squat on the ground, and shrewdly evading swords of the cavalry, they hamstrung horses, bringing riders to the ground.' The survivors were too used up, and the horses too blown, to crown the victory, which came almost at once, as the infantry advanced on the main enemy position.

'Great, black masses of Soudanese rose from their shelters in one wild rush for the square, determined to reach and to smash it. We stood ready with our Martinis, and at the right moment we opened fire. The great masses flattened like waving grain in a hail-storm, while the few that reached the square met our bayonets. Even after having been pierced with bayonets, they continued to fight, inflicting wounds with their double-edged swords. In bravery, I am bound to record, the enemy was a match for any army in the world. They were religious fanatics; every man who took the life of an infidel was thereby assured that upon his own death he would be given immediate entrance into Paradise.' Time after time the bloodied remnants of the enemy gathered together again behind shelter, and then bounded forward for one more hopeless charge, every much as wild as the first, but each one delivered with dwindling forces. The battle began at about 10.30 in the morning and lasted until about two o'clock in the afternoon, when the staccato Martini volleys had swept away all opposition in front and the hammering machineguns of the Naval Brigade had cleared the sugar mill. Given unblown, unbroken cavalry, the defeat they had inflicted on the Mahdi's forces in the district would have been final. As it was, they buried more than 2,000 enemy dead in their own rifle pits; and went on to rescue the Egyptian garrison of Tokar — the first time the Mahdi had met with a check in his meteoric career.

But not as great a check as it could have been, for the force commander, General Sir Gerald Graham, V.C., was just as big a bonehead as Brigadier Stewart, an old parade-ground stamper who would have been bumping his mental ceiling in the rank of Regimental Sergeant-Major. When the march was resumed, the first thing he did was to plan the route right across Baker's battlefield of El Teb, where 2,500 corpses, hideously and obscenely mutilated by the enemy, had lain rotting in the heat since the 5th of February. It was 'ghastly', wrote Corporal Gordon. 'Our indignation rising into anger, we could not for weeks shake from memory.'

The force was then re-embarked and landed further down the coast for an advance from Suakim to Tamaai, where another part of Osman Digna's army had just wiped out an inland Egyptian garrison as it was being evacuated to the coast. Osman Digna commanded this force in person, and intended to wipe out the British; while the British objective was to open the coast route to Berber, closed by the uprising. Just before the march-off, General Graham sought out the Black Watch. 'He informed us that he was not satisfied with the way we had fought at El Teb; he said he expected us to charge the enemy's position and fight hand to hand instead of meeting the enemy's advances by rifle fire. A more astounded lot of men could hardly be imagined than our regiment as we listened to this speech; it had not occurred to us for one moment that our work in that engagement was not praiseworthy. I am sure that if the number of dead had been counted in that part of the enemy's position taken by us, it would have been clear that a large percent of the killing was by the accurate shooting of the Black Watch.' As Gordon put it, 'burning within, sun scorched without', they set off for Tamaai, their corned beef rations, in typical army style, being in tins too large to carry in such circumstances so that many were simply dumped in the desert.

The General's thought-processes are impossible to understand; not even the popular German dictum that a modicum of stupidity is an essential requirement for success in a military career, properly explains it. This is true, in a sense, for toughness and courage are more valuable properties in the field than, say, sensitivity and imagination. But hand to hand fighting, which he advocated, puts indigenous and civilised soldiers on almost the same footing, apart from the superior discipline of the latter; a quite fatal proceeding when the latter are enormously outnumbered by the former. It is to throw away the advantage of the rifle, which General Gordon had already seen as the dominating weapon of the battlefield; a lesson constantly repeated, but always ignored, right up to 1914, by one army or another. The British, it is only fair to say, learned their lesson earlier than this, in the Boer War; but they took a very long time to grasp the proposition, obvious enough to Gordon and to Wolseley many long years before. The whole point of Wolseley's night march at Tel-el-Kebir had been to nullify by darkness the devastating effect of rifle fire from prepared entrenchments.

On 12th March the force halted at sunset 1,000 yards from Osman Digna's position, centred on a wide, deep watercourse strewn with stones and boulders and surrounded by trenches dug into the sandhills. The enemy began to snipe at them, and a daring party dashed forward, only to be swept by machinegun fire. At dawn on the 13th, the day Kipling was to immortalise with the lines: *An' 'ere's to you, Fuzzy-Wuzzy, with your 'ayrick 'ead of 'air — You big black boundin' beggar — for you broke a British square!* — at daybreak of this day, Drum-Major Clark of the Black Watch collected all the buglers in the force, and posted them on a knoll for a concerted and theatrically effective call to fight. 'There they sounded the "long reveille",' wrote John Gordon, 'the grandest, most sublime sound as it pierced the clear, pure air and from the hills where the enemy lay concealed echoed back to us its stern significance, the last slow notes lingering and finally trembling out into eternity.'

Breakfast was mixed with bullets, as the enemy snipers opened fire, the men bolting as much food as they could, for they knew not when the next meal would be. Two brave men, John Miller and John Cains, ate nothing, saying they could not understand why they had no appetite. 'Both these men were buried just after sunset, and all the soldiers believed it to be fulfilment of a presentiment,' commented Gordon.

This day, 13th March, there were two squares, and the Black Watch formed the front and left face of the leading square. As they advanced, the command rang out: 'Fix bayonets!' Then 'Charge!' The soldiers dashed forward, keeping their tight formation, then halted as the Sudanese came leaping out from concealment in the ravine. On command, the front rank knelt down, rifles to their shoulders, so that the rear rank could fire over their heads. Firing was by controlled volleys, one rank firing while the other reloaded, alternately. Swarms of black warriors poured across the river bed, with more coming on behind, seemingly in endless numbers. 'Picturesquely formidable they were, led by their sheiks on horseback. We soon discovered that if we killed or wounded a sheik, eight men would leave the fighting line to carry him off the field. We took advantage of this, picking off every sheik we could and firing volleys at his attendants, thus making a new set of eight attendants leave the line to carry him off.' Then a lone figure was seen to break ranks and dash forward into the midst of the Sudanese; it was Sergeant Ronald Fraser, under open arrest for some offence, and seeking to clear himself by an outstanding act. A number of his opponents fell, then the black tide closed round him, and over him.

'It was impossible to shoot down the hordes surging upon us from the ravine,' wrote Corporal Gordon. 'The struggle developed into a wild hand to hand contest between swords, spears, crooked knives and boomerangs on the one side and bayonets on the other, a veritable hell. The smoke from our Martinis hung over us, a dense cloud, not a breath of air stirring to carry it away. Just how long this mad contest had raged I do not know — time was of no consequence — when suddenly our officers and N.C.O.s forming the supernumerary rank, were attacked from the rear. Great God, the centre of our square was filled with the black fiends! Clean them out, and with the bayonet; to fire would be to shoot our own men. Foes in front, foes in rear. We fell back, with the rear rank and officers fighting those in the centre of the square while the front rank engaged those still pressing hard, sticking to us like burrs. We kept trimming their ranks; in their frenzy they unintentionally gave advantage, for when they stopped to mutilate our dead, we shot and bayoneted.'

The second square moved up on their right, and began sweeping away with rifle fire the enemy gathered there, while the cavalry brigade and the mounted infantry came up on their left. 'Without this help from outside,' wrote Gordon, 'I think there would not have been a man of our square left; we were pitted against fearful odds.' They had lost 60 officers and men killed, apart from wounded. 'Now we were an entirely different regiment; the strain, the tenseness, of close action, had used up all reserve power. I remember feeling utterly weak from incessant use of the bayonet. We had been at it two hours; from nine to eleven the struggle of the broken square of the Second Brigade lasted.' This brigade was so exhausted that it was unable to take part in the follow up, and once again, although Osman Digna's camp went up in flames, the result was short of total victory, and Rudyard Kipling was to write:

> Then 'ere's to you, Fuzzy-Wuzzy, an' the misses and the kid;
> Our orders was to break you, an' of course we went an' did.
> We sloshed you with Martinis, an' it wasn't 'ardly fair;
> But for all the odds agin' you, Fuzzy-Wuz, you broke the square.

Excellently descriptive of such a battle as the ballad was, it contained one major historical inaccuracy. 'Fuzzy-Wuz' did *not* break the square. That superlative feat was performed by General Sir Gerald Graham. The order to 'Charge!' was wrong in any case, as a square is not designed for that purpose; and secondly, the order was given to the Black Watch only, and not to the York & Lancaster alongside them. The General had ripped his own square apart, and in the face of a mass enemy. The men knew it, and the officers knew it, and for once they were united.

'The broken square was rankling in Captain Stevenson's mind,' wrote Corporal Gordon. 'He called all non-commissioned officers together and had us re-fight the battle. At the order which opened up the square, imaginary hordes of Soudanese rushed in from behind. He criticized freely the General's orders; and he was absolutely right. Never should command to charge have been given; an open doorway was offered the enemy; it was an unspeakable blunder.'

But the most serious thing about it was the consequence for that other Gordon, in Khartoum. The two battles of El Teb and Tamaai had taught 'Fuzzy-Wuz' that, while he might do what he liked with Egyptians, it was mass suicide to fight British troops. Osman Digna had been wounded; many thousands killed. He withdrew and refused to fight; he never gave Graham another chance to wipe him out completely. Therefore, considerable forces still remained to him in the interior, and Graham failed to push home the drive to Berber, when a rapid and complete victory might have transformed the whole situation, frightening the Mahdi and putting life into the English politicians. For Gordon had decided that any mass evacuation must be a massacre; instead, he advised that the Mahdi could be, and must be, 'smashed up'. The politicians were horrified, for that would be unprovoked aggression, it could be construed as intervention in the Sudan, and this they would never do. True, they had just smashed up Osman Digna to the tune of many thousands of dervish corpses, but then this had been forced upon them by public opinion after the defeat of Baker, and anyway, if looked at in the correct light it was not *really* intervention in the Sudan. As Lord Hartington was able triumphantly to point out, the Red Sea area of the Sudan was only technically a part of the Sudan; practically, however, it might well be regarded as a totally separate district. The old lady had very nearly wrung the chicken's neck, with blood and feathers all over the place, and the best of intentions, but her humanitarian principles utterly prevented her from going any further and making a meal of it. Self-righteously seizing a broom, primly she swept the remains under her skirt.

Meanwhile, a torrent of cables had been pouring out of Gordon in Khartoum, reporting on the realities of the situation as he found them; couched in blunt, racy language, quite horrifyingly so. Also a flow of refugees, for he was sending down as many as he could of the women and children and the Egyptian soldiers. But always, he pointed out, there could be no final settlement without settling the Mahdi; and as the prophet's religious principals made peace impossible, the settlement would have to be by force. If they did not do this, then they would be responsible for the massacre of all those in Khartoum and all the outlying garrisons. This had little effect on politicians intent only on the London political scene. But Gordon's continual requests for Zobeir did disturb them, for Gordon told *The Times* correspondent in Khartoum, and *The Times* told the world; and the Liberal press and the Anti-Slavery Society were affronted to the point of hysteria. Only Gladstone was in favour, and he was out of action, ill. Then, on 12th March, the flow of communications from Khartoum stopped. The Mahdi had moved in and the local tribes had risen for him.

Rumour reached London that Gordon was cut off and surrounded in Khartoum. This was authoritatively and weightily denied by Mr. Gladstone. It was quite untrue, Gordon was only 'hemmed in'. Thousands sighed with relief and murmured, '*Dear* Mr. Gladstone knows best.' And, indeed, dear Mr. Gladstone could prove it, for now and then a message from Gordon did get through. But these messages contained no references to matters they had mentioned in their own communications; and as they could not bring themselves to believe that the Mahdi was reading H.M. Government's official correspondence, they simply assumed that Gordon had them, but chose not to answer. There was no doubt that the old lady had been gravely wronged by the chicken.

CHAPTER FOURTEEN: 'WE HEAR HIS DRUMS FROM THE PALACE'

'It is, of course, on the cards that Khartoum is taken under the nose of the expeditionary force, which will be *just too late*. The expeditionary force will perhaps think it necessary to retake it; but that will be of no use, and will cause loss of life uselessly on both sides. It had far better quietly return, with its tail between its legs; for once Khartoum is taken, it matters little if the Opposition say "You gave up Khartoum", etc., etc., the sun will have set. If Khartoum falls, then go quietly back to Cairo, for you will only lose men and spend money uselessly in carrying on the campaign.' — *Gordon, Khartoum*, 13 October 1884.

The siege of Khartoum lasted 317 days, nearly as long as that of Sebastopol. At first, the investment was loose. On 11 March 1884, Gordon wrote to his sister Augusta: 'This may be the last letter I send you, for the tribes have risen between this and Berber and will try and cut our *route*. They will not fight us directly, but will starve us out.' On 13th March, the Mahdi's men were closer. 'We are all right. The enemy has established himself some six thousand strong nine miles from here, and we hear his drums from the Palace. We are well off for food, and the people are in good spirits.' It was not until 12th October that he wrote: 'The Mahdi has come down to pay us a visit — and he has brought all his guns; he means to starve us out, not to attack directly.'

There were four inflexible factors in the tragedy. There was Gordon himself, who wrote on 5th November: 'I expect Her

Majesty's Government are in a precious rage with me for holding out and forcing their hand.' He was prepared to die rather than abandon — to 'rat' on — the people he now felt committed to save. 'Not that (D.V.) I will ever be taken alive.'

There was the Mahdi, continually sending in letters to Khartoum, trying to get Gordon to surrender, who had proclaimed his revolt in the words: 'Let us all show penitence before God, and abandon all bad and forbidden habits, such as the degrading acts of the flesh, the use of wine and tobacco, lying, bearing false witness, disobedience to parents, brigandage, the non-restitution of goods to others, the clapping of hands, dancing, improper signs with the eyes, tears and lamentations at the bed of the dead, slanderous language, calumny, and the company of strange women.' In Gordon's view, the Mahdi's grasp of the Koran was shaky, but there was no doubt that he understood the desert and its peoples better than anyone else. He was an outstanding military leader in the local conditions, but more than this, he represented government of a sort; a fact not appreciated by Europeans at the time, for they thought of him as a mere desert gangster.

There was Garnet Wolseley, Gilbert and Sullivan's 'model of a modern Major-General', the finest soldier in the British Empire, and a friend and admirer of Gordon since Crimea days, who had said he was 'not worthy to pipe-clay Gordon's belt'. Back in the 1860s there had been a time when Wolseley rather than Gordon was being considered by Whitehall for the post of commander of the 'Ever Victorious Army'. Afterwards, Wolseley had told Gordon, jokingly: 'How differently events might have turned out had I been sent on that mission instead of you. I should have gone there with the determination of wiping out the rebellion and becoming myself Emperor of China!' This was a hit at his own intensely ambitious nature, where the contrast to Gordon was strongest. What he said now was: 'If you contemplate sending an expedition in the autumn to Gordon's relief, the sooner he is informed the better it will be for him and for our interests.' And, he added, ominously, 'The English people will force you to do it whether you like it or not.' They did, but it was not until 5th August that Gladstone voted £300,000 for a Gordon relief expedition, 'in case it might be necessary'. And it was Wolseley who was to command it, commenting on the delay, in writing, with the bitter words: 'We have been anxiously looking out for Gladstone's death...' And it was he who was to reverse 'G.O.M.' to 'M.O.G.', branding Gladstone, not the Mahdi, as 'Murderer of Gordon'.

The fourth inflexible factor was the Nile, as Wolseley had reminded the Government as early as 8th April, before Gordon was cut off. 'All the gold in England will not affect the rise and fall of the Nile or the duration of the hot and cold seasons in Egypt.' The first vital point was that Khartoum was sited at the junction of the White and the Blue Nile, surrounded by water on three sides; as long as the river was high, forming a formidable moat, Khartoum was easy to defend, but when the water-level fell at about Christmas time, the town could be approached by land from almost any direction. The second vital point was that Khartoum lay 1,500 miles up the Nile, and most of that distance was desert; the only practical route for Wolseley's relief expedition of 7,000 men and the vast amount of supplies they needed was by water and those waters were becoming navigable by May. Even so, there was nothing easy about it; quite the reverse. There were rock-strewn rapids, or 'cataracts', studding at intervals the entire course of the river. To pass some of them, the boats would have to be unloaded, then both boats and stores would have to be manhandled overland for great distances.

It was in fact, writ very large, the problem of 'portage' on the Canadian rivers; and Wolseley, who had waged just such a campaign in Canada some years before, decided to employ the same methods. But first, both boats and boatmen had to be obtained. The building of 800 specially designed whalers was put out to contract among a number of firms in England; they were 30 feet long, with a beam of 6½ feet and a shallow draught of 2½ feet, and each carried ten soldiers and two boatmen. The boatmen were specially recruited *voyageurs*, mostly French and British Canadians, with a few Iroquois Indians, who were experienced in this type of critical water-work. All the Nile steamers were requisitioned, including those belonging to Cooks, the tourist agency; and vast dumps of coal had to be established for them, which was the work of Redvers Buller, the later Boer War general. Another general of the future, Ian Hamilton of Dardanelles fame, was with the force, and commented that they felt like 'Boy Scouts dressed up like Red Indians let loose in a flotilla of canoes'. The main forward base was to be at Wady Haifa, immediately nicknamed 'Bloody Half-way'. When established, it looked as if 'the goods station of a London terminus, a couple of battalions of infantry, the War Office, and a considerable proportion of Woolwich Arsenal had been all thoroughly shaken together, and then cast forth on the desert'. At Wady Haifa the force was to divide into two — the River Column and the Desert Column, the latter being a Camel Corps organised for a rapid dash across the desert for Khartoum.

On 18th September the Black Watch were warned that they had been selected to take part in the Nile Relief Expedition, and Wolseley inspected them at Kasr-el-Nil Barracks. 'He made a short, impressive address,' recollected Corporal Gordon. 'I distinctly remember his eyes, which seemed to have depth of controlled emotion. He told us he did not think there would be much fighting in the campaign, but there would be plenty of hard work,' They left on 25th September, first by rail, then by steamer; they were to transfer to the new whalers at the Second Cataract, where the going became difficult. But they were held up on the way by a shortage of coal for the steamers; and instead of doing a comfortable stretch of 220 miles in three days by steamer, they took nine days to cover the distance. Buller's under-estimate of the coal required cost the whole expedition some three weeks delay.

Meanwhile, fantastic rumours were afloat in besieged Khartoum; but, on 17th September, the day before the Black Watch were notified, General Gordon wrote in his Journal: 'I have the strongest suspicion that these tales of troops at Dongola and Merowé are all gas-works, and that if you wanted to find Her Majesty's forces you would have to go to Shepheard's Hotel at Cairo.' And on 24th September, the day before the expedition started, he wrote: 'I cannot too much impress on you that this expedition will not encounter any enemy worth the name in an European sense of the word; the struggle is with the climate and destitution of the country.' Corporal Gordon would have endorsed that, for one 38-mile stretch of the 1,500 miles they had to traverse took them eleven days. General Gordon was also at one with Wolseley in his estimation of the effect of the operations against Osman Digna on the Red Sea coast earlier in the year; to fight two battles, then evacuate, must tend to make the Mahdi think the British were afraid of him. Wolseley summed up this instance of Gladstone's wavering policy in the Sudan as: 'Butcher and bolt.'

Gordon protected the landward side of Khartoum with a triple minefield. The mines were improvised and the fuses were matchboxes, but it was a distinctly modern touch which had exactly the same effect on wild dervishes then as it has on anyone else now: fear out of all proportion to the danger. The Mahdi's men never did breach the minefields, although they had artillery. Khartoum became a city of explosions, shells falling into the town hour by hour, day by day, month by month. The wing of the Palace occupied by Gordon was a particular target. Distinct among the daily noises was the Nordenfeldt they had captured from Hicks; a kind of manually operated pom-pom, it made a sort of grunt at half-second intervals, and Gordon lightly supposed that 'the Arabs put a slave boy to turn the handle'. Keeping records of ammunition expenditure for the first six months, he recorded that the defenders had shot away some 3 million Remington rounds, apart from 1,570 shells from the Krupp gun and 9,442 from the Mountain gun. As far as he could, he kept a record of what the Mahdi's men fired back, and calculated how much could still remain to them from the horde of ammunition taken from Hicks. Food was not yet critically short, and Gordon's main limitation was the quality of his troops; apart from the black Sudanese, they were mostly terrible braggarts and terrible cowards. He was prepared, he wrote to 'back them against any troops in the world for cowardice!' The local tribesmen were the worst: 'a cow would have taken their fort, though there were 1,200 men in it.' With better troops, he could have worried the Arabs with offensive sorties at night; 'but it is no use, we are not up to it'.

Gordon managed to get a number of communications through to Cairo, but Kitchener's spies were less successful in penetrating the ring of besiegers — partly perhaps because, while many were eager to leave Khartoum, few were keen to go there. Those that did get through to Gordon were all too often typical Civil Service screeds, asking for precise returns. For instance, a letter from Mr. E. H. Egerton, standing in temporarily for Baring in Cairo, arrived in late September, asking 'to be informed exactly when he expects to be in difficulties as to provisions and ammunition'. Gordon noted this in his Journal (which went down to Cairo in due course for Egerton to read), and remarked: 'Now I really think if Egerton was to turn over the "archives" (a delicious word) of his office, he would see we had been in difficulties for provisions for some months. It is as if a man on the bank, having seen his friend in the river already bobbed down two or three times, hails, "I say, old fellow, let us know when we are to throw you the life buoy, I know you have bobbed down two or three times, but it is a pity to throw you the life buoy until you really are *in extremis*, and I want to know *exactly*, for I am a man brought up in a school of exactitude."'

He was becoming convinced, perhaps unfairly, that the Government hoped that Khartoum would fall before they were put to the trouble of sending an expedition. 'If a boy at Eton or Harrow acted towards his fellows in a similar way, I *think* he would be kicked and *I am sure* he would deserve it.' Into the Journals he poured not only the day-to-day record of the siege, the political and military situations and so on, but also light-hearted little essays and asides. Some of the reasons given for the award of the Victoria Cross, he wrote, 'are really astounding'. With an only half-concealed reference to his own position, he added: 'A man defends a post, if he loses it his throat is cut; why give him a Victoria Cross? and if given, why not give it to all who were with him? they equally with him defended their throats.' And, concluding a report of a dervish night attack on his isolated fort of Omdurman across the river, he noted: 'The cock turkey has killed one of his companions, reason not known. (Supposed to be correspondence with Mahdi, or some harem infidelity.)' These asides were his emotional release from strain; not the strain from fear of death, but of appearing completely confident and capable all the time, so as to buoy up the spirits of the craven troops and the scared population. At this time, for the first time, he inspired fear; men shook in his presence. And at the same time, he could note: 'At the Mahdi's camp they had another "church parade" today. I suppose they are working up their fanaticism.' It was a humorous comment on the central fact that the basic danger to be feared was not any one shell or rifle bullet, but defeat itself — the fall of Khartoum.

As well as turning out 50,000 rounds of ammunition a week, he had workshops building steamers, and one of these he playfully named the *Zobier*, to annoy the humanitarians of the Anti-Slavery Society, who did not appreciate that the Mahdi used pressed men, including Sudanese, in his front rank of attack, pressed on by the Arabs from behind, a particularly deadly form of slave-driving. The Khartoum Journals have a serenity missing from the questing religious preoccupations of much of Gordon's writing at other times; only at one point, and over one incident, does he show worry and alarm. This was the fate of the party under his senior assistant, Colonel J. D. H. Stewart, an old friend from Crimean days, which he had sent out of Khartoum with important documents in the steamer *Abbas* on 8th September. The documents included a Journal, the official cipher, a full statement revealing the desperate position of Khartoum, and an appeal, via Baring to the Government, for immediate help: 'How many times have I written asking for reinforcements? No answer at all has come to us, and the hearts of men have become weary at this delay. While you are eating and drinking and resting on good beds, we and those with us are watching night and day, endeavouring to quell the movement of this false Mahdi. The reason why I have now sent Colonel Stewart is because you have been silent all this while and neglected us, and lost time without doing any good.'

Had Baring received these messages, an impetus would certainly have been given to Wolseley to take desperate measures to get at least a small force through to Khartoum. On the Government, of course, they could have no effect. But their effect, if they fell into the hands of the Mahdi, would probably seal the fate of Khartoum. Gordon therefore took the most elaborate measures to make sure that the *Abbas* got through. She was specially fitted out with buffers below the waterline, to minimise damage in case of collision with rocky reefs; she was to be escorted past the principal danger points by other steamers, and was to tow two sailing boats as lifeboats. Above all, Stewart was warned not to land on the river bank, for fuel or anything else, if there were natives in the vicinity. In fact, Stewart disregarded all orders for his safety and when, on 18th September, the *Abbas* ran on a rock 100 miles short of safety at Dongola, where Major Kitchener was, he had already cast loose the lifeboats and landed unarmed on the bank, to get help from local Arabs, who, pretending friendship, waved a white flag; once ashore, he and his companions were murdered. 'I feel somehow convinced that they were captured by treachery — the Arabs pretending to be friendly,' noted Gordon on 5th November, when he knew no details except what he had from the Mahdi, who had made another proposal for surrender, based now on a deadly accurate knowledge of the weakness of the defenders.

Five months after the tragedy, Corporal John Gordon actually walked out across the dried-up river bed of the Nile to where the remains of the *Abbas* lay perched on a rock which, back in September, would have been an island in a rocky and dangerous part of the river. The wreck had been gutted of everything except its ¾-inch armour plate, and it was much larger than they had supposed, 70 feet long with a beam at the paddle-boxes of 22 feet. The odd thing was, that there was no need for her to have chosen the rocky channel as there was a much better one at the same point. They suspected treachery, and yet to guard against this a squad of a dozen highly-paid Greek soldiers had been put aboard her by General Gordon. But certainly, there had been treachery ashore. They learned the details at length from a survivor, Hassein Ismail, who had been a stoker in the steamer and who was interrogated by General Brackenbury. Stewart had contributed to the disaster, first by casting off the two lifeboats prematurely, then by going ashore to bargain for camel transport, and finally by going ashore unarmed. They had been cut down while drinking coffee, at the order of Sheikh Suleiman Wad Gamr. The British soldiers, on learning this, made sure that he and his chiefs would have no homes to come back to, laying them waste with gun-cotton.[8] Among those who had been murdered were the British Consul in Khartoum, Mr. Power, who had also been correspondent for *The Times*, and the French Consul, as well as some refugees, male and female.

Gordon had taken every precaution to see that the *Abbas* should get through, and even if she did not, that the party

---

[8] Hassein Ismail's narrative, which is long and detailed, may be found in full in *My Six Years with the Black Watch*, by John Gordon, LL.B. (Harvard), and published by Samuel Usher, Boston, in 1929. At this time, 1884, his brother, George A. Gordon, had just been installed minister of the Old South Church, Boston, U.S.A.

could still make safety in the sailing boats she towed behind her. Now, Stewart's trust in, or may it have been contempt for? the native people, had ensured the worst. The Mahdi now knew the desperate straits he was in, but the Relief Expedition did not. Gordon worried over the whys and wherefores for days, doubting at first the truth of the news; but was soon overwhelmed by the task of single-handedly putting heart into, and at the same time actually conducting, almost every detail of the defence of Khartoum. Soon, with the hot season over, and the level of the river beginning to fall in November, the siege took a more serious form. The Mahdi made his headquarters a short distance away, bringing with him his chained European prisoners, some of whom were governors of garrisons which had now surrendered and had saved their lives by becoming Moslems, including Rudolf Slatin, an Austrian. There was another Austrian, Father Owhrwalder, some Greek Orthodox priests, and a party of nuns. A nun who would not change her religion was staked out on the sand in the burning sun, a theological argument of some force in that climate.

The political and military arguments, between Gordon in Khartoum and (via Baring) Gladstone in London, were made farcical because of the difficulties of communicating with a besieged town 1,500 miles from nowhere; and very often, if the messages got through, they got through garbled. The basic facts were that Gladstone had ordered Gordon to evacuate Khartoum, but, as Stewart noted, what seemed straightforward to begin with, increasingly appeared more difficult, and then finally became impossible. The reality was that if the inhabitants could not be evacuated, or if government could not be handed over to Zobier, then thousands must succumb to the razor-cut agony of the knives. Gladstone, a stubborn old man and a Liberal with a capital 'L', specialising in calls to humanity, had the enviable ability to draw a welcome curtain over this aspect of the matter.[9] After Khartoum had been besieged for six weeks, he was able to assure the House that: 'We see no reason to modify, in any respect, the statements previously made, that there is no military or other danger threatening Khartoum.' In May, although Gladstone was being hissed in public, he was able to state that he was not then contemplating a relief expedition, because this would be in effect to wage an aggressive war of conquest against a people 'struggling rightly to be free'. This statement of far-seeing humanitarian principle was enunciated some months *after* he had initiated the policy of 'butcher and bolt' against Osman Digna and his freedom-loving locals.

It was not until 29th July that a Gladstone communication of 23rd April reached Gordon. It was stiff with displeasure, asking him to 'state cause and intention of staying in Khartoum'. Gordon replied humorously: 'I stay at Khartoum because Arabs have shut us up and will not let us out.' On 18th September, the day the crew of the *Abbas* were slaughtered, Gladstone received a Cairo telegram giving garbled news from Gordon which was some four months out of date. A plan for a raid by steamers on the besieging force was mentioned, plus requests for Turkish intervention. To Gladstone, it seemed that Gordon was attempting to involve him in some scheme to 'smash up the Mahdi', another of those bankers' wars. A witness, who saw him read the telegram, stated: 'His face hardened and whitened, the eyes burned as I have seen them

---

[9] To be fair, the phenomenon was not confined to Gladstone or the Victorians; for it was humanitarians and peace-lovers who evacuated India so precipitately that many hundreds of thousands, possibly millions, were cut to pieces in internal struggles. Gordon, incidentally, was in favour of the evacuation of India, except for some ports, in the 1880s. He was neither a Jingo nor an Empire-builder.

once or twice in the House of Commons — burned with a deep fire as if they would have consumed the paper on which Gordon's message was printed.' Gladstone's actions were immediate, massive, and impressive; he at once gave instructions that Gordon was to be relieved as Governor-General of the Sudan; henceforth, his powers would be reduced to that of simple Governor of Khartoum and its immediate neighbourhood. And nothing could, as it turned out, have been more appropriate to the situation, for when this disciplinary instruction at last reached Gordon it was anyway unreadable and the date was 25th November. Gordon controlled with certainty only Khartoum; his outlying fort of Omdurman, across the river, had been under continuous attack since 12th November and was cut off.

CHAPTER FIFTEEN: 'HIS SUFFERINGS ARE OVER'

'If you send out a soldier to run away from those at whose head you have placed him you must not send a Gordon.' — *J. L. Garvin.*

The first sign of the coming assault on Omdurman was when, on 8th November, a herd of cows appeared. Gordon sent down the steamer *Ismailia* to help the garrison repel them. 'I expect the Arabs will drive the cows on to the fort, and try to explode the mines,' he wrote, and that evening could add: 'The rockets from Omdurman drove back the advance of the cows; it was an ingenious attempt, if meant.' To the Mahdi's repeated attempts to get him to surrender (and become a Moslem), Gordon was replying with claims to have a method of causing earthquakes by electricity. Better still, the starving garrison captured 41 cows. On 12th November came the assault, with heavy firing all day, except for a half-hour lull in mid-morning. Two of Gordon's mobile fortresses, the armoured paddle-steamers, were hit; one went aground; then the telegraph between Khartoum and Omdurman went dead.

'This is our *first* encounter with the Mahdi's personal troops,' wrote Gordon. 'One tumbles at 3 a.m. into a troubled sleep; a drum beats — tup! tup! tup! It comes into a dream, but after a few moments one becomes more awake and it is revealed to the brain that *one is in Khartoum*. The next query is, where is this tup, tupping going on. A hope arises it will die away. No, it goes on, and increases in intensity. The thought strikes one,

"Have they enough ammunition?" (the excuse of bad soldiers). One exerts oneself. At last, it is no use, up one must get and go on to the roof of the palace; then telegrams, orders, swearing, and cursing goes on until about 9 a.m. Men may say what they like about glorious war, but to me it is a horrid nuisance. I saw that poor little beast the *Husseinyeh* (a Thames launch) fall back, stern foremost, under a terrific fire of breechloaders. I saw a shell strike the water at her bows; I saw her stop and puff off steam, and I gave the glass to my boy, *sickened unto death*, and I will say my thoughts turned on (BLANK) more than anyone, and they are not beneficent towards him. No Royal Navy vessels would have behaved better than the *Ismailia* today; she passed and repassed the Arab guns upwards of twenty times, when any one well-placed shell would have sunk her. I must say the Arabs today showed the greatest pluck; over and over again they returned to the attack, though overwhelmed with musketry fire of the castellated *Ismailia*. I think they must have lost heavily, for at times they were in dense groups.'

Next day, Fort Omdurman had its flag flying, and Gordon knew that, although cut off, it had not fallen yet. At intervals, there were continuous rolls of fire as the Arabs blazed away at the weak points in Gordon's defences. Musket 'balls fell like water' on the road up to the Palace, as the Greek Consul put it. During the lulls, bugle calls rang out from Khartoum, and were answered from Omdurman, a temporary form of communication while Gordon organised a flag system. On 22nd November, Gordon noted that he had had between 1,800 and 1,900 killed and 242 badly wounded since the start of the siege, 255 days before. Most of the fatal casualties had been incurred early on, when he had tried to break the siege-ring with soldiers who, as he at once discovered, would rather die than fight. He could, personally, have escaped at any time in one of the steamers, as Mr. Gladstone indeed wished him to do; but then the town would fall, and the people who had helped him resist would suffer a terrible fate at the hands of the Mahdi's men, who had many casualties to avenge. Gordon did not, any more than Mr. Gladstone, wish to occupy the Sudan permanently, but they must, he insisted in his Journal, form some stable government before getting out; and he suggested as Governor-General for that period, not himself, but Major Kitchener, of whom he had a high opinion, in spite of the inadequacies of his intelligence service. Although Kitchener spoke Arabic, his knowledge of the Sudan was naturally not on a par with Gordon's, which affected his task in organising a spy network.

Corporal Gordon, too, thought highly of the future Field Marshal. 'I remember well his appearance; over six feet in height, with a soldierly bearing, an austere countenance, almost hard, yet as I watched him in conversation I saw his face light up, his reserve disappear for the moment in his keen interest. No one could fail to note something extraordinary about Kitchener; he was distinct from other men; the great power in him, even while only potential, made itself felt.'

General Gordon was already preparing the steamer *Bordeen* for a passage down river through the Mahdi's lines, with his last Journal and a final request, not for an expeditionary force, but for 200 men to attack the rear of the Arabs, which, he thought, would raise the siege. It would be, not their numbers, but the proof that England had intervened, which would sway the Mahdi. 'During our blockade,' he wrote, 'we have often discussed the question of being frightened, which, in the world's view, a man should never be. For my part I am always frightened, and very much so. I fear the future of all engagements. It is not the fear of death, that is past, thank

God; but I fear defeat, and its consequences. I do not believe a bit in the calm, unmoved man. I think it is only that he does not show it outwardly. Thence I conclude no commander of forces ought to live closely in relation with his subordinates, who watch him like lynxes, for there is no contagion equal to that of fear.' Every drumbeat, every 'church parade' in the Mahdi's lines, every crowd of women calling out to him for food for their children, now reinforced his deep fear of defeat and its dreadful consequences for the people he had come to Khartoum to protect. Hence he strode about, cold and aloof, a stern and apparently unmoved figure; on whose outward appearance of calmness the fate of Khartoum now depended.

On 14th December, with the *Bordeen* due to flee from the town next day, he closed up his last Journal after writing the words:

'Now MARK THIS, if the Expeditionary Force, and I ask for no more than two hundred men, does not come in ten days, *the town may fall*; and I have done my best for the honour of our country. Goodbye, C. G. GORDON.'

Ten days, Gordon had said on 14th December. And ten days later, on 24th December, 1884, Corporal John Gordon was marooned with a Black Watch boat's crew in the middle of the Third Cataract of the Nile. Their Regiment was lying second in the race for Khartoum. 'What a weather-beaten, forlorn, reckless-looking crew we were on this lonely island twelve hundred miles from the sea. We figured out the date: it was Christmas Eve. What could we do to celebrate? We never had enough to eat. Underneath our supply of daily rations in the boat were packed solid and secure provisions we were forbidden to touch. Did we dare steal a treat? The thought of the cheese made our mouths water,' They broke it open, and had cheese and Navy biscuits for Christmas pudding. 'We lighted our pipes, chatted by the fire for an hour or more, then fell back on the sand, all hard struggle, all loneliness, forgotten, and soon we were in a deep sleep, and I do not recall that any of us had bad dreams.'

A few days later they reached Korti, where the Expeditionary Force was divided into two parts — the River Column which, because the Nile went into a gigantic bend before turning again towards Khartoum, had the greatest distance to go — 400 miles; and the Desert Column, which was to strike overland across the neck of the bend direct for Khartoum, a distance of only 180 miles. The state of affairs in Khartoum was not fully realised, and there was no urgency. Instead, the boats of the River Column were hauled up, inspected, and repaired. The Desert Column, coming in to Korti across the desert, were in a bad way already. 'The camels on this march through the desert,' wrote Corporal Gordon, 'owing to lack of numbers, were overworked, underfed, abused,' As an economy measure, their numbers had been reduced; and they were simply dying in protest. On the outskirts of Korti alone, nearly a hundred corpses of camels were to be seen, as Corporal Gordon well knew, for he was given the job of helping to bury them. These losses half-crippled the Desert Column. It was not until 8th January 1885 that General Wolseley reviewed them before their dash to Metemmeh, a place on the river just before Khartoum, where they were supposed to rendezvous with Gordon's steamers, which would convey some of them quickly into Khartoum, as proof that the siege was about to be raised.

Corporal Gordon, who was with the River Column, was surprised to find no opposition from the Mahdi's forces during the treacherous passage of the rapids at Birti; he, with half the battalion, were put ashore to clear out the defenders and they all expected a hard fight; but the dervishes pulled back without firing a shot. The reason was that the Mahdi's covering force had been very roughly handled by the Desert Column at the wells of Abu Klea on 17th January. News of what had happened to Osman Digna when he encountered British troops must have got around, for the dervishes, instead of unleashing their usual series of wild rushes, went on to the defensive and tried to get the British commander, General Sir Herbert Stewart, to attack them. As Stewart was expecting to be attacked and had bivouacked in defensive formation the night before, there was some conflict of intention and a considerable delay, before the British accepted the new order of things, and advanced in square.

Letting the British march steadily up to them, the dervishes charged at close quarters the front of the square; and were simply swept away by the drilled volleys. They then swung round the sides of the square, to the rear, searching for a weak spot to dash at; and found it at the left rear corner where Colonel Burnaby, the second-in-command, had wheeled his section outwards to help repel the initial assault on the front face. The dervishes were incredibly quick to spot his error of judgement, and in a flash they were piling into the centre of the square, Burnaby being killed in a gallant attempt to remedy his blunder. As at Tamaai, there was no question of the square *being* broken, but the consequences were almost as serious as if it had been. Most of the 126 British casualties occurred as a result of simple miscalculation, combined with the swiftness with which the enemy took advantage of it, pouring into the momentary opening. But the British stubbornly beat them down, hand to hand, and then continued their steady advance, flailing the dervishes with fire. More than 1,100 enemy dead were afterwards counted; the number of their wounded not being known.

Burdened by their 61 wounded, the British did not reach the Nile until dawn on 19th January where, at the wells of Abou Kru, or Gubat, they had another fight, losing 36 killed and no less than 107 wounded, which brought the total of wounded to 168, an immense impediment to such a column. Worse, among the mortally wounded was the commanding officer, Sir Herbert Stewart. The leadership now devolved on Sir Charles Wilson, an Intelligence officer, who had never commanded troops in the field before. The dervish losses were again very heavy.

Next day, 20th January, although Khartoum was still holding out, the fort at Omdurman had fallen, and the level of the Nile was very low, uncovering the defences along two-thirds of the perimeter; the defenders, from strain and starvation, were in an almost trance-like state and unable to properly extend the minefields along this immense new area. Now was the moment for the Mahdi to assault. And when, that day, the guns in his camp began to thunder, many thought their hour had come. The dervish guns fired slowly, at regular intervals, 101 shots — a salute for victory, presumably over the relief expedition. Gordon went up to the roof of the palace and scanned the dervish lines with his powerful telescope. *The Arab women were weeping.* What they had received was the news of Abu Klea, and their thousands of dead. The victory salute was just a stratagem to cover up the imminence of relief. That night, according to Father Owhrwalder, held prisoner in the Mahdi's camp, the Mahdi had a vision — that he must retire into the interior, give up the siege of Khartoum. It would have taken very little to confirm the truth of the vision. The critical day was 21st January. Realising that part of the relief force must be nearing

Metemmeh, Gordon had sent down-river some of his steamers, carrying his last Journal, and up-to-date messages, and they arrived as Wilson was actually attacking Metemmeh and gallantly joined in the battle. Originally, with Stewart commanding on land, Wilson was to have boarded one of the steamers with some soldiers, sailing at once to Khartoum. Now that Wilson was in sole charge, he could not go himself, but he could have delegated someone else, Lord Charles Beresford for instance. However, the mud houses of Metemmah were impervious to his artillery (because the shells went right through), and an assault appeared costly; he was worried about his wounded; and, as an intelligence officer, accustomed to careful weighing of evidence, he found the information as to the state of Khartoum contradictory. He could have had no idea of the wavering in the Mahdi's camp; but, above all, he was the bearer of a letter to Gordon which he had to deliver personally. Therefore, instead of sending part of his force quickly down-river to Khartoum, he made slow, methodical preparations, and did not leave until 24th January, by which time the Mahdi was on the brink of another vision. This, sparked by a spy's report that the falling Nile had choked with mud part of the southern defences of Khartoum, produced next day the decision to act swiftly before the lagging relief force could come up. And to attack just before dawn instead of, as was the Arab custom, just after it. Gordon himself always advocated attacking Arabs in the last darkness, because normally their horsemen were vital to them; but in this assault, no horsemen would be required. Ironically, the confidential message for Gordon which was the main reason for Wilson waiting until he could deliver it personally, in effect relieved Gordon of his command and placed him under Wolseley's orders. At the last, it was Mr. Gladstone who, with the best of intentions, struck the fatal blow.

On 25th January, therefore, the Mahdi was as unobtrusively as possible moving 50,000 warriors towards the weak point of the defences where the falling of the Nile had uncovered them; with the intention of relieving Gordon of his command most abruptly. While, the same day, Wilson was steaming up the Nile in the *Bordeen*, in order to relieve Gordon of his command in somewhat different fashion. He had no luck, for the steamer went aground that day on a rock in the shallowing water, and hung poised there all night, 'with water running like a mill-race all round her,' wrote Wilson. These steamers, if they had remained with Gordon in their usual role of guarding the river frontage of Khartoum, might just possibly have repelled the assault, or at least detected it in time. As it was, at about 3 o'clock in the morning of 26th January, 1885, the white prisoners in the Mahdi's camp heard a very brief burst of fire, which almost instantly dwindled away. Then silence. The spearhead of the 50,000 dervishes had burst through the defenders at one bound, and were rushing through the streets, screaming *Kenisa! Saraya!* To the church! To the palace!

On 28th January, when Wilson's steamers reached the point where the Nile divides to flow past Khartoum on both sides, all speculation was at an end. 'Not only were there hundreds of dervishes ranged under their banners, standing on the sandspit close to the town ready to resist our landing,' wrote Wilson, 'but no flag was flying in Khartoum and not a shot was fired in our assistance. The sight at this moment was very grand; the masses of the enemy with their fluttering banners near Khartoum; the long rows of riflemen in the shelter trenches at Omdurman; the groups of men on Tuti island; the bursting shells, and the water torn up by hundreds of bullets and occasional heavier shot, — made an impression never to be forgotten. Looking out over the stormy scene, it seemed almost impossible that we should escape.' The Sudanese crew and gunners were appalled, stricken. Their homes and families were in Khartoum. They no longer cared whether they lived or died. The captain of the *Bordeen*, Khashm el Mus, 'rolled himself in a rug, and then coiled himself in a corner, oblivious to all that was going on'.

Wilson realised at once that Gordon was dead. 'I never for a moment believed he would allow himself to fall into the Mahdi's hands alive,' he wrote. Morale went to pieces among the crews, the steamers repeatedly ran aground in their panic flight; both eventually were lost, the *Talahawiyeh* sunk, the *Bordeen* wedged immovably upon a rock.

The proof did not come in until 11th February, when a soldier of the River Column found a donkey's saddle lying in a ditch on the bank. Inside a black saddle-bag was a soiled and crumpled letter written in Arabic, from an Emir in Berber to an Emir in Dar Monassir, announcing the fall of Khartoum and the death of 'the traitor Gordon'.

The Europeans in the Mahdi's camp had evidence much sooner. On the morning of 26th January, some 48 hours before the relief force arrived, a party of whooping dervishes came triumphantly up to where Rudolf Slatin, associated with Gordon during his Governorship of the Sudan, lay in chains. They were carrying a round object in a blood-stained strip of cloth. 'Is not this,' they jeered, 'the head of your uncle, the unbeliever?'

The blue eyes in the severed head were half-open, and the hair was white.

'What of it?' answered Slatin. 'A brave soldier who fell at his post. Happy is he to have fallen; his sufferings are over.'

Wolseley heard the news of the fall of the town on 4th February, prayed that Gordon had met a swift death, and sent off a telegram which reached London early the next day.

Queen Victoria learned the news at her retreat in the Isle of Wight. Trembling, she burst in on Lady Ponsonby, crying, 'Too late!' And then she sat down to send an open telegram to the Prime Minister. 'These news from Khartoum are frightful, and to think that all this might have been prevented and many precious lives saved by earlier action is too frightful.'

Gladstone duly noted in his diary that 'The circumstances are sad and trying,' adding, what was really important, 'It is one of the least points about them that they may put an end to the Government.'

For two days, Khartoum was a hell. Gordon's body was jabbed at by every passing spearman, then the remnants thrown down a well; his head was placed in the fork of a tree, so that every passerby could spit at it. Four thousand others, men, women, children, were slashed to death by the dervishes; flogging, torture, rape went on in an orgy of pent-up emotion and hate. The living, men and women alike, were stripped naked and driven across the river to Omdurman, now a slave compound; but left in the boiling sun, many died. The Mahdi came first, to make his choice of the women, and took the pick of the younger ones, from the age of five upwards, for his now substantial harem. Then the other chiefs followed, in order of seniority. The dervishes were wildly exultant; all waverers would now come over to them; the Sudan was theirs. And to drive home their victory, parties of them began to move down to where the River Column was still struggling, far from Khartoum. They would harass them at the most difficult places, drive the white soldiers back into Egypt.

One of these positions was the Shukook Pass, overlooking a cataract, where the razorback hill of Kirbekan ran at right-angles to the river. The River Column were still coming on, the order still was to get to Khartoum; and this time, instead of being outnumbered between five and ten to one, the forces were approximately equal — six companies of the Black Watch and six companies of the Staffordshires against an estimated 800 dervishes holding an almost impregnable position among the rocks and ravines. General Earle, commanding the attackers, decided that frontal attack was out of the question, and carried out a neat series of encircling movements which culminated in an assault on the main position. Bagpipes playing, the British infantry went forward, bayonets flashing, as they flushed out the enemy riflemen hiding among the rocks, until finally all that still resisted was a stone hut, with a small window and a barricaded door, like a primitive pillbox. 'As we were about to attack this, General Earle came among the soldiers, patting our backs, delighted with the way we had carried the position,' wrote Corporal Gordon. In spite of all that had happened, they were perfectly prepared to take the last defenders prisoner; but the Sudanese never gave quarter and probably expected none. Their fire was accurate, one soldier was killed, then the British rushed the hut, were all around it, but could not get in because the only opening was the 18-inch square window in the stone walls, through which the defenders were firing.

Corporal Gordon was standing by this; some soldiers were actually standing on top of the walls, while others tried to set fire to the thatched roof, and others still were firing down through the roof from the rocks above. At this moment, General Earle walked up past Corporal Gordon, fired through the window into the hut, then looked in. A dervish bullet took him in the forehead and he fell dead at the Corporal's feet. 'The fate of the hut, with its last unyielding occupants, I do not record,' he wrote. 'Any true soldier with red blood in his veins knows that it was promptly sealed by the death of our commander.'

This was the true calibre of Mahdism; a deadly ferment spreading outwards from the desert, which was to drain still further the bankrupt exchequer of Egypt by the continual need to fend it off. Corporal Gordon wrote a word picture of March 1885, when it was planned to renew operations in the autumn, when the hot season would be over. 'At Khartoum, flying banners of the triumphant imposter, Mohammed Achmet the Mahdi, he and his hosts in full command, sending emissaries far and wide to win over, by bribes of eternal salvation, or by threats of death, all infidels, to the Moslem faith, and all tribes to a belief in him; in the provinces along the upper Nile, the Monassir tribes, strong for him, constantly plotting and killing; wavering tribes, especially the Shaggheihs, wanting to be on the winning side, but having no faith in the imposter, willing to fight with us against him, yet never to be trusted, now yielding, now going over to him by the thousands, because elsewhere they saw no hope, no advantage to themselves; vultures preying on dead bodies strewn on the sand where battles had raged; in the Eastern Soudan huge slaughter at McNeill's Zareba, and men wielding pick and shovel, laying ties and rails, actually completing some eighteen miles of the planned narrow gauge railroad from Suakim; and we at Abu Dom, an advanced guard, building a fort and barracks, preparing to settle down till autumn when, reinforced by ample troops, we are to push forward to Berber and Khartoum and knock the very foundation from under this inferno in the Soudan.

'Who could have predicted the disappointment which came like a thunderbolt and practically stunned us; so eager were we to get a sight of the place where Gordon had miraculously held out against the enemy, so crazy we were to avenge his death. A crestfallen regiment we certainly were as, on May 26th, we started down river for Wadi Haifa; a complete withdrawal.' Soon, they were back where they had started from, Kasr-el-Nil barracks, Cairo, hotly discussing the expensive and deadly farce in which they had been engaged. 'We were in the very place where nine months earlier General Wolseley's address, just before we set out for Khartoum, had inspired us to determined action; and now —

What was the end of all the show?

...

Ask my Colonel, for I don't know.'

CHAPTER SIXTEEN: 'A FAR MORE SERIOUS AFFAIR'

'If Egypt is to be quiet, Mahdi must be smashed up. Once Khartoum belongs to Mahdi, the task will be far more difficult; yet you will, for safety of Egypt, execute it. If you decide on smashing Mahdi, then send up another £100,000 and send up 200 Indian troops to Wadi Haifa. I repeat that evacuation is possible, but you will feel the effect in Egypt, and will be forced to enter into a far more serious affair in order to guard Egypt.' — *Telegram from Gordon to Government*, 26 February 1884.

The Mahdi survived Gordon by only five months, dying of smallpox and harem excesses on 20th June 1855. But Mahdism was not dead. The 'Guide' was succeeded by a new chief, the Khalifa Abdullah-el-Taeshi, who thought in terms of further conquest and the same year began to advance towards Cairo. It took a force of 5,000 British troops to check him, and this was done only with difficulty, for large areas which had formerly been friendly had now gone over to the victors of Khartoum. On 30th December 1855, was fought the battle of Guinniss. Two British brigades, supported by British cavalry and mounted infantry, met a dervish force only slightly larger — some five or six thousand men, a mere raid. Corporal Gordon was almost a spectator for this battle, because he had joined the mounted infantry and they were not properly used to follow up the retreat of the raiders, who left only 800 dead behind them. And this was to be the pattern for years to come: comparatively large and expensive forces employed merely to check dervish raids, with no decision achieved or even attempted. 'Butcher and bolt.'

When the Mahdi had first raised his standard of revolt in 1881, the Egyptians had thought two companies sufficient to bring him in. In 1884, General Gordon had thought that 200 Indian troops would be sufficient as the lynch-pin of a basically political answer, the hand-over of power to the influential Arab leader Zobier, slave-dealer though he was. As the Government would give him neither, he failed. It was not until a dozen years had passed that a Conservative administration entered into the 'far more serious affair' which he had predicted; and by then the fighting force thought necessary numbered some 25,000 highly-trained British and Egyptian troops, supported by the resources of industrial England. For this campaign was as unlike the cheap colonial method favoured by Gordon as it could possibly be. He had advocated a small force of lightly-equipped regulars as the backbone to large irregular forces recruited from the local inhabitants. But this was to be a direct confrontation of civilisation with barbarism; fighting it, not with the methods of savagery, but of civilisation — the mechanical, machine-powered civilisation of nineteenth-century Britain. Its leader was the same Herbert Kitchener, now General Sir Herbert Kitchener, Sirdar of Egypt, who had served as Gordon's tenuous link with the outside world in 1884; and among his very junior officers were a cavalryman called Winston Spencer Churchill and a naval gunboat commander named David Beatty, both destined for fame in the twentieth century.

The deadliest weapon he employed was the Sudan Military Railway, a single, narrow-gauge track pushed steadily across the desert 400 miles from Wady Haifa to the Atbara. It was also deadly slow — the campaign took two years, which silences all criticism of Wolseley's terrible, improvised struggle up through the jagged cataracts of the Nile. Rails, sleepers, water, all had to be brought in and pushed up forward, with the enemy still holding the next intended terminus. For the desert, not the dervishes, was the real enemy, refusing food and water, straining all transport by sheer distance. The railway killed the distance and supplied the food and water; journeys of long and desperate weeks became a day's trip by Bradshaw. Where Cambyses and his army had died and disappeared, vanished without trace, the railway struck far, fast, and hard. But after each strike, there had to be a pause, while supplies were built up again, for the railway had also to carry with it the means of its own extension. As the young war correspondent, G. W. Steevens, put it: 'Dervishes wait and wonder, passing from apprehension to security. The Turks are not coming; the Turks are afraid. Then suddenly at daybreak one morning they see the Sirdar advancing upon them from all sides together, and by noon they are dead. Patient and swift, certain and relentless, the Sudan machine rolls conquering southwards.'

So it was at the Atbara, when two Mahdist commanders, the veteran Osman Digna from his home near the Red Sea and the young general from Omdurman, the Emir Mahmud, converged in the spring of 1898 to crush the head of the Christian serpent. Not that Kitchener's army was entirely British — far from it. For years the British had been training Egyptian officers and black Sudanese soldiers in the machine-like methods of civilised warfare; turning natural irregulars into a passable imitation of themselves. Now, they had 12,000 men at railhead, British, Egyptian, Sudanese; against 18,000 of the Khalifa's men, Arab horsemen and Sudanese infantry. 'The wretched peasant, with that filthy cloth, which you see, is a determined warrior, who can undergo thirst and privation, who no more cares for pain or death than if he were a stone,' Gordon had written from Khartoum in September 1884. 'They are in their own land; the pains of war are their ordinary life; and they are supported by religion of a fanatical kind, influenced by the memory of years of suffering at the hands of an effete set of Bashi Bazouks. No; if our Kentish or Yorkshire boys are to come up to help me, it is not with my wish, unless with the greatest precaution.' Now, they were on their way, fourteen years too late.

The method, however, made sense in the context of the political plan; and this was perhaps the greatest difference, for previously there had been no long-term aims at all, merely a reluctance to get involved which had resulted in haphazard, expensive, useless operations of the 'Butcher and Bolt' sort. It was not a policy; the government had no policy; they merely reacted to whatever the dervishes cared to do. So much so, that the Khalifa had at one point demanded the instant submission of a number of European rulers, including Queen Victoria. Kitchener's campaign was different: it was for the conquest and occupation of the Sudan on Roman lines. The results were to be permanent; the lives that were lost would not be merely thrown away as in the past, when, as Mr. Bennet Burleigh, war correspondent of the *Daily Telegraph*, wrote: 'The exigencies of home politics proved to be of more weight than pledged compacts with friendly natives, or the conservation of soldiers' triumphs and lives.' After Kitchener's victory, there would be no more victories; because there would be no more dervish army and no more wars to fight. And after the army of conquest would come the administration which alone could really abolish slavery. Government marched behind the guns.

But before the war correspondents could get to the battle, they had first to battle Baring, now Lord Cromer, and

Kitchener. Baring had tried to ban all press representatives except one man from a certain press agency, who was in his pocket, which could also have been a most advantageous arrangement financially for the favoured one; and the *Daily Telegraph* declared war. Burleigh saw Baring, who manoeuvred his specious arguments 'rather prettily', but had eventually to give way when further press reinforcements marched up. Kitchener, also interviewed, was much more reasonable, but thought that their presence at battles only should suffice, when, provided they did not speak to the staff, they could do what they liked. He clearly did not understand the importance to morale of continuous newspaper coverage. More, there was an emotional resentment of newsmen, expressed in the order permitting them to advance in front of the troops if they wished. It is not known if any availed themselves of this generous offer, but Burleigh was able to advance at the battle of the Atbara just behind the crack-shooting Camerons, who played a vital part, advancing in line and firefighting the way for the rest, into, through, and out the other side of, Emir Mahmoud's zariba-fenced, trench-mazed battle position, with the dry bed of the Atbara River at its back.

Mahmoud had moved on the Atbara, supported by the Haddendowa Arab horse under Osman Digna, in the belief that he faced an Egyptian army, which he could destroy. When he found that half only were Egyptian, the rest British, he formed a roughly circular defensive camp, with a high mound in the centre where he had his own bomb-and-bullet-proof command post dug in. Everything was dug in, from the transport animals with their own slit trenches, to the ten 7-pounder howitzers in individual palisaded emplacements loopholed for the 20 to 40 riflemen allotted to defend each gun. Around the entire defensive hedgehog he threw a zareba, or thorn fence, the desert equivalent of barbed wire. Here, he settled down to wait for reinforcements from Omdurman. When they arrived, he intended to move out and destroy the railway line. He launched no harassing night raids, to which Kitchener's army was vulnerable, presumably because he did not want to give away his exact position. Although it took Kitchener some time to fix this, the British general's preliminary moves cut off all lines of retreat except one — across a waterless desert virtually impassable for a man on foot, particularly if wounded.

On 7th April 1898, the 'Soudan machine' made a night approach march to the zareba. During a few hours halt in the desert, Burleigh overheard a muttered conversation in the bivouacs of the Seaforth Highlanders.

'Ah, Tam, how many thousands there are at hame across the sea thinking o' us the nicht!'

'Right, Sandy, and how many millions there are that don't care a damn. Go to sleep, you fool!'

The march was resumed, timed to bring them on to the zareba with the dawn. As the horizon behind them steadily lightened, and the sun rose, they saw ahead the misty dream shapes of the palm trees along the river beginning to stand out against the sky; and men moving about there; and other menacing figures which somebody declared must be a line of dervish skirmishers but which turned out to be, on closer inspection, rows of storks and vultures waiting for breakfast. In front of the position among the grey-green palms was a smoke-grey line, the zareba, and behind the battle flags of the Baggara, white, pale blue, yellow, pale chocolate. The Anglo-Egyptian Army halted at a distance of half a mile. 'Thud! went the first gun, and phutt! came faintly back, as its shell burst on the zariba into a wreathed round cloud of dust, smoky-grey,' wrote Steevens, the *Daily Mail* man. 'I looked at my watch, and it marked 6.20.

'Now, from the horse battery and one field battery on the right, from two batteries of Maxim-Nordenfeldts on the left, and from a war-rocket which changed over from left to right, belched a rapid, but unhurried, regular, relentless shower of destruction. The round grey clouds from shell, the round white puffs from shrapnel, the hissing splutter of rockets, flighted down methodically. And all over the zariba we saw dust-clothed figures strolling unconcernedly in and out, checking when a shell dropped near, and then passing contemptuously on again. But when it had lasted an hour or more, not a man showed along the whole line, nor yet a spot of rifle smoke. All seemed empty, silent, lifeless, but for one hobbled camel, waving his neck and stupid head in helpless dumb bewilderment. Presently the edge of the storm of devastation caught him too, and we saw him no more.'

Shortly before eight o'clock the barrage stopped. 'Advance!' yelled a staff-major, galloping up from the rear towards the little Maxim-Nordenfeldt assault guns. Mules were whipped into motion and the Maxims began to bump forward, rolling past the halted infantry who were waiting for their bugle. Then the infantry call sang out, and, bugles blaring, Highland bagpipes wailing, Egyptian brass bands playing, the war-machine went forward. And the emotion of the men, one half of them black, the other half white, went up in a roaring cheer. As it died, back at them from behind the zariba thorn, came the high call: 'Allah, el Allah, el Akbar!'

In one long line the Cameron Highlanders formed the front of the British advance; the line, as it went forward, was like a ruler laid across the sand; the attack was like a parade, with the Union Jack held high in the centre and the men steadily marching with their rifles at the 'slope', bayonets glittering. The rifles were Lee-Metfords, with defective ammunition and defective magazine-springs; the bullets they had filed, to turn them into manstoppers, the springs they had discarded because they caused jams. The latest British rifle was no better than the enemy's Remingtons, except that the cartridge powder was smokeless. As the Camerons crested the ridge 300 yards from the zariba, they halted and knelt down. 'Volley-firing by sections,' came the command as the enemy bullets whined and whipped overhead. Then the deliberate, drilled crash of rifles fired simultaneously on the word of command, the belch of yellow heat, the thump of the kicking butts. Crash, crash, crash. Volley after volley.

A cry of astonishment. 'O!' A soldier reared up, then pitched over on his back. Stretcher-bearers dashed forward, knelt, shook their heads; turned to another victim. Bullets now came hissing out from behind the zariba; the bugle sang again; the line rose up and went forward. 'It never bent nor swayed,' wrote Steevens, 'it just went slowly forward like a ruler. The officers at its head strode self-containedly — they might have been on the hill after red-deer; only from their locked faces turned unswervingly towards the bullets could you see that they knew and had despised the danger. And the unkempt unshaven Tommies, who in camp seemed little enough like Covenanters or Ironsides, were now quite transformed. Whether they aimed or advanced they did it orderly, gravely, without speaking.' The Union Jack went tumbling down, Staff-Sergeant Wyatt rolling on the ground with a bullet from an elephant gun in the knee. An orderly grasped the fallen flag, and it rose again, bobbing about to mark the centre of the Camerons' advance, checkered with holes and rents. Then they were at the zariba, only a loose, low hedge of camel-thorn, not half as formidable as rumour had said it would be. But still, it stopped them. 'Pull it away,' said someone.

To show how it should be done, Major-General Gatacre, C.B., the Brigade Commander, strode forward, seized a thorn-bush, and began to wrench it out of the hedge; and instantly a dervish leapt out of cover with a throwing spear, deadlier than a sword. 'Give it him, my man,' said the General, with hauteur, to Private Cross. And while the General laboured, the private fired, then thudded his bayonet home in the brown body. Almost in an instant, the zariba was gone, half the men pulling it away, the other half firing steadily into the trenches and palisade behind. Then, front and rear ranks firing alternately, they marched on, the hail of bullets kicking up puffs of dust among a maze of trenches and emplacements so haphazard that the battle plan had to be discarded. It was a honeycomb, holding everything.

In the front trenches were rows of black Sudanese, handcuffed together, but not so tightly that they could not use the rifles the Arabs had given them. Others again, had been manacled and chained behind their guns. In another might be a camel, and in another Sudanese slave women and their children; and among them all, the fighting men who fired and fired until they were shot or bayoneted, and even then might pretend death for another shot from behind. Captain Urquhart was shot through the body in this fashion; one of his men bayoneted the dervish, and as they stooped over the mortally wounded captain, he muttered, 'Never mind me, lads. Go on, Company F.' General Gatacre was in the second trench, engaging, army sword to dervish spear, a single opponent. Parrying a blow, he drove the point in, withdrew it from the fallen man, and marched on. Private Chalmers was engaging an Emir holding a dervish banner; the Baggara chief fell, clasping the rifle muzzle. There were small forts, holding the brass 7-pounders and their parties of desperate riflemen; each to be cleaned out with bullet or bayonet. 'It was like clearing out by hand a nest of live hornets,' wrote Burleigh of the *Telegraph*, who had mounted his horse, and from that elevation was able to save one trenchful of Sudanese women from death, for it was hard to tell the men from the women in the dust, smoke, confusion, and shouting.

No prisoners were taken, the wounded were killed off; for it was death to your comrade to leave one behind alive. Even the children fought, if they could. Standing by the body of his dead father, a black, pot-bellied ferocious little hero ten years old did not desert the corpse as the dreadful war-machine ground on, but waveringly lifted an elephant gun to his shoulder, which blew him over backwards as he pulled the trigger. It was fair fight, except for the Maxim-Nordenfeldts, which were bounced up with the infantry on the flanks, where they could get through. What told was the superior march and fire-discipline of the Anglo-Egyptian army; for when Osman Digna and the 4,000 Arab horsemen bolted, the flank battalions were able to come up to help the centre, and, wrote Steevens, 'the Warwicks were volleying off the blacks as your beard comes off under a keen razor'. They drove on remorseless across the position until they came to the central *dem* or keep, the battle headquarters of Mahmoud, in front of which lay stretched on the ground, in chains, three of Mahmoud's prisoners, their heads rammed to the soil by forked sticks placed across each man's neck.

There were 2,000 riflemen inside that keep. A company of the 11th Sudanese charged at once, and simply vanished, suffering a hundred casualties in a few seconds. Piper Stewart, of the Camerons, stood on a knoll, playing *March of the Cameron*

Men to rally the battalion. After sixty seconds, he fell. But all around the keep, on both sides, the remorseless tide of white and black soldiers was driving steadily forward, behind a blaze of bullets. Ahead, the dervishes were beginning to stand up and move back; at first, they were merely getting up and walking away. And stopping to fire as they did so. 'For,' wrote Steevens, 'the running blacks — poor heroes — still fired, though every second they fired less and ran more.' Then, suddenly, they were at the dried-up river — the Atbara. As the fugitives scrambled away, the soldiers flopped on their faces and picked them off; one man of the Lincolns knocked four over in succession, like rabbits. Some were hiding in the ravine, and the black Sudanese soldiers went down with a rush and finished them off. Ahead of the fugitives, whole or wounded, stretched only the deadly desert wastes. The battle was over, and it had lasted precisely 25 minutes. 'Very good fight, very good fight!' the Sudanese were shouting.

Kitchener had lost more than 550 men killed and wounded; but the dervish army was ruined. Inside the circle of the zareba were probably 3,000 of their dead; they were not exactly counted, for no one was anxious to linger in that slaughterhouse in the passionate heat of the sun. What they saw there was a horror. Wrote Steevens: 'Black spindle-legs curled up to meet red-gimleted black faces, donkeys headless and legless, or sieves of shrapnel, camels with necks writhed back on to their humps, rotting already in pools of blood and bile-yellow water, heads without faces, and faces without anything below, cobwebbed arms and legs, and black skins grilled to crackling on smouldering palm-leaf — don't look at it.' Pinned to a palm tree was an extraordinary corpse, noted Burleigh. One of the 24-pounder rockets fired by Lieutenant

David Beatty's Naval detachment had nailed him through the chest to the palm trunk behind.

The army reformed away from that horrible place, leaving small parties to search it thoroughly. In Mahmoud's bomb-proof keep the Sudanese soldiers found, hiding under a bed, the enemy commander, Emir Mahmoud Abu Achmed. Burleigh was waiting for the censor to pass his press despatch, when he heard this news. 'As the prisoner came limping along over the rough pebbles, I went forward to meet him, and he gave me the impression of a man who thought that his last hour had come. He was dazed and yet dogged when brought before the Sirdar. Tall, standing some 6 ft., as much black as Arab in feature, about thirty years of age — this was the Taaisha Baggara, and nephew of the Khalifa.[10] He held his head up and scowled at his guard.'

Kitchener, the unlovable, efficient, emotionless, unbending general, in high boots and khaki, gazed at his stalwart opponent dressed in the ornate, gold-embroidered *jibbeh* which had replaced the deliberately spartan, patched shirt worn originally by the Mahdi and his followers.

'Are you the man Mahmoud?'

'Yes; I am Mahmoud, and I am the same as you.' He meant that he was a general, too.

'Why did you come to make war here?'

'I came because I was told — the same as you.'

The Emir was taken down for full interrogation by Rudolf Slatin, who had turned Moslem to save his life and had spent many years in chains as a prisoner of Mahdi and Khalifa. Now the tables were turned, but still Mahmoud was defiant. 'The

---

[10] The Taaisha were the ruling clique, or 'Establishment', of the dominant Arab master race, of which the Baggara were the senior tribe.

Khalifa has men like the sands of the sea. They will meet you at Shabluka and Omdurman, and you cannot conquer, for my master has 60,000 soldiers, many guns, and holds strongly fortified positions, utterly unlike my poor zariba.' Omdurman was indeed next on the list. But in the autumn, after the hot season had come and gone. Kitchener was in no hurry, he was going to make sure.

There are two postscripts. The Emir went down the line by train and was fascinated, particularly when the engine was detached at a station. 'Where has it gone, for water?' he asked. 'Does it drink and eat, too, like men? Is it always a great smoker? Strange devil! does it never get tired? Are there many other such wonders in Cairo?' Already, Western technology was beginning to gain a victory. Nevertheless, he was rightly impatient. When his photograph was taken, he wanted to see the picture at once, a technicality not to be solved for another half century.

The final postscript is the power of the press, revealed by the wounded to Steevens. 'It was difficult to be sorry for most of the men who were hit,' he wrote, 'they were so aggressively not sorry for themselves. One face was covered with a handkerchief; one man gasped constantly — just the gasp of the child that wants sympathy and doesn't like to ask for it; one face was a blank mask of yellow white clay. The rest, but for the red-splashed bandages and the reek of iodoform, might have been lying down for a siesta. Their principal anxiety was to learn what size of deed they had helped to do that day.'

'A grahn' fight? The best ever fought in the Soudan? Eh, indeed, sir; ah'm vara glahd to hear ye say so.'

'Now, 'ow would you sy, sir, this'd be alongside them fights they've been 'avin' in India? Bigger, eh? Ah! Will it be in tomorrow's pyper? Well, they'll be talkin' about us at 'ome.'

CHAPTER SEVENTEEN: 11,000 LIVES FOR ONE

'Another brigade, sir? Why it makes me sick to see all this preparation against such an enemy. We had 1,500 men at Abu Klea, and now we've got 20,000. Despise the enemy; yes, I do despise them; I despise them utterly. Rifles are too good for them. Sticks, sir, we ought to take to them — sticks with bladders on the end.' — *Senior Captain.*

'...so the wretched man started off with the water-bottles of the whole half-company to fill them at the mirage...' — *raconteur.*

'Wottermi doin' that for? Doncher know? To kerry the bleed'n' Grenadier Gawds to Khartum.' — *Thomas Atkins.*

'You may call the show barbaric, if you like; it was meant for barbarians. The English gentleman, if you like, is half barbarian too. That is just the value of him.' — *G. W. Steevens.*

'Were a smart contractor to take up the job (of running canteens), the War Office and the country might, on those lines, succeed in making campaigns pay for themselves. At any rate, they would recover every farthing of the soldier's pay, and a trifle over.' — *Bennet Burleigh.*

'Get out of my way, you drunken swabs.' — *General Kitchener, to the war correspondents.*

In August 1898, by road, river, and rail, Kitchener began to concentrate within striking distance of Khartoum, an army of almost twice the size of that which had won the Atbara in twenty-five minutes. Two infantry divisions — one British, one Egyptian; eleven cavalry squadrons — one British, ten Egyptian: five batteries of field guns — one British, four Egyptian; one Egyptian horse battery, one British howitzer battery, two British siege-guns; twenty Maxim machineguns — ten British, ten Egyptian; eight companies of Egyptian Camel Corps; and six fighting gunboats on the Nile, armed with Nordenfeldts and machineguns. On 1st September they arrived before Omdurman; on 2nd September the Khalifa attacked them, and by evening the Mahdist empire was 'smashed up'. As Gordon had wished, 'the greatest precaution' had been used; and also, the utmost speed. Wolseley had started in September; his main force never saw Khartoum; had they continued, it would have been March before they arrived. The difference was Kitchener's railway — the weapon that won the Sudan. In four weeks, it put 22,000 fighting men in front of Khartoum.

But it was not such an unequal combat as might appear. There were some 25,000 riflemen, mostly armed with Remingtons, among the Khalifa's 50,000 men; he had available, but chose to make little use of, the eight or ten Maxim machineguns and the battery of big Krupp guns which he had; he did use, and not without effect, the extraordinarily rapid pace of his infantry — estimated at 7 m.p.h. In the hills around Omdurman they were to out-run camels; and even gave chase to cavalry. His men had an instinctive knowledge of war which made them anything but machine soldiers. All this he threw away, for two reasons. Firstly, impressed by the superficial aspect of Western civilisation, expressed in the drilled, ordered tactics of its regular armies, he had reorganised the Mahdi's forces as a carbon-copy of his opponents'; but had failed to

247

grasp the methods by which the fruits of technology, the improved artillery, were integrated with the infantry. Secondly, over-impressed by the prowess of his own men, the Khalifa, instead of waiting to be attacked like Mahmoud at the Atbara, deliberately put his soldiers through the 'mincing machine', with the result that he inflicted, with 50,000 men, no greater casualties than had Mahmoud with 16,000 For the losses of the Anglo-Egyptian armies at the Atbara and at Omdurman were identical — between five and six hundred killed and wounded.

'I incline to the belief that the Khalifa and his men, true to their crass, credulous notions, were overweeningly confident in themselves,' wrote Burleigh. 'A fatal fault, they underrated their opponents. His Emirs, Jehadieh, and Baggara had so often proved themselves invincible in their combats against natives of the Soudan, that they had come to hold that none would face their battle shock. There was pride of countless triumphs, and the long enjoyment of despotic overlordship that hardened their wills and thews to win victory or perish.' Burleigh knew them well, having been present as war correspondent at Tamaai and Abu Klea, fourteen long years before. It was, in fact, their courage that brought them defeat. Had they fought as guerrillas, particularly by night, and never concentrating, there would have been no force for Kitchener to smash. Barbarism tried to meet civilisation on the latter's terms, and inevitably was with ease destroyed. A part-explanation is that the ruling caste, the Arabs, were superb cavalry, far better than the bulk of the Anglo-Egyptian horsemen; and that cavalry actions could not be fought at night, the time when superior fire-power is almost nullified, for want of seen targets. Even so, the Khalifa would have benefited by a study of Gordon's doctrines on guerilla war.

In 1898, Mahdism was not quite what it had been; it was beginning to fray at the edges, in face of the steady advance of the white men. The grasp of the Arabs on their black infantry was loosening; Kitchener was able to raise dervish units from among the deserters and prisoners taken in the Atbara campaign, and these fought against the Khalifa at Omdurman. The British, on the other hand, were becoming recognisably twentieth century, with 'pin-up' photographs from the *Graphic* on the walls of the mess. 'Coloured them ourselves — helps you through the day you know,' said a Subaltern to Steevens. 'That's a well-developed lady, isn't it?' The men were extremely short of reading material, books and magazines, and were elated to see reports of their activities in the newspapers, it being easier to risk death in an important matter than in an affair which settles nothing. Letters from home were important. Regiments were touchy about their sickness figures, and Steevens sparked a volcano of educated fury when he suggested that the Guards' ratio of sickness to strength returns was poor. Molten lava poured forth from the Horse Guards, Whitehall. But nobody loved the cossetted Guards, and one popular and unkind suggestion was that they should be refrigerated down in Cairo, unpacked and de-frosted in front of Omdurman, then packed in ice again for return to base, immediately after having done their stuff. The war correspondents kept putting their feet in it, literally, and the worst fears of Baring and Kitchener were confirmed. They all picked on the boots, but Steevens was the worst; his brutal exposures produced a storm in the House of Commons and a hurricane of official denials, very much later watered down to the admission that, although it was true that the boots wore out in a month (Burleigh said two weeks), they were nevertheless very good boots; only, one shouldn't use them for marching in the Sudan. Burleigh was merciless on the fleecing of the men by the contractors who ran the canteens; and his reports on the defects of the Lee-Metford rifle were disturbing. Both the propellant in the cartridges and the magazine springs were weak, minor matters when seen from England maybe, but by no means unimportant when you were being rushed by a couple of healthy dervishes. The soldiers had offset the former defect by doctoring the ammunition, careful filing of the bullet-tips producing a projectile which broke up on impact with flesh and mushroomed inside the organism in many tiny, tearing fragments: 'dumdum' bullets. For Omdurman, the men were ordered to use their magazines for the first time, because the newly-issued hollow-nosed bullets were less likely to jam in the badly-designed breeches and magazines.

Kitchener, of course, was furious. All these revelations damaged the 'public image' of his army which he had so carefully constructed, even to rationing the home leave allowances for officers so that too many at one time should not be seen in Piccadilly; most of them had to take local leave in lieu. He was probably genuinely afraid also of the effect on the 'liberal' section of public opinion of the 'no quarter' rule and the necessary slaughter of the dervish wounded in action. A 'do-gooder' in Golders Green was unlikely to realise that leaving live dervishes behind you in a hand-to-hand hot combat was tantamount to doing 200 m.p.h. on the M.1 in dense fog. You might survive, but somebody was going to get killed. This was wise, for the cast-of-thought in England which had been overjoyed to hear of the Mahdi's triumph at Khartoum, and the death of Gordon, still existed, were vocal, and did in fact subsequently brand the British forces as brutalised murderers. The reason was, that the 'do-gooders' knew as much about the Soudan of 1885, or 1898, as they did about the M.1 of 1965.

On 21st August Steevens was with a column moving south, which to its delight came across a new-built military road sign-posted to METEMMEH. It was then the only military signpost in the Sudan and, wrote Steevens, 'the caravan set out at least half a mile an hour the better for it'. The day of the centre-line oasis of boards — POL, HH, FORWARD AREA STRAIGHT ON, THIS ROAD UNDER OBSERVED FIRE, NACH PARIS, ACHTUNG MINEN — was not yet; nor yet the strange Western pictorial writing, post-Pharaoh in date, left to puzzle the archaeologists of A.D. 4004 as to the precise nature of the tribe which obviously pursued its prey, the desert rat, through Africa into France. But the other signs were there — the contorted corpses of the dead animals; here, camels and donkeys with their throats cut, already mummied, speaking plainly the message that this was Mahmoud's work. A year ago, the Jaalin tribe of Metemmeh, reluctant to attack the Anglo-Egyptian army, had opened correspondence with Kitchener in order to get rifles and so break away from Mahdism. They had been detected; their swords and spears proving no match for the rifles of Mahmoud's punitive expedition. The smell of death still lingered in the ruins of Metemmeh, strewn with bones and skulls; and, wrote Steevens, 'between Mahmoud's camp and the town, stand a couple of crutched uprights and a cross-bar. You wonder what, for a moment, then wonder that you wondered. A gallows! At the foot a few strands of brown palm-fibre rope and one, two, four, six, eight human jawbones. Just the jawbones, and again you wonder why; till you remember the story that when Sheikh Ibrahim, of the Jaalin, came here a week or two ago he found eight skulls under the gallows in a rope-netting bag. When he took them up for burial the lower jaws dropped off, and lie here still.' A dreadful silence lay over the ruined town. 'The stillness and the stench soak into your soul, exuding from every foot of this melancholy graveyard — the cenotaph of a whole tribe, fifteen years of the Soudan's history read in an hour. Sun, squalor, stink, and blood: that is Mahdism.' At Metemmeh, the strong had vanquished the weak: rifles against spears. And now, the stronger were about to vanquish the strong: the batteries, the machineguns, the drilled volleys against massed, unarmoured advance, foretaste of 1914.

The object of the Khalifa was to fight on the plain between the Kerreri hills and the heights of Gebel Surgham, drawing the attention of the enemy with his main body, while two other corps, using the high, rocky ground for concealment and surprise, worked round to their rear on both sides. Good tactics, bearing in mind that rocky hills and ravines suited the ability of his men admirably, apart from offering necessary cover. Also, Kerreri had an Armageddon-type legend attached, as the coming 'death field of the infidels'. This area was variably distant between seven and ten miles from his stronghold of Omdurman, on the opposite side of the Nile to Khartoum.

Kitchener's object was to fight on the plain, if he could get the Khalifa to come on, because this area could easily be swept with fire. In short, broken ground — good dervish fighting country; open ground — good European firing country. But, above all, Kitchener and all his generals were agreed that the dervish army must be cut off from all possibility of retreat into Omdurman, because house by house fighting in that rabbit warren would be very costly, greatly favouring the defence. In case this should happen, his siege guns had already been tried, in Cairo, against a wall specially built to duplicate that of Omdurman. These careful tests had shown that the howitzers, firing shells containing the new high explosive, lyddite, were inadequate; because the fuses were instantaneous and the muzzle-velocity low, they merely scratched the outer face of the wall, as a modern field gun would do. The two old 40-pounder Armstrong guns, firing shells filled with the old low explosive, gunpowder, were more efficient, because their high velocity ensured penetration before explosion.

On 1st September 1898, the British moved forward to occupy part of the range of low hills, to reconnoitre, and to emplace the siege artillery. And so, they had their first view of Omdurman. 'It was a purple stain on the yellow sand,' wrote Steevens, 'going on for miles and miles on every side. A great city — an enormous city — a city worth conquering indeed!' The tomb of the Mahdi, white and glittering, rose cone-shaped above the mud houses. 'The distant view of Omdurman,' asserted Steevens, 'would have disgraced no European capital: you might almost expect that the hotel omnibus would meet you at the railway station. In front of the city stretched a long white line — banners, it might be; in front was a longer, thicker black line — no doubt a zariba or trench. Then they did mean to fight after all. Only as we sat and ate a biscuit and looked — the entrenchment moved. The solid wall moved forward, and it was a wall of men. Whew! What an army! Five huge brigades of it — a three-mile front, and parts of it eight or ten men deep. It was beginning to move directly for our hill, and — turn, turn, turn — we heard the boom of a war drum. Now they seemed to halt; now they came on. The five corps never broke or shifted, the rigid front never bent; their discipline must be perfect. And they covered the ground. The three miles melted before them.' At that point, 'We'll go back now,' observed the leader of the British cavalry. 'It was a perfect reconnaissance,' wrote Steevens, 'not a man lost, not a shot fired, and everything seen,' A heavier boom echoed across the heat-hazed plain, the siege-guns had opened fire from their emplacements on the far side of the Nile. Volcanoes of flame and smoke spurted upwards from Omdurman; and after a short while it was seen that the Mahdi's tomb had a ragged look, like a boiled egg which has been cracked open with a spoon. But there was no battle that day; it had been only the dress rehearsal.

The command performance began at dawn next day, a battle where only distance blurred; the Lee-Metford cartridges were smokeless, and perhaps the breeze blew away the drifting smoke of the Egyptian Martinis and the dervish Remingtons. There had never been anything like it in the world before, and there never will be again. 'The noise of something began to creep in upon us,' wrote Steevens. 'It cleared and divided into the tap of drums and the far-away surf of raucous war-cries. A shiver of expectancy thrilled along our army, and then a sigh of content. They were coming on. Allah help them! they were coming on!'

'I heard a rumbling as of tempestuous rollers and surf bearing down upon a rock-bound shore,' wrote Burleigh. 'Few will ever see again so great and brave a show. A vast army, with a front of three miles — warriors mounted and a-foot, clad in quaint and picturesque drapery, with gorgeous barbaric display of banners, burnished metal, and sheen of steel — came sweeping upon us with the speed of cavalry.[11] Who should

---

[11] 'Brigades must be so trained that each battalion and individual soldier must know how to get into the best formation with the least possible delay for meeting the attack of the spearmen, who, it must be remembered, *can move at last three times as quickly as a British soldier can double.*' — para. 6 of Major-General Gatacre's instructions.

count them? They were compact, not to be numbered. It was a great, deep-bodied flood, rather than an avalanche. The sound grew every instant louder and more articulate. It was not alone the reverberation of the tread of horses and men's feet, but a voiced continuous shouting and chanting — the dervish invocation and battle challenge, "*Allah el Ellah! Rasool Allah el Mahdi!*" Emirs and chiefs on horseback rode in front and along the lines, gesticulating and marshalling their commands. Mounted Baggara trotted about along the inner lines of footmen. Khalifa Abdullah's great black banner, black-lettered with texts from the Koran and the Mahdi's sayings, was upheld by his Mulazimin. It flaunted the wind, acclaimed by his followers. There were apparently as before five great divisions in the dervish army.'[12]

'They came very fast,' wrote Steevens, 'and they came very straight; and then presently they came no farther. With a crash the bullets leaped out of the British rifles. It began with the Guards and Warwicks — section volleys at 2,000 yards; then, as the Dervishes edged rightward, it ran along to the Highlanders, the Lincolns, and to Maxwell's Brigade. Shrapnel whistled and Maxims growled savagely. From all the line came perpetual fire, fire, fire, and shrieked forth in great gusts of destruction. And the enemy? No white troops would have faced that torrent of death for five minutes, but the Baggara and the black fighters came on. The torrent hurled them down in whole companies. You saw a rigid line gather itself up and rush on evenly; then before a shrapnel shell or a Maxim the line suddenly quivered and stopped. The line was yet unbroken, but it was quite still. But other lines gathered up again, again, and yet again; they went down, and others rushed

---

[12] 'Dervish' was the popular general term; but they referred to themselves as 'Ansar', or Servants of God.

on. Sometimes they came near enough to see single figures quite plainly. One old man with a white flag started with five comrades; all dropped, but he alone came bounding forward to within 200 yards of the 14th Sudanese. Then he folded his arms across his face, and his limbs loosened, and he dropped sprawling to earth beside his flag. It was the last day of Mahdism, and the greatest. It was not a battle, but an execution.'

'The field was white with jibbeh-clad corpses like a landscape dotted with snowdrifts,' wrote Burleigh. 'Viewed from our side, so far it had been the least dangerous battle ever soldier bore part in.' A few men fell, mostly British, because their general had insisted that they stand up to fire behind a zariba instead of, like the Egyptians, lying down in shelter trenches. A few explosions in front, which they mistook for 'shorts' from their own guns, was actually the dervish artillery in action, poorly served; but most of it was then lying in the arsenal at Khartoum. The British artillery, on the other hand, was doing deadly work. 'The long 15-pounder English field cannon hit with the precision of match rifles,' wrote Burleigh, 'and were discharged as though they were quick-firing guns. As for the stinging Maxim-Nordenfeldts, they bucked and jumped like kicking horses, yet were fired so fast that the barrels must have been well-nigh red hot.' But they cannot have fired for long, for each gun used only approximately 100 rounds. As a British artillery major had predicted, after field-firing exercises: 'Nothing will come within 800 yards of that and live,' But for some reason the Maxim machineguns (the prototype of the Vickers familiar to soldiers of two world wars) were disappointing. 'I closely watched the effect of their fire through my glasses,' wrote Burleigh. 'I am compelled to say that they often failed to settle upon the swarming foe. At any rate, their effectiveness was not equal to what might have been expected.'

Steevens agreed, checking the dead afterwards, and coming to the conclusion that rifle fire had accounted for most, with artillery a good second. And yet Captain Smeaton's detachment alone, of six Maxims, fired 54,000 rounds. The infantry fire was not on this scale, and much of it was at hopelessly long ranges. Seeing the dervishes still coming on, despite the artillery punishment, the Grenadier Guards were ordered to fire section volleys at 2,700 yards, which had no effect, not surprisingly, as the extreme effective range for an aimed shot with a modern rifle is not much more than 700 yards — beyond that distance, without a telescopic sight, a man is an impossibly small dot. The ranges gradually came down to 1,700, 1,500, 1,200, 1,000 yards. Some of the infantry fired on average between 32 and 34 rounds. One complete battalion, the Northumberland Fusiliers, got off only 1,000 rounds, and the Lancashire Fusiliers fired an astounding total of 400 rounds, less than one shot per man. That, presumably, was the front rank; and, firing by sections, might have taken less than six seconds to deliver, or one second firing simultaneously (for the British volleys were so good that there was one split-second sound when they fired — a single crash).

But this first attack was delivered by a part only of the 50,000-strong dervish army, some 12-14,000 men. The other two corps were moving round, mostly out of sight, round the rear of the Anglo-Egyptian forces, which for the moment appeared already completely victorious. Before the general advance was sounded, two things happened: the 21st Lancers were ordered out to prevent the enemy remnants retiring in the direction of Omdurman, and Bennet Burleigh had a skirmish with a dervish. A group of camp followers went out from the halted battle line to collect souvenirs from the dead dervishes, spears, swords, and so on; and some of the war correspondents followed them. Mr. Burleigh assures us that he was merely 'curious to see the effect of our fire'. A single wounded dervish easily routed the lot. He leapt up, spear in hand, and the camp followers bolted. One, a native N.C.O., dropped to one knee, to aim his Martini-Henry. It missed fire. He tried again, and apparently missed; at that, he got up and bolted after the rest. Burleigh, on his horse, cantered on, (although another correspondent turned back), because Mr. Bennett Stanford, another newsman, was now the object of the dervish's attack. Stanford waited until the warrior was close, then fired a four-barrelled Lancaster pistol point-blank, which had no observable effect on the dervish. Stanford spurred sharply away to safety. To save the black N.C.O., the *Telegraph*'s man-on-the-spot, Burleigh, rode between him and the dervish. 'I pulled up my rather sorry nag and took deliberate aim. I fired and believe hit him, and as my horse was jibbing about fired a second shot from my revolver with less success, then easily got out of the dervish's reach. The camp followers by then were all safe, and so was the native soldier, Mr. Dervish having the field very much to himself.' Then out galloped a proper soldier, Lieutenant Smyth, firing from the saddle as he rode past. 'Checking his horse, Lieutenant Smyth wheeled it about, and he and the dervish collided. The man, who by this time appeared somewhat weak, grabbed the Lieutenant and strove to drive his lance into him. With great hardihood Lieutenant Smyth fired his revolver in the dervish's face, killing him instantly. An examination of the dead dervish showed he had received four bullet wounds.'[13] An examination of Lieutenant

---

[13] This little comedy is very much to the point, illustrating why the soldiers used dum-dum bullets in their rifles and what big game

Smyth revealed that he had received a spear gash in the arm, although in the excitement he had not felt it and, streaming blood, kept declaring that he was untouched.

Fortunately, the dervish had been too weakened to throw his spear, either at Burleigh or Smyth, because although a revolver is a poor, crude, wild, soft-hitting weapon, the scientifically-designed throwing spear is a man-stopper. The weight is at the tail, the point of balance far forward; this impels a quite unexpected velocity to the heavy weapon, which thuds home with transfixing force. The weight of the tail and protruding shaft is then likely to drag a man from his horse; at any rate, anyone with four feet of heavy spear sticking out of him is temporarily incapacitated for further operations. At close range — but only at close range — the weapons of barbarism are effective indeed. This was to be demonstrated almost immediately by the 21st Lancers, in their dash to cut off the retreating dervishes from Omdurman.

The future Prime Minister, Lieutenant Winston Churchill, was among them, and also a war correspondent, Hubert Howard, representing the *New York Herald* and *The Times*. Burleigh had just waged a war of the war correspondents with him, because, as a double reporter, he got a double ration of words down the telegraph, and most of them seemed to leak into *The Times*, which had another full-time representative in

---

hunters really mean when they talk about 'stopping power'. The present author has seen two Canadian soldiers empty their revolvers into a large calf without bringing it down. It may be argued that modern service rifles and ammunition are far superior; true, but not much. The present author has seen a .303 rifle bullet drill a British steel helmet through-and-through; and yet has fired four shots into a wild boar, achieving both a spine-hit and a brain-hit, which halted the animal but did not bring it down; it fell over only when someone else fired a dum-dum round and its intestines promptly dropped out on the snow.

the field anyway; but he soon put a stop to the tricks of old auntie *Times* and a British shell put full-stop to Howard's career later that day, depriving us of a brilliant despatch of a unique event — the clash on unequal terms of British troops armed with lances and dervish troops armed with spears. The weapons were equally primitive, the inequality lay in the numbers. There were less than 400 Lancers, and the dervish fighting group they unexpectedly burst upon numbered 500, according to a Lancer officer interviewed by Burleigh; 1,500, according to Burleigh himself; and 2,700, according to Winston Churchill, writing in his book *The River War*, first published in 1899. One thing is sure: no one actually stopped to count them. The Lancers fell into a typical dervish trap, a large force hidden in a khor or ravine, and even when perceived vulnerable only to the 15-pounders firing shrapnel, to be driven out only by infantry — and at some cost, because hand-grenades and light mortars were not available.

Burleigh afterwards got a description from one officer, Steevens from another. The Lancer interviewed by Burleigh said: 'We moved along to the left — i.e., east of Surgham — following up the enemy on that flank. Our object was to prevent them retiring into Omdurman, or, at any rate, delay their retreat. A body of dervishes were seen crouching not far off to the right. Colonel Martin determined to push the enemy back and interpose between them and the town. The regiment, of four squadrons, was wheeled into line. When 300 yards off we started to charge, and were met by a heavy musketry fire from the enemy. At first it was ill-directed, but very soon casualties occurred in our ranks from it. Instead of a few dervishes, we tumbled upon over 500 hidden in a fold of the ground. They were in a khor or nullah, into which we had to drop, and they lined it twenty deep in places. The dervishes, when we struck them, did not break, but "bunched" together, showing no fear of cavalry.' Indeed, there was no reason why they should; they knew from boyhood how to deal with them, lie down and ham-string the horses.

Slap! 'It was just like that,' said a Lancer captain to Steevens, striking an open hand with one fist, to illustrate the impact. Then, said Burleigh's witness, 'there was half a minute's hacking, cutting, spearing, and shooting in all directions; then we cleared them, and rallied on the far side.'

'Rally, No. 2!' yelled a sergeant, so mangled across the face that his body was a cascade of blood, nose and cheeks flapping hideously.

'Fall out, sergeant, you're wounded,' said his troop subaltern.

'No, no, sir; fall in!' shouted the sergeant hoarsely, reeling about in his saddle. 'Fall in, No. 2; fall in. Where are the devils? Show me the devils.' And No. 2 Troop fell in, four unwounded men out of twenty.

The wounds inflicted by the primitive weapons were savage. Slashed faces and severed wrists or arms were the least of them; some men came reeling out, with their viscera tumbling out of their bodies and wreathing down round their saddles, but still in the saddle, still riding. Behind, the dervishes were hacking at any fallen body that still quivered, and men went back into the nullah to try to bring out a fallen or reeling comrade in a ring of circling savages. Wrote Burleigh: 'Lieutenant Montmorency, having got through safely, turned back to look for his troop-sergeant Carter. Captain Kenna went with him. Lieutenant T. Connally and Winston Churchill also turned about to rescue two non-commissioned officers of their troops. They succeeded in their laudable task.'[14]

---

[14] To Burleigh, Churchill was just another Lieutenant and rival author when his book *Khartoum Campaign 1898* was published by Chapman

According to Burleigh, there had been 320 Lancers, of whom 22 were killed and 50 wounded, besides many dismounted, 119 horses being lost. The Regiment was ruined, unable to carry on with its task, and this was probably a major reason why the Khalifa managed to escape by a few minutes. Once through, the Lancers stopped and got their revenge with firearms, blazing away with carbines at the dervishes. An officer estimated the enemy's losses as 60 from the charge, 100 from the fire-fight; but this may have been optimistic. Whether it was or not, the arithmetic was bad, and the Lancers had made a large and unnecessary addition to the casualties of the Anglo-Egyptian army.

This second phase of the battle, following the decimation of the dervish frontal attack, had included another unnecessary disaster on the right flank, in the Kerreri hills, on the opposite end of the line to the Lancer's charge in front of Jebel Surgham on the left flank. Both were, in fact, occurring simultaneously. The sacrificial frontal assault had been not exactly a feint, but designed to draw all attention to the front, while two other equally large forces of dervishes enveloped both the right and the left flanks of the Anglo-Egyptians, and lapped round behind them. Osman Azrak had led and died with the frontal charge; but Ali Wad Helu and the Khalifa's eldest son, Sheik-ed-Din, were inconspicuously occupying the Kerreri heights; while the Khalifa and his brother Yakub lay hidden out of sight behind the low hills of Surgham, ready either to envelop the

---

the following year. His previous book *Sirdar and Khalifa: The Reconquest of the Soudan*, covering the Atbara, was at this moment on the bookstalls. Churchill's own book owes something both to Burleigh and to Steevens's *With Kitchener at Khartoum*, published by Nelson, because the Lancers were not at the Atbara, and only arrived in the final stages of the Khartoum concentration.

left flank or make one more effort to bar the way into Omdurman, according to the way the battle went.

When the British-commanded Egyptian Camel Corps and cavalry moved up the slopes of Kerreri, some 2,000 men, they found at the top some 12-15,000 dervishes, on rocky, sloping ground ideally suited to the fastmoving enemy foot soldiers. The Camel Corps, in any case, was really fit only for reconnaissance in the desert, not for fighting on hills. First they retired, and then they ran, leaving some of their guns behind them as it became apparent that a dervish on foot could outpace a camel on that ground. Their losses were, comparatively, heavy; they were saved only by coming within range of three of the naval gunboats lying on the Nile, which punished the dervish force with the concentrated fire of Maxim-Nordenfeldts and Maxims from their high gun-towers. The dervishes were not beaten, but they were beaten off.

Placidly ignoring this threat to his right, Kitchener ordered his whole force forward, advancing to fulfil the master intention — get between the dervish army and Omdurman, so that they could not retreat into it and cause him days of bitter street-fighting. They began to advance over the debris of the first dervish attack. 'The bodies were not in heaps, bodies hardly ever are,' wrote Steevens, 'but they spread evenly over acres and acres. And it was remarkable, if you remembered the Atbara, that you hardly saw a black; nearly all the dead had the high forehead and taper cheeks of the Arab. The Baggara had been met at last, and he was worth meeting. It was now twenty minutes to ten. Suddenly from rearward broke out a heavy crackle of fire. The crackle became a crashing, and the crashing waxed to a roar. Dervishes were firing at us from the top of Gebel Surgham. Macdonald's brigade, still facing northward, was a sheet of flashes and a roll of smoke. What was it? Had they come to life again?'

Kitchener had not merely left his right open, but his left also — and behind Jebel Surgham on the left were another 12,000 or so dervishes, led by the Khalifa in person. This by itself, remembering the terrible firepower at Kitchener's disposal, did not matter much; but in the advance, a wide gap opened between the bulk of his forces and the Egyptian brigade commanded by Colonel H. A. Macdonald. The dervishes were quick to see and take advantage, and they came pouring on, 12,000 of the master race of the Sudan, against drilled black Sudanese soldiers and drilled Egyptians. Not long ago, a thousand Sudanese or Egyptians would have run from one Baggara horseman, so dread was their fighting reputation. And then, as the dervish forces came in on the left rear, so those from Kerreri heights swarmed down also from the right rear, and all driving for Macdonald, threatening him from three sides almost, but not quite, simultaneously. Of this fault in co-ordination Macdonald made full use, switching the bulk of his fire-power to meet each in turn, his brigade performing precise, parade-ground manoeuvres under pressing attack. A British brigade would have been in little danger; not merely were they steady, but their fire was drilled, accurate, devastating. Whereas the blacks and the Egyptians were notorious for wild, reckless fire when pressed; not merely ill-aimed, but un-aimed, the bullets going up vertically into the clouds or whining into the sand a few yards ahead.

The nearest help was a mile away, but, as Burleigh remarked, 'the dervishes were wont to move so that ordinary troops seemed to stand still'. This brigade, Lewis's, anyway did not move at all, though help came from other quarters, and also a panic order, possibly from the divisional commander, for

Macdonald to retire, which must have meant a shattering blow to shaky morale, a run, and then annihilation. 'I'll no do it. I'll see them damned first. We maun must fight,' grunted Macdonald, and disobeyed. As each successive assault came in, uncoordinated, from a different direction, he turned to meet it, his firing line facing first south, then west, then north, his black and Egyptian soldiers performing their drill-movements impeccably, with men falling under the dervish fire, and their replies surprisingly steady and accurate. The British artillery swung round to their help, and the last dervish army disintegrated.

'The honour of the fight must still go with the men who died,' wrote Steevens. 'Our men were perfect, but the Dervishes were superb — beyond perfection. It was their largest, best, and bravest army that ever fought against us for Mahdism, and it died worthy of the huge empire that Mahdism had won and kept so long. Not one rush, or two, or ten — but rush on rush, company on company, never stopping, though all their view that was not unshaken enemy was the bodies of the men who had rushed before them. A dusky line got up and stormed forward: it bent, broke up, fell apart, and disappeared. Before the smoke had cleared, another line was bending and storming forward in the same track. Their horsemen led each attack, riding into the bullets till nothing was left but three horses trotting up to our line, heads down, saying, "For goodness sake, let us in out of this".'

After it all was over, for there was no more dervish army after this to come on, the great black flag of the Khalifa stood up lonely on the plain, surrounded by bodies. Kitchener shut up his glasses, remarked that he thought they had been given 'a good dusting', and the advance was resumed. The black flag was gathered in, and raised beside Kitchener's red and white

Egyptian banner, whereupon the gunboats promptly shelled it, unaware of the change of possession. Red flag flying, black flag now discreetly furled, Kitchener rode on into Omdurman, on the heels of the fleeing Khalifa.

'Over 11,000 killed, 16,000 wounded, 4,000 prisoners — that was the astounding bill of Dervish casualties officially presented,' wrote Steevens. 'It was a most appalling slaughter. The Dervish army was killed out as hardly an army has been killed out in the history of war. It was simply unavoidable. Not a man was killed except resisting — very few except attacking. It was impossible not to kill Dervishes: they refused to go back alive.' The Anglo-Egyptian loss was approximately the same as at the Atbara — 524 killed and wounded, most of them quite unnecessarily, through the stupid order for the British to fire standing instead of lying, the recklessly rash charge of the Lancers, the incredible over-estimation of the fighting powers of the Egyptian Camel Corps, the gap that was allowed to open between the main body and Macdonald's brigade. Far worse were the errors on the dervish side, though few were tactical. The error was major — to attempt massed cavalry and infantry attacks, in daylight, against the fire-power of the almost-twentieth century. Poor Khalifa, he was not alone; the Western generals were to try it, too, sixteen years afterwards, having learned nothing from his defeat, passing it away as a mere colonial affair, against mere ignorant black people of no account.

Gordon was avenged; and Gordon would not have approved, neither of the methods, so awkward, so cumbersome, so expensive, nor of the extermination of the Baggara, for he liked and admired them.

CHAPTER EIGHTEEN: 'WITH MAXIM AND BIBLE WE BURIED HIM…'

'Them dervishes are good uns, and no mistake. They came on in thousands on thousands to lay us out, but we shifted them fast enough.' — *Thomas Atkins.*

Omdurman had looked splendidly impressive from a distance in the haze, the Mahdi's tomb glittering white and jewelled in the sun, a sight out of the Arabian Nights. Closer inspection, as the troops and newsmen moved into the town after the fleeing Khalifa, revealed a warren of fouled mud-structures that pigs would be ashamed to inhabit, even when due allowance is made for the circumstances in which they were seen, defeat being an untidy affair always. 'There were no streets, no doors or windows except holes, usually no roofs. As for a garden, a tree, a steading for a beast — any evidence of thrift or intelligence, any attempt at comfort or amenity or common cleanliness — not a trace,' wrote Steevens. 'Omdurman was just a planless confusion of blind walls and gaping holes, shiftless stupidity, contented filth and beastliness.' And this under the passionate glare of a sun that makes a European glad not merely to strip off all his clothes, but to wish that he could remove the flesh as well, and just sit there, sweating in his bones; for preference, packed in ice.

But these were just the suburbs. At last they burst on to the main thoroughfare of the Khalifa's capital. 'The rude semblance of a street,' wrote Steevens. 'Only it was paved with dead donkeys, and here and there it disappeared in a cullender of deep holes where green water festered.' Wrote Burleigh: 'Vile beyond description is Omdurman. Beasts pay more regard to sanitation than dervishes. Pools of flush and stagnant water abounded. Dead animals in all stages of decomposition lay there in hundreds and thousands.' And besides these, the newly-bled beasts and men fresh fled from the battle, with Maxwell's brigade, the Maxim guns on their light wheeled carriages, Kitchener and his staff, coming on behind. 'Dead and wounded dervishes lay in pools of blood in the roadway,' wrote Burleigh. 'Several of the dying enemy grimly saluted the staff as we passed. An Emir who, horribly mauled by a shell, lay pinned under his dead horse waved his hand and fell back a corpse.' Among the dead were slave girls and children, presumably cut down by their masters when trying to escape. 'We saw worse things,' said Steevens, 'horrors such as do not sicken in the mass on the battlefield — a scarlet man sitting with his chin on his knees, hit by a shell, clothed from head to foot in his own blood; a woman, young and beautifully formed, stark naked, rolling from side to side, moaning. As yet we saw not one fighting man, and still we could feel that the place was alive. We pushed on between walls, we knew not whither, through breathing emptiness, through pulsing silence.'

The 3,000 soldiers, hurrying on to nail the Khalifa, somewhere in this mud-warren, were impeded by the welcome of the inhabitants, mostly slaves of the Baggara, who had grasped with wonderful rapidity that the town was being 'liberated', not sacked. The notables, tactfully, wore their patched Mahdist gowns inside out, so that the patches were largely concealed; this was in token of their change of allegiance. Slatin, who had been in chains near Omdurman when Gordon was killed, was with Kitchener, and he was widely recognised and greeted. 'Yet more wonderful were the women,' wrote Steevens. 'There were at least three of them to every man. Black women from Equatoria and almost white women from Egypt, plum-skinned Arabs and a strange yellow type with square, bony faces and tightly-ringleted black hair; old women and little girls and mothers with babies at the breast; women who could hardly walk for dyed cotton swathings, muffled in close veils, and women with only a rag between themselves and nakedness — the whole city was a huge harem, a museum of African races, a monstrosity of African lust,' Those who were not already busy looting the town granary pressed in on the troops, tried to mingle with them, and nearly halted pursuit altogether. 'One flat-nosed black lady forgot propriety so far as to kiss my hand,' admitted Steevens.

It was not as bad as Brussels in 1944, when the populace, headed by their younger women, brought an armoured division to a grinding halt; but, combined with the superior-styled rabbit warren which was his 'palace', it helped the Khalifa slip away at one entrance, while the troops with rifle butts were breaking in at the other. Meanwhile, armed dervishes by the thousand were being over-awed by a bold and confident front, and were unwillingly laying down their arms, except for the occasional flat bang of a rifle shot which told of a desperado more stubborn than the rest. Everything else was disappointment. 'The Mahdi's tomb was shoddy brick ... the Khalifa's house had a dead donkey putrefied under its walls ... the mosque was a galvanised shed, and would have repulsed the customers of a third-rate country photographer. Everything was foul. They dropped their dung where they listed; they left their brothers to rot and puff up hideously in the sun. The stench of the place was in your nostrils, in your throat, in your stomach. You could not eat; you dared not drink. Well could you believe that this was the city where they crucified a man to steal a handful of base dollars,' wrote Steevens. 'The army moved out to Khor Shamba during the 3rd. The accursed place was left to fester and fry in its own filth and lust and blood. The reek of its abominations steamed up to heaven to justify us of our vengeance.'

Burleigh of the *Telegraph* was busily taking dervish prisoners, and after dark reached the prison compound, which was simply a pestilential swamp, flanked by a row of rough gallows (with a man swinging from one of them), and the prisoners heavily chained amidst the filth. They included a European who had been there, in chains, for eleven years. His name was Charles Neufeld, captured on a diplomatic mission, and his chains were so strong that it was not until next day, with the workshop resources of one of the gunboats, that they could be knocked off. Burleigh found that Neufeld, unlike Slatin, took a semi-favourable view of the departed Khalifa. For an Arab, not exceptionally cruel; certainly not a monster. Apparently, he was pro-Western, which was his reason for keeping, not killing, white captives, so that he could have long talks with them. This made his section of the Baggara tribe, the Taaisha, 'absurdly suspicious'; and their 'jealous, narrow fanaticism annoyed him'. But his power was limited and he could not afford to defy them too far.

The day after the battle, Saturday, 3rd September, Burleigh toured the Mahdi's tomb. It was splashed with blood where the lyddite shells had killed some of the many people who had crowded there for sanctuary, and part of the dome had fallen in. It was believed by the faithful that the Mahdi was not there, having ascended bodily to heaven, and that the tomb represented simply his place of departure for paradise. But he was there. To prove it, Kitchener had the roughly-embalmed corpse with its still recognisable features taken out of the ornate tomb; then he had the head cut off, the body broken up and thrown into the Nile — the symbolism clear. Burleigh heard that the head was to be given to a medical college, but apparently Kitchener had some idea of using the skull as an inkstand or drinking cup.[15] Behind the iron-hard visage, this matter went very deep with him.

Next day, 4th September, was Sunday, fitting for a funeral. Gordon's funeral. It was held, not in miserable, stinking Omdurman, but in the green setting of Khartoum, in the grounds of the palace where Gordon had fallen, and in the wreck of its garden, amid the dark-green palm and blooming orange trees, fronting the waters of the Blue Nile. Representatives of all units were formed up there, backed by the chaplains of the Presbyterian, Church of England, Roman Catholic, and Wesleyan faiths. Their appearance was a triumph, for one of these, Burleigh would not disclose which one, had refused to attend if the others did. Only an abrupt order from Kitchener, for him to embark forthwith for Cairo, obtained his reluctant submission.

The palace of Khartoum looked very like a grave. The untended garden, the windows bricked up (a relic of the siege), and, more signs of what had happened here, the marks of musketry, of shell and cannon-ball, scarred on the splintered walls. ''The bones of murdered civilisation lay before us,' wrote Steevens. Inside was a courtyard, with stairs running down into it; on those stairs, Gordon had been murdered.

At 10 a.m., the drilled ranks outside snapped to attention, the band crashed into 'God Save the Queen'; little-by-little, as it played, the Union Jack crept up the flagstaff, to whip smartly in the breeze above re-conquered Khartoum. Drilled cheering

---

[15] *The White Nile*, by Alan Moorehead (World Books, 1960), P. 346.

commenced, for the Queen, for the Khedive, above the steady thunder of a 101-gun salute fired by the Maxim-Nordenfeldts of the gunboat *Melik*, moored in the Blue Nile. All heads were uncovered, and the Guards band played the 'Dead March in Saul'. Count Calderai, the Italian Military Attaché, stood there, face working; Count von Tiedmann, the German Attaché, was openly weeping. The Presbyterian Chaplain — for Gordon had been a Presbyterian — said a brief prayer: 'Our help is in the name of the Lord who made heaven and earth,' then read the 15th Psalm. After the other chaplains had followed him, with muffled drums rippling eerily, the Highland pipers played a spine-chilling lament, dying away into the dull boom of minute guns. As the officers, by seniority, stepped forward to shake Kitchener's hand in congratulation for his victory, then, wrote Steevens, 'there were those who said the cold Sirdar himself could hardly speak or see'. In any event, he was unable to dismiss the parade, and had to ask one of his officers to do it for him.

Then permission was given for the men to break ranks and look round the Palace, if they wished. Everyone did so. 'They filled the roofless rooms and packed the stairway where Gordon was struck down,' wrote Burleigh. 'I was surprised to find that even the youngest, most callow soldiers knew their Khartoum and the story of Gordon's fight and death. There were speculations and suggestions as to how the end exactly came about that were a revelation to me, so full of information and pregnant of observation were many of the men's remarks.'

'Thus with Maxim-Nordenfeldt and Bible we buried Gordon after the manner of his race,' wrote Steevens. 'We came with a sigh of shame: we went away with a sigh of relief. The long-delayed duty was done. The bones of our countrymen were shattered and scattered abroad, and no man knows their place;

none the less Gordon had his due burial at last. So we steamed away, and left him alone again. Yet not one nor two looked back at the mouldering palace and the tangled garden with a new and a great contentment. We left Gordon alone again — but alone in majesty under the conquering ensign of his own people.'

POSTSCRIPT

The Khalifa got clear away into the wastes of the Sudan, back to El Obeid, where the Mahdi had started from nineteen years before. In November 1899, another British expedition brought him to battle. When his attack failed, the Khalifa gathered his surviving chiefs around him, and they sat ceremoniously down in due order according to rank, behind their bodyguard, to await death from the withering fire of the advancing British. The white men were awe-struck when they realised what the close-knit group of huddled corpses meant.

Osman Digna, who had been there almost from the first, was also the last to be taken, being captured in January 1900. The man whom the Sudanese called the 'Grand Master of the Art of Flight', had had a run of twenty years, out-fighting them all with his unspoken creed, that a dead soldier is a bad soldier.

There was an outcry about the Mahdi's skull, Queen Victoria was particularly shocked, believing that the affair 'savoured too much of the Middle Ages'; and Baring had it quietly buried in the Moslem cemetery at Wadi Haifa, 'Bloody Halfway'. Baring himself wrote his memoirs, and attacked the 'Gordon cultus' at last.

Mr. Gladstone died respected, so did Mr. Disraeli. England got the Sudan only just in time, dislodging the French from Fashoda immediately after the capture of Khartoum. The race for Africa had begun, and the Sudan covered the river route into the heart of the Dark Continent. England also got the Suez Canal.

Bennet Burleigh wrote another book, and conducted an oddly oblique correspondence with a Mr. E. N. Bennett,

274

attacking that gentleman's article in *The Contemporary Review* with articles in the *Daily Telegraph*. E. N. Bennett had got hold of an undoubted fact, when he wrote: 'It is, of course, an open secret that in all our Soudan battles the enemy's wounded have been killed.' The astonishing thing was, that Burleigh denied this, although it was in fact no secret and he himself, on pages 41-2 of the book he was just bringing out, told how he saved the life of Mousa Digna when that rebel, shot through the stomach, but still waving his spear, was being shot at by Sudanese soldiers. E. N. Bennett, a particularly virulent 'do-gooder', had never been in the Sudan, thought that the Geneva Convention applied, and grossly misunderstood and exaggerated. Nevertheless, instead of explaining, Burleigh retired behind a pompous smokescreen. 'There is not and never was a scintilla of truth for the charge of wholesale slaughtering of wounded dervishes,' he wrote. 'I certainly never heard of the matter until Mr. Bennett made the accusation, and I cannot trace its authorship beyond himself.' But if the word 'inevitable' was substituted for 'wholesale' (with its implications of after-battle), the charge was true, amply borne out by Burleigh's own despatches, as well as those of Steevens. The 'do-gooders' were still vocal, still capable of carrying terror far beyond the point that their numbers warranted.

General Kitchener was to die, a Field Marshal, in the bitter cold sea off the grim and barren Orkneys, aboard the sinking H.M.S. *Hampshire*; but long before, he had pointed out, tactfully, that there was in the Sudan a population of three million, 'of whom it may be said that they are wholly uneducated'. He suggested, with all the force of a man who was now Lord Kitchener of Khartoum, that the city should become an educational centre for the whole of the Sudan. 'I accordingly propose,' he wrote, 'that at Khartoum there should be founded and maintained with British money a college bearing the name of the Gordon Memorial College, to be a pledge that the memory of Gordon is still alive among us, and that his aspirations are at length to be realised.'

The college was built, has trained many generations of native rulers of the Sudan, and still stands. How long it will stand, now that a new chaos is engulfing Africa, no man may say.

A NOTE TO THE READER

If you have enjoyed this book enough to leave a review on **Amazon** and **Goodreads**, then we would be truly grateful.
Sapere Books

Sapere Books is an exciting new publisher of brilliant fiction and popular history.

To find out more about our latest releases and our monthly bargain books visit our website:
saperebooks.com

Printed in Great Britain
by Amazon